IMAGES
*of America*

# Around Lake Memphremagog

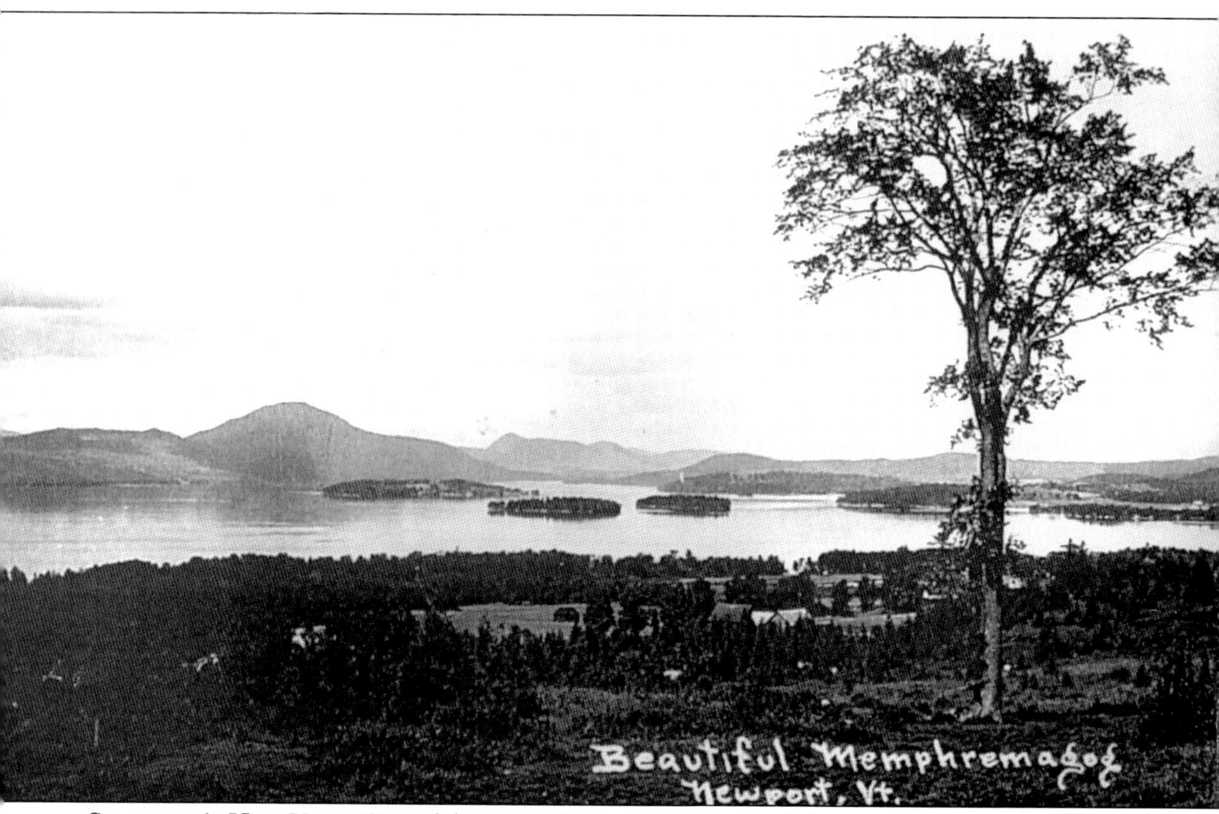


**SHATTUCK'S HILL VIEW.** One of the most photographed and well-known views of Lake Memphremagog, on the American side of the line, is from Shattuck's Hill in Derby. The pull-off spot is popular for noon-hour lunches, evening sunsets, parking by moonlight, and wedding photographs in the field. Lake Memphremagog, with its islands and nearby mountains, is the Northeast Kingdom's "Great Lake."

*Dedicated to the folks who have a fond connection to Lake Memphremagog and who honor its history. For those who have gone before and those who are yet to come. For the Seven Generations.*

IMAGES
*of America*

# AROUND LAKE MEMPHREMAGOG

Bea Aldrich Nelson
and Barbara Kaiser Malloy

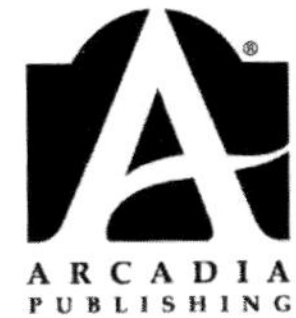

Copyright © 2003 by Bea Aldrich Nelson and Barbara Kaiser Malloy
ISBN 978-0-7385-1250-1

Published by Arcadia Publishing
Charleston, South Carolina

Printed in the United States of America

Library of Congress Catalog Card Number: 2003112430

For all general information, contact Arcadia Publishing:
Telephone 843-853-2070
Fax 843-853-0044
E-mail sales@arcadiapublishing.com
For customer service and orders:
Toll-free 1-888-313-2665

Visit us on the Internet at www.arcadiapublishing.com

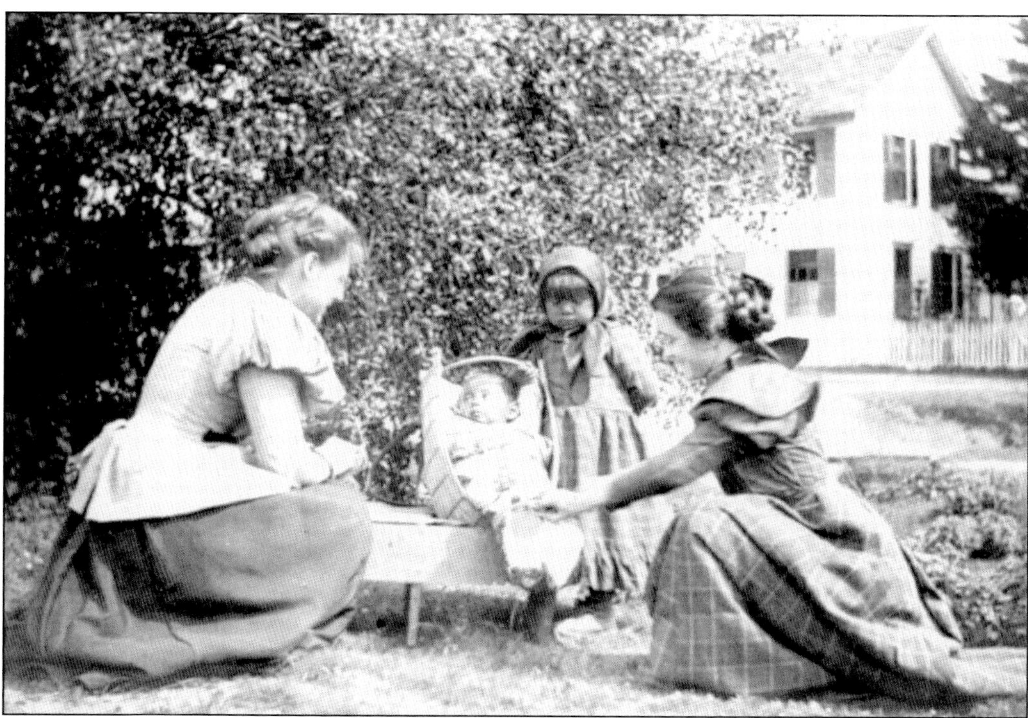

**A Family Visit.** Abenaki children have walked to their auntie's house in town to make a visit. Intermarriage between the native population and Europeans was common, especially during the 1800s, when assimilation was one of the methods of survival for the Abenaki people. The history and development of the villages and towns around Lake Memphremagog cannot be told without an acknowledgment of this combined heritage. Many of the area's traditions and family customs are a result of this interaction.

# RESOURCES

Byrd, Thomas, and Jerry Miller. *Around and About Cary*. Ann Arbor, MI: Edwards Brothers, 1994.
Cary Elementary School. http://caryhs.wcpss.net/site/index.php?id=53
Cary High School. http://caryes.wcpss.net/ces/history.php
Cary Fire Department.
The *Cary News*, Cary, NC.
Legeros, Mike. http://www.legeros.com/ralwake/wake/history/yrac.shtml. (10/5/2010)
Page-Walker Arts and History Center, Cary, NC.
Van Scoyoc, Peggy. *Just a Horse Stopping Place: An Oral History of Cary, North Carolina*. Cary, NC : Passing Time Press, 2006
United Methodist Church, Cary, NC.

## Discover Thousands of Local History Books Featuring Millions of Vintage Images

Arcadia Publishing, the leading local history publisher in the United States, is committed to making history accessible and meaningful through publishing books that celebrate and preserve the heritage of America's people and places.

Find more books like this at
**www.arcadiapublishing.com**

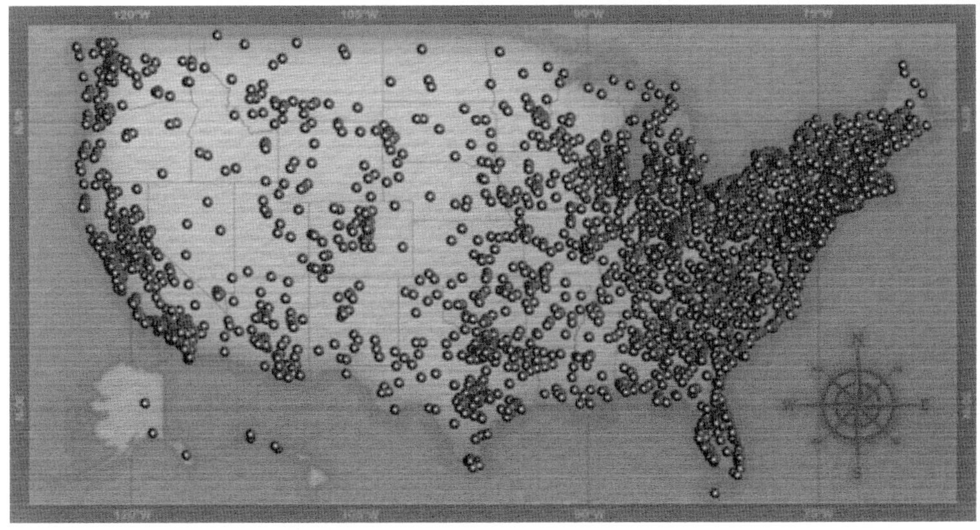

Search for your hometown history, your old stomping grounds, and even your favorite sports team.

Consistent with our mission to preserve history on a local level, this book was printed in South Carolina on American-made paper and manufactured entirely in the United States. Products carrying the accredited Forest Stewardship Council (FSC) label are printed on 100 percent FSC-certified paper.

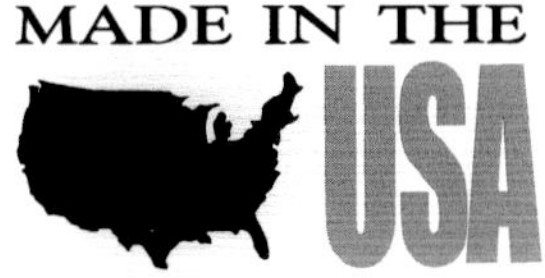

# Contents

# Acknowledgments

We want to sincerely acknowledge our appreciation for our local organizations: the Memphremagog Historical Society of Newport and the Alnobak Heritage Preservation Center. Without their archival and photographic collections, we would not have been able to pull this project together or to include the joint Abenaki, French, and English heritage that makes the Northeast Kingdom and the Eastern Townships around Lake Memphremagog unique. Last but not least, we want to give a special *wliwini* (thank you) to our families and friends for their patience, understanding, encouragement, and support when we needed it.

Memphre is a copyrighted name courtesy of coauthor Barbara Malloy.

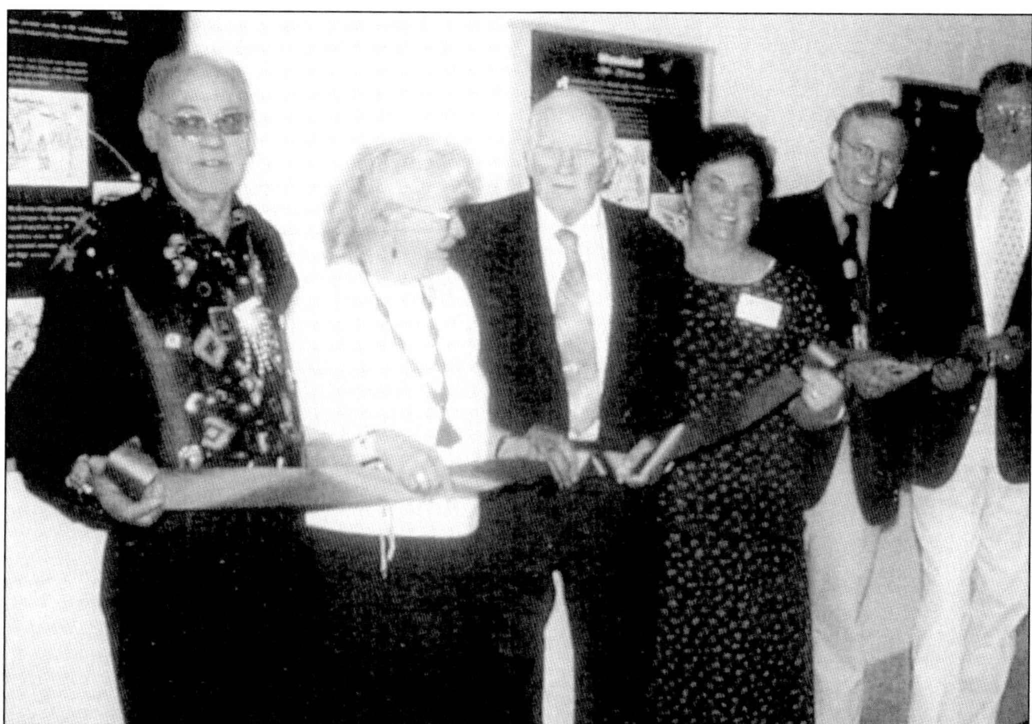

**Cutting the Ribbon.** This photograph was taken in July 2001 at the dedication of the permanent exhibition Mamlabegwok: The Crossroads, located in the second-floor hallway of the Emory-Hebard State Office Building in Newport. The exhibit was the result of an unprecedented collaboration between local organizations and departments of the Vermont state government. The Memphremagog Historical Society of Newport, the Alnobak Heritage Preservation Center, the Vermont Department of Buildings and General Services, and the Vermont Division for Historic Preservation, with financial help from the state legislature, enabled the walk-through timeline of the Memphremagog region to be accessible to the general public. By means of sketches, text, and photographs, the history can be viewed from the last Ice Age to contemporary times.

# Introduction

Welcome to the pages of *Around Lake Memphremagog*. This is an historical thumb-through timeline, a key to unlocking the door of a journey into the past. Lake Memphremagog is a 30-mile-long lake that lies in what are now two countries: Canada and the United States. For thousands of years before the white man came to this area, the lake and its shores and waterways played an important role in the lives and history of the Wabanaki people. This pictorial history begins from these earliest of times after the last Ice Age and through the prehistoric periods. When the first Europeans arrived and "discovered" the lake, Mamlabegwok was the waterway crossroads at the heart of the Western Abenaki homelands and was well traveled by Native Americans, French traders and trappers, and Jesuit priests.

In the early 1600s, Samuel de Champlain was the first to document a visit to this large lake. Since the late 1700s and the 1800s, when more and more settlers came into the area, Lake Memphremagog has been important to the history and development of the towns and villages around its shores in northern Vermont and southern Canada. This pictorial history continues with the settlement, industry, tourism, and people of these towns and villages as we travel through time around the lake. It is the combined history and cultural heritage of Native Americans and Europeans that makes the traditions and customs of the Memphremagog region so unique; and it is this combined cultural history and heritage that is recalled through sketches, vintage photographs, and postcards, all with interesting captions. We hope that this publication will serve as a link to the before and a record for the beyond.

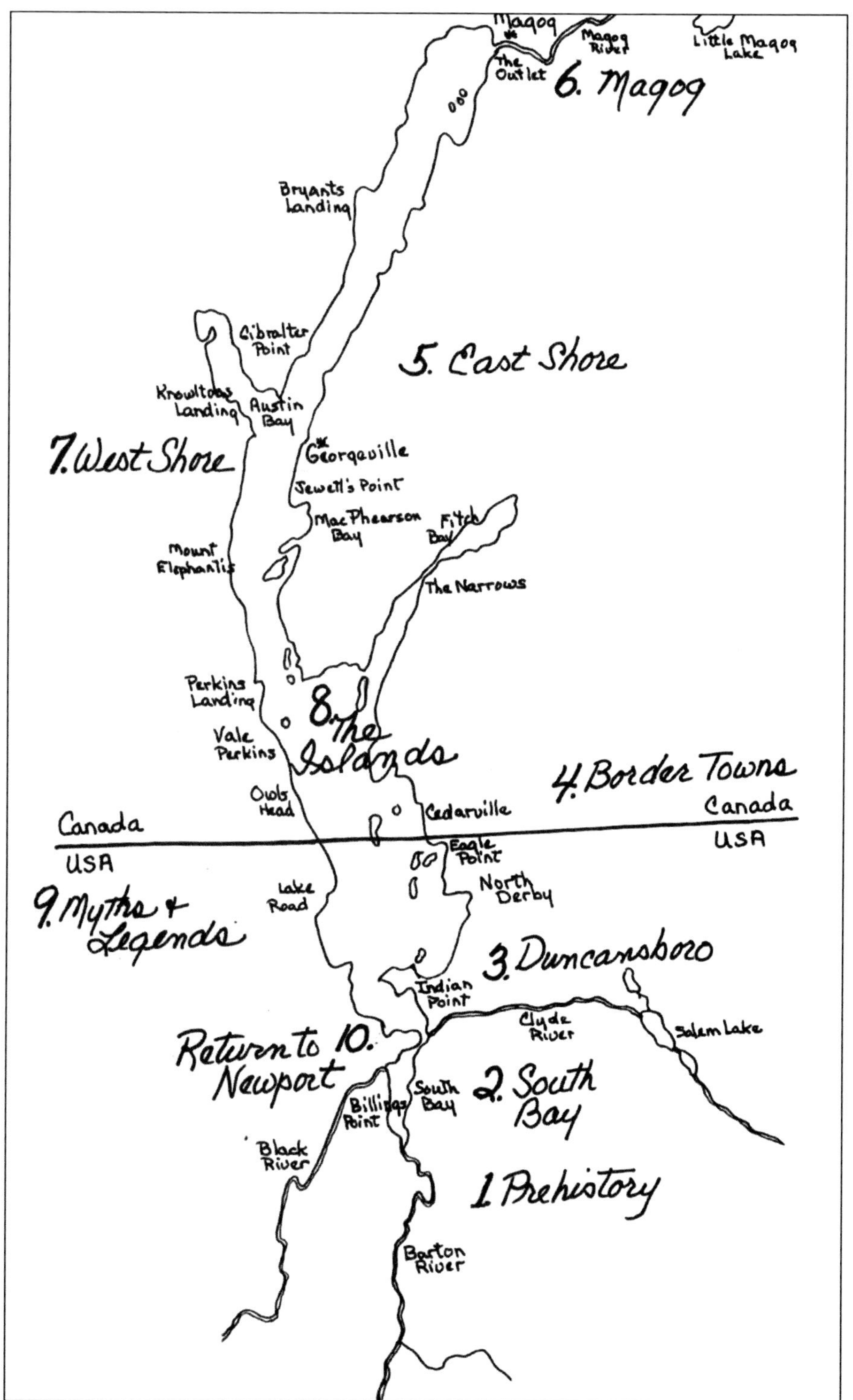


**THE MAP.** This map will help you on your journey around the shores of Lake Memphremagog. The chapter numbers and area locations serve as a guide to your pictorial travels through history.

# One

# Mamlabegwok and Its Prehistory

Mamlabegwok is an Algonquian word that means "at the big waters" and is where the name Memphremagog comes from. The Abenaki, the Native American people whose homeland includes Lake Memphremagog at its center, are just one of the many Algonquian speaking nations. "Abenaki" comes from the Algonquian word *Wabanaki*, which translates as "east land" or "dawn land," and the Abenaki call themselves *Alnobak*, which means "ordinary people" or "human beings." Therefore, Alnobak Wobanakiak are the "people of the dawnland," shortened and modernized to Abenaki. Those of us west of the White Mountain range and south of the South Lawrence River in Canada are Western Abenaki. The Abenaki people did not recognize boundary lines separating the ownership of countries or nations; to them it was homeland. The land belonged to the creator, and they were here to care for it while on their earth walk, not to claim ownership. It is the history of these people and their philosophies that is closely linked to Lake Memphremagog and its waterways, and has been for thousands of years. This history, according to the geological and archaeological record, begins at the end of the last Ice Age (12,000 to 14,000 years ago) when the ice sheet receded and left glacial lakes, rivers, and ponds dotting the landscape. It is soon after this period that the prehistoric cultural history begins and Lake Memphremagog, or Mamlabegwok, meaning "big waters," is formed.

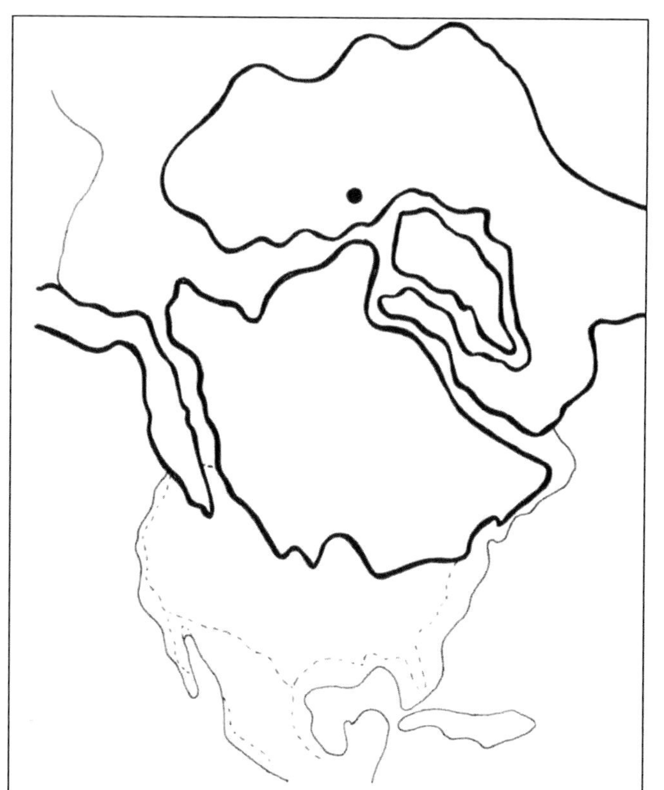

**The Ice Sheet.** During the last Ice Age (16,000 to 18,000 years ago), an ice sheet covered most of the land in the northern hemisphere. The tons of ice pressed the land down and caused it to reach out beyond what is now coastline. As the glacier moved, high volcanic mountaintops like Owl's Head were ground down. By 15,000 years ago, a warming climate caused the ice sheet to recede.

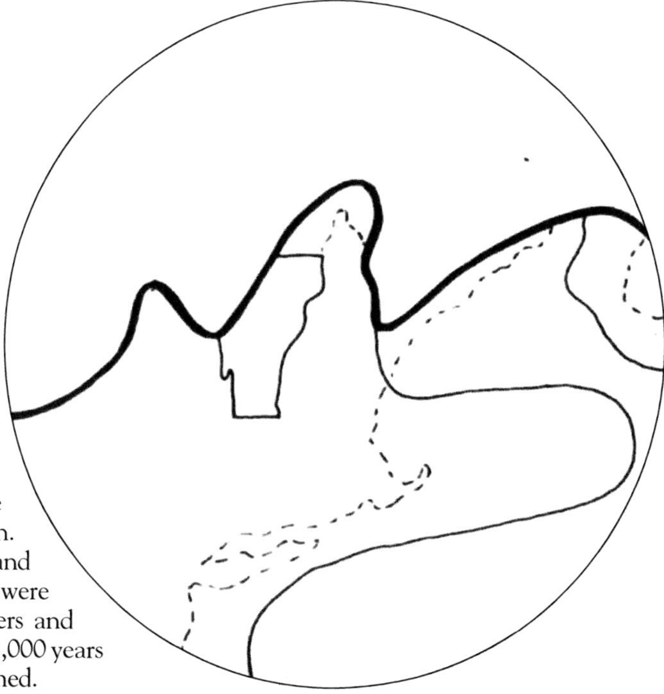

**Land Is Exposed.** As early as 12,000 years ago, the ice sheet had receded, and meltwater formed a large lake from the Memphremagog region down to the Connecticut River Valley. With no more melting ice to feed it, the Hitchcock-Upham Lake eventually diminished and left glacial lakes and river valley wetlands, which became the Memphremagog drainage basin. The Connecticut River Valley and the Memphremagog watershed were then open to Paleo-Indian pioneers and traveling hunter-gatherers at least 2,000 years before the Champlain Sea was formed.

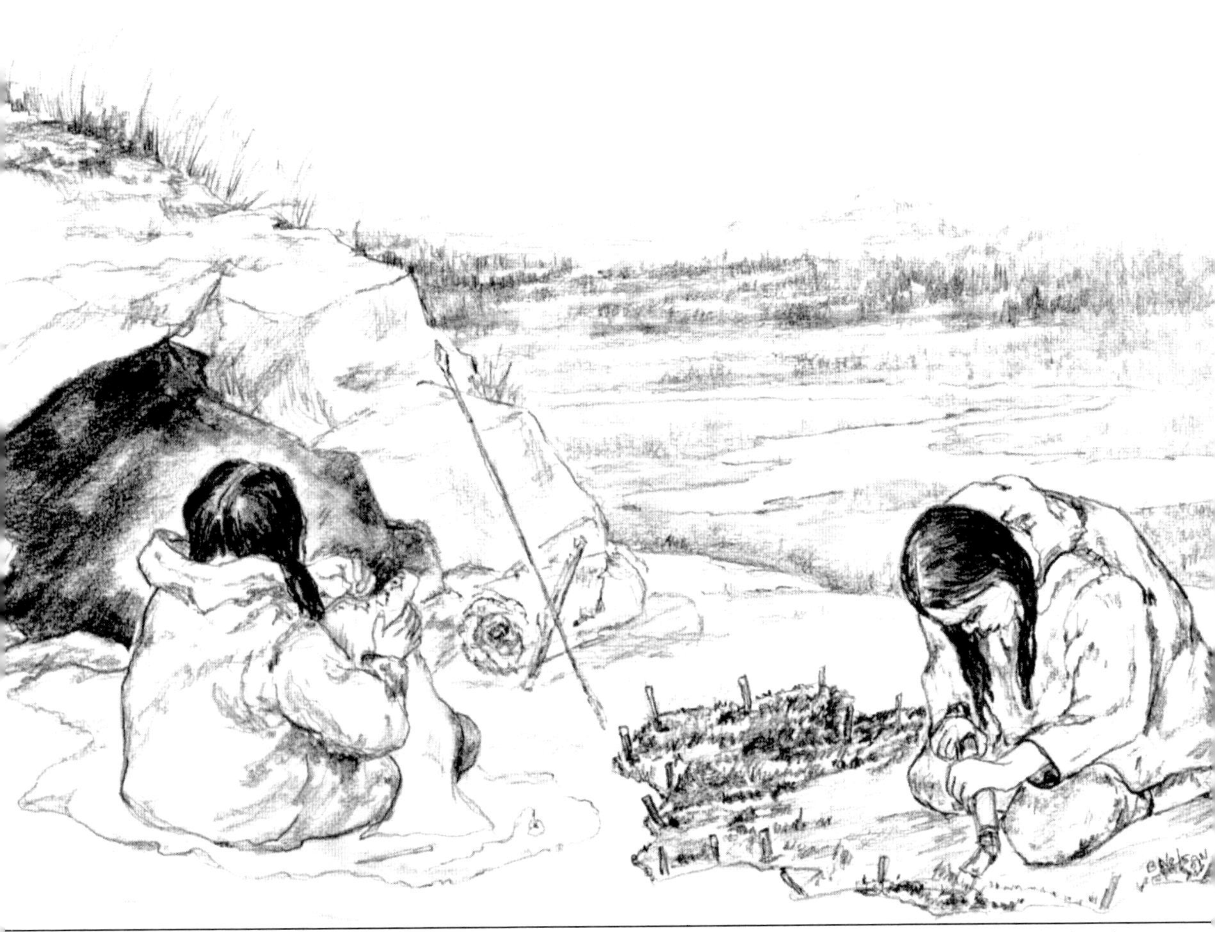

**A Paleo-Indian Campsite.** During the Paleo-Indian period (8500–6000 B.C.), mobile family groups of early pioneer Paleo people explored the ice-free land. Small residential camps were chosen on high terrain with a good view of the surrounding territory, usually in close proximity to wetlands. Temporary open-air sites were used while following migrating herds of caribou on their seasonal circuits of hundreds of miles. Paleo diets were supplemented with fish, waterfowl, small mammals, and plants. Housing and clothing were made from hides, tools and weapons were made of stone and bone, and travel was by foot, carrying or dragging burdens. Permanent sites were not utilized, and very little archaeological evidence for this ancient time period exists in Vermont. Only 30 Paleo-Indian sites have been identified throughout the state, and only one in the Memphremagog region.

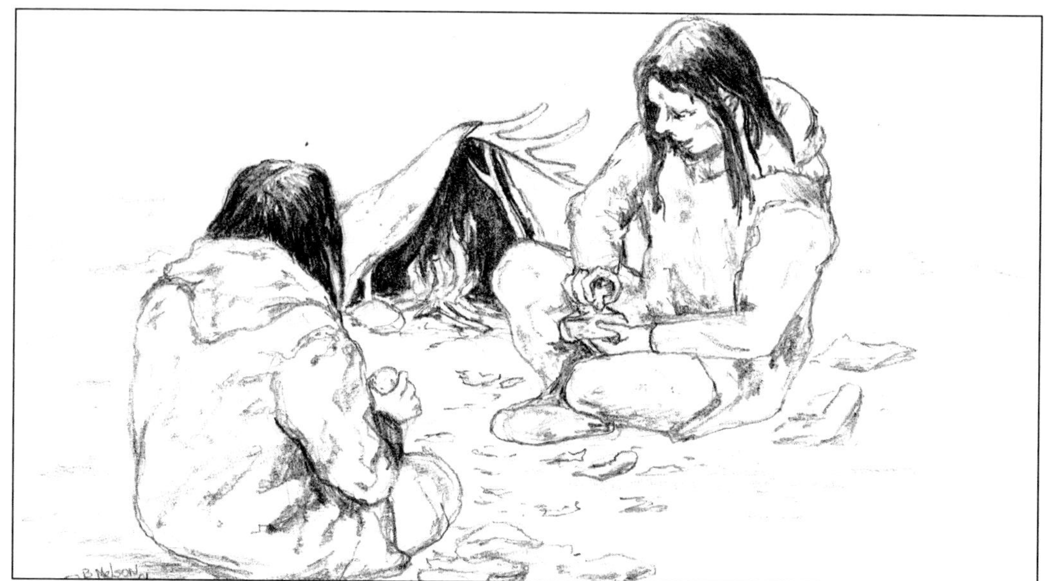

**Making Stone Tools.** It seems reasonable to assume, due to archaeological research, that the earliest inhabitants, called Paleo-Indians, might very well have been the precursors to the northeastern Algonquians, the ancestors of the Abenaki people. One of the archaeological signposts of this time period, at least 10,000 years ago, is the distinctive fluted stone projectile point, often made from exotic lithic materials. Such a point has been found in Derby, Vermont, within the Memphremagog and Clyde River watershed.

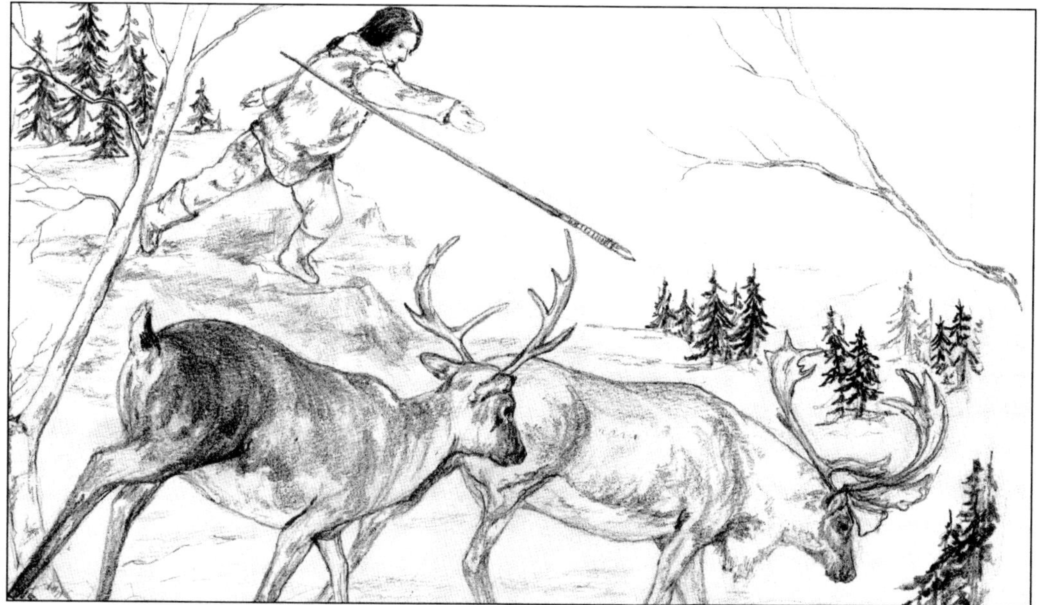

**Hunting Caribou.** The land, supporting herds of large animals, became a park tundra with spruce, fir, and birch trees. The Paleo-Indians followed these herds, particularly the caribou, on their seasonal migrations to grazing and calving grounds. They hunted with a range of hand-held spears: lightweight killing lances with bone, stone, or tusk points; heavy thrusting spears with detachable foreshafts; and lightweight throwing spears. Barbed bone or antler harpoons were used for fish, and throwing sticks were used for waterfowl.

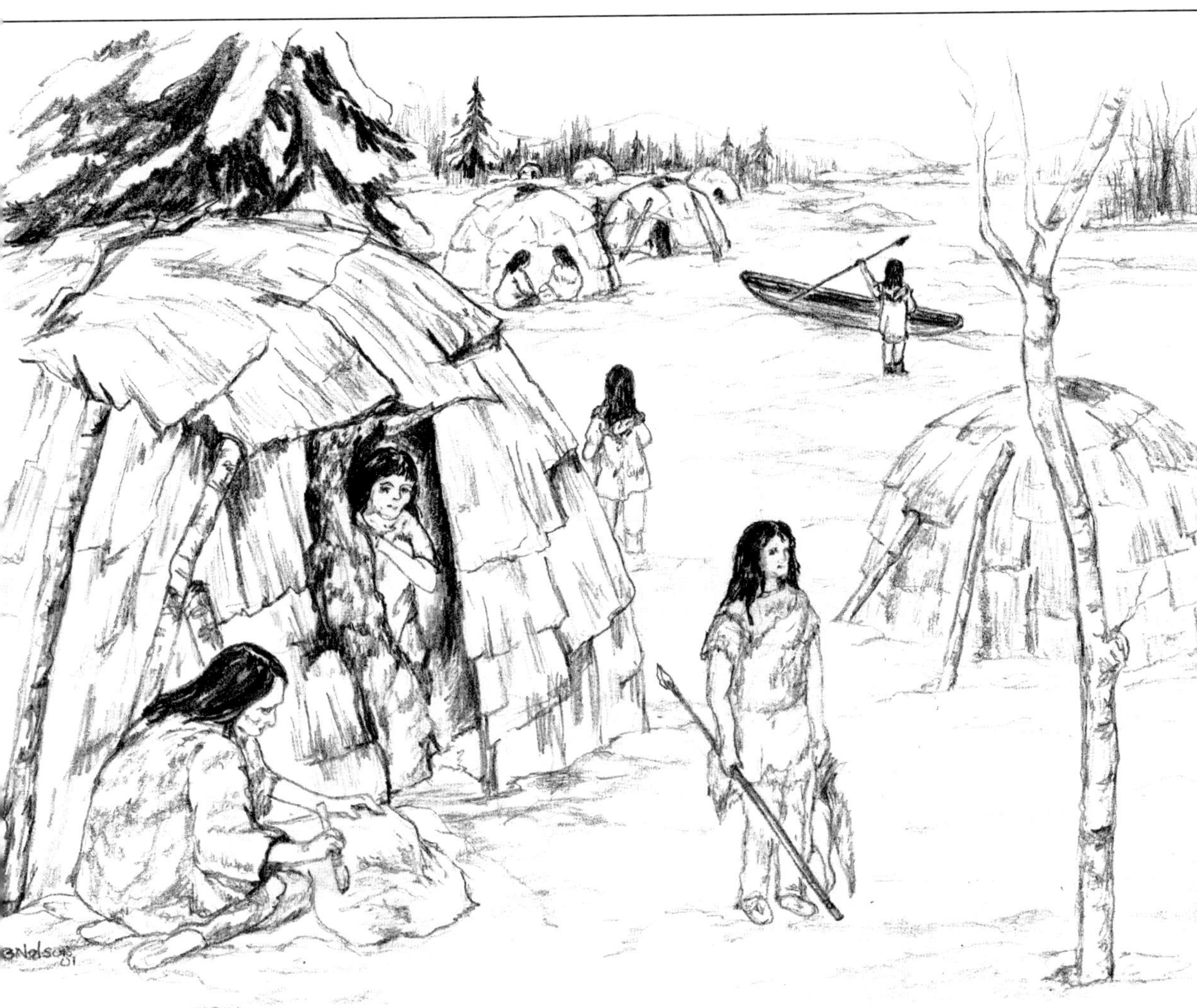


**An Archaic Village.** This cultural time period (8000–900 B.C.) is divided into three time spans: Early, Middle, and Late Archaic. Over this long period of time, many adaptations and cultural changes occurred. With a warming climate, changing forests, and a larger variety of animals, plants, and roots, populations gradually increased. By the Late Archaic period (4000–900 B.C.), the dog had become domesticated, and burdens were carried by dog travois. The people lived in small base villages with seasonal encampments for various activities within the Memphremagog drainage basin. Families frequented these same areas season after season. Local lithic materials, including slate, quartz, and flints, were used for tool-making. Some archaeological evidence indicates that the southern end of Lake Memphremagog had an occupation during the Archaic period.

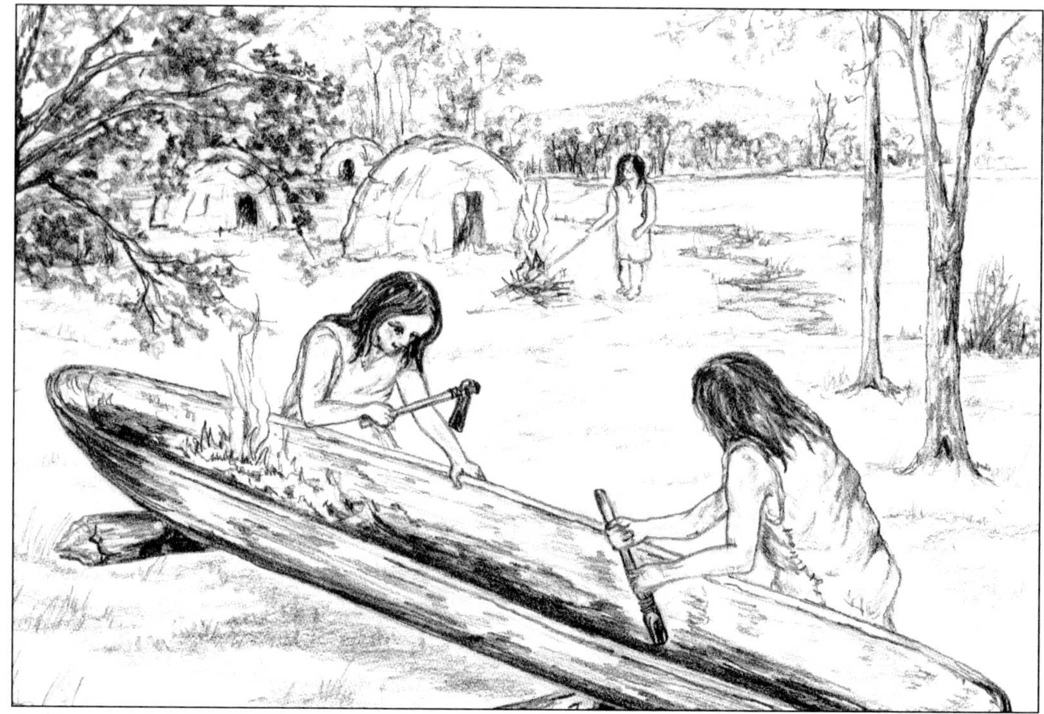

**A Dugout Canoe.** Archaeological evidence of highly specialized ground slate tools for woodworking suggests that the dugout canoe became an important mode of transportation in the Late Archaic period. It was the custom to submerge the canoes underwater at semipermanent base camps for preservation and protection while the band was away on its seasonal rounds of hunting and fishing. At least one example of a dugout has been found in Lake Memphremagog.

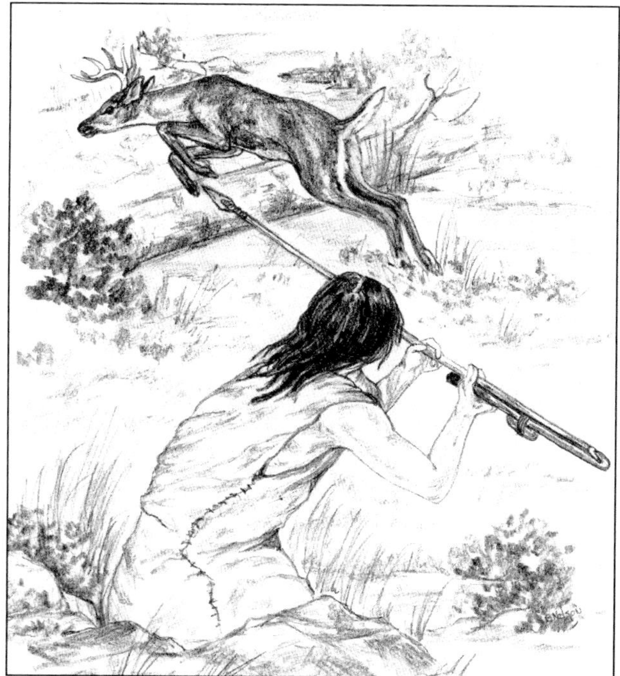

**The Atlatl.** During the Archaic period, hunting shifted from herds to solitary animals such as deer, moose, and bear. Hunting occurred at shorter distances from the fall camps, where the game was butchered and processed. The atlatl, or spear thrower, lengthened the distance and force of the throw and was the hunter's main hunting weapon.

**The Leister.** Other Archaic period innovations were the use of nets, weirs, and specialized fishing spears called leisters. Shells and exotic materials were used for decoration and tools, some coming from great distances such as copper from the Great Lakes area. This and other evidence suggests wide-ranging exchange and trade networks. Lake Memphremagog became a crossroads on main northeastern waterway routes.

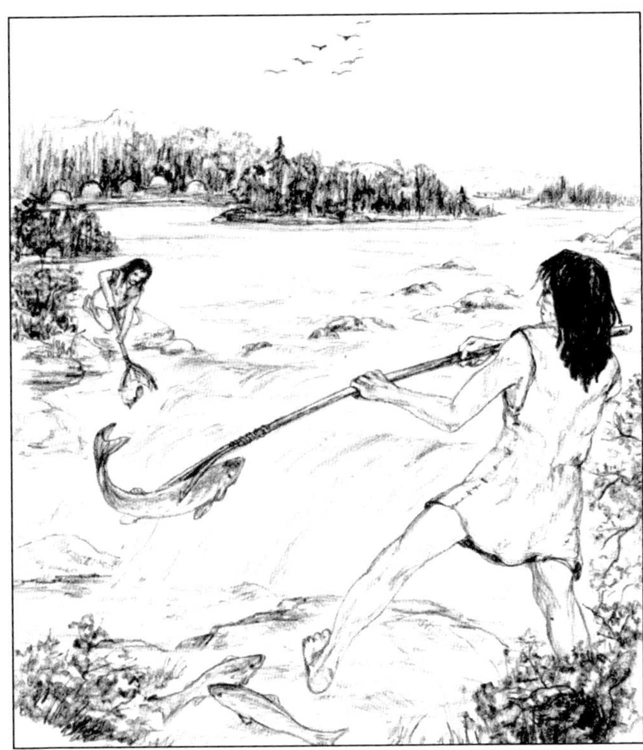

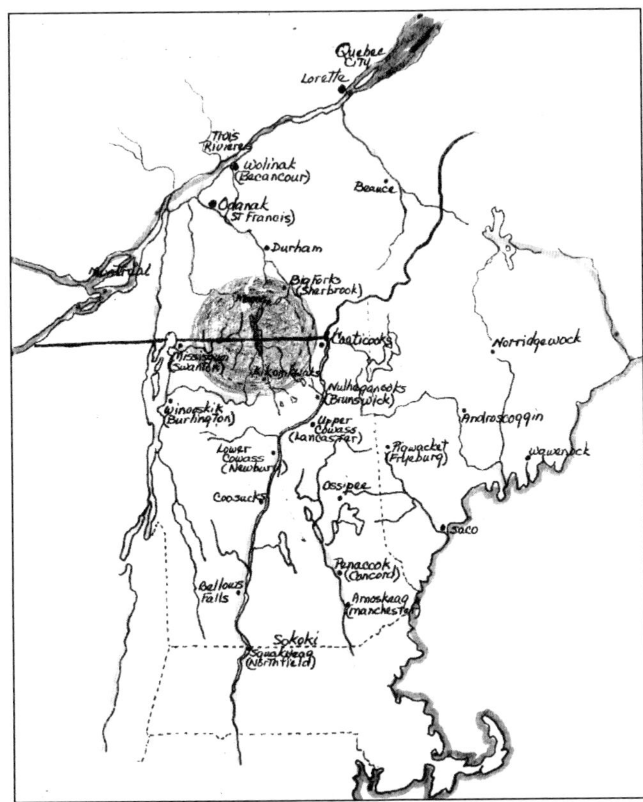


**A Crossroads.** Lake Memphremagog is located at the heart of the Western Abenaki homeland. The lake was well traveled due to its location and proximity to waterways that flowed toward the Atlantic coast, the St. Lawrence seaway, the Great Lakes, and southern New England via Lake Champlain, the Hudson River, and the Connecticut River. Lake Memphremagog's shores saw many an Indian campsite. The lake was a crossroads and focal point for extensive exchange networks between Native nations.

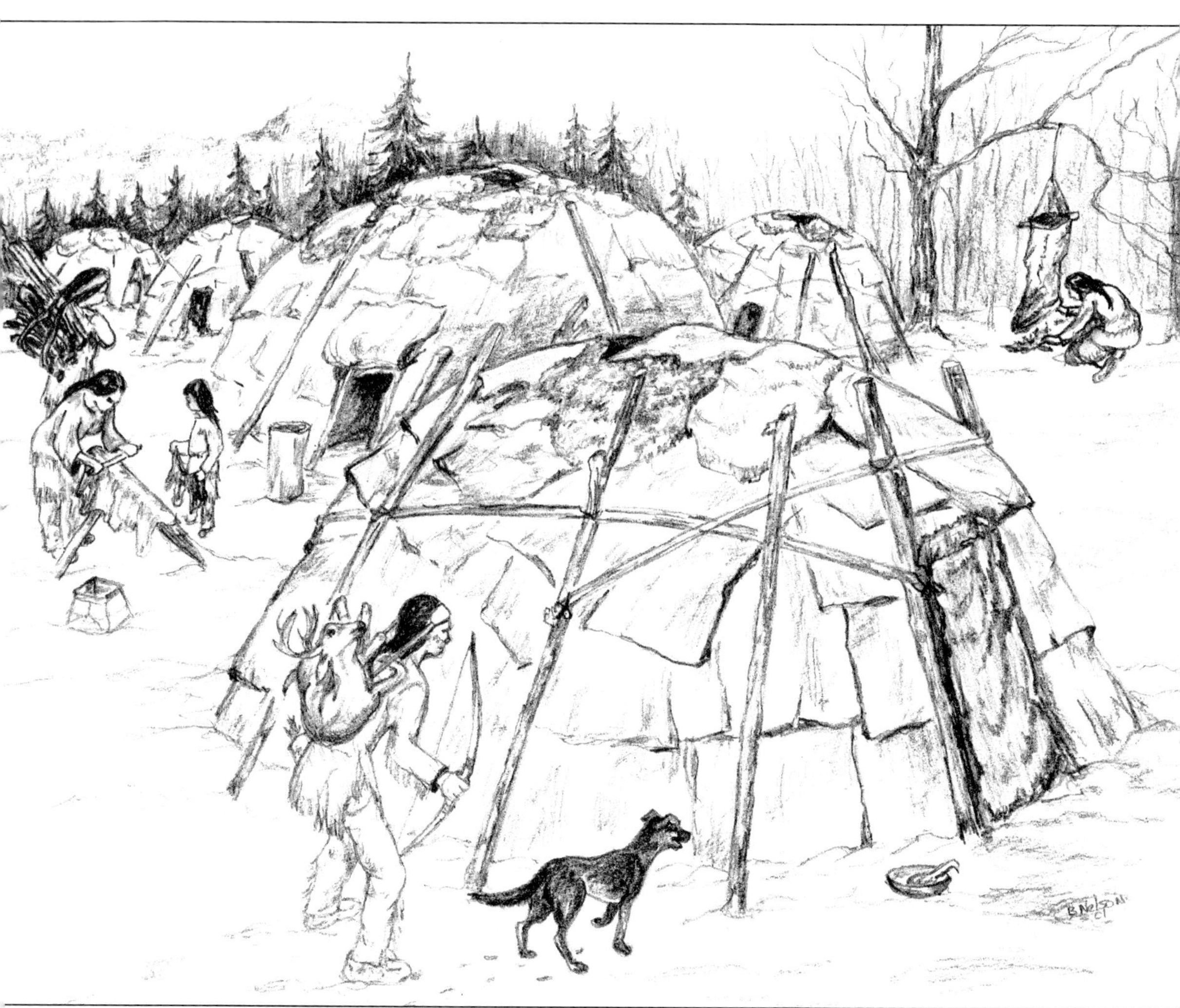

**A Woodland Winter Village.** During the Woodland cultural time period (900 B.C. to A.D. 1600), major cultural changes and adjustments were made for the Algonquian-speaking Wabanaki people around Memphremagog's shores. Regionalism between watershed populations began to be established, and the Memphremagog basin and Clyde-Nulhegan areas were no exceptions. By 1050, extensive semipermanent settlements of circular, dome-shaped houses—wigwams (or wigwoms)—could be found in virtually all of Vermont's lake and river systems. Population growth necessitated a variety of habitats, and diversification became a strategy in not overtaxing game or food resources. Cultivation and harvesting supplemented the seasonal cycles of hunting, fishing, and gathering. Trade and exchange networks played an influential role in cultural innovations and advancements. Many of these lifeways and innovations were later adopted by the early settlers and became standard practices throughout the Northeast Kingdom of Vermont and the Eastern Townships of Quebec, the Western Abenaki homeland.

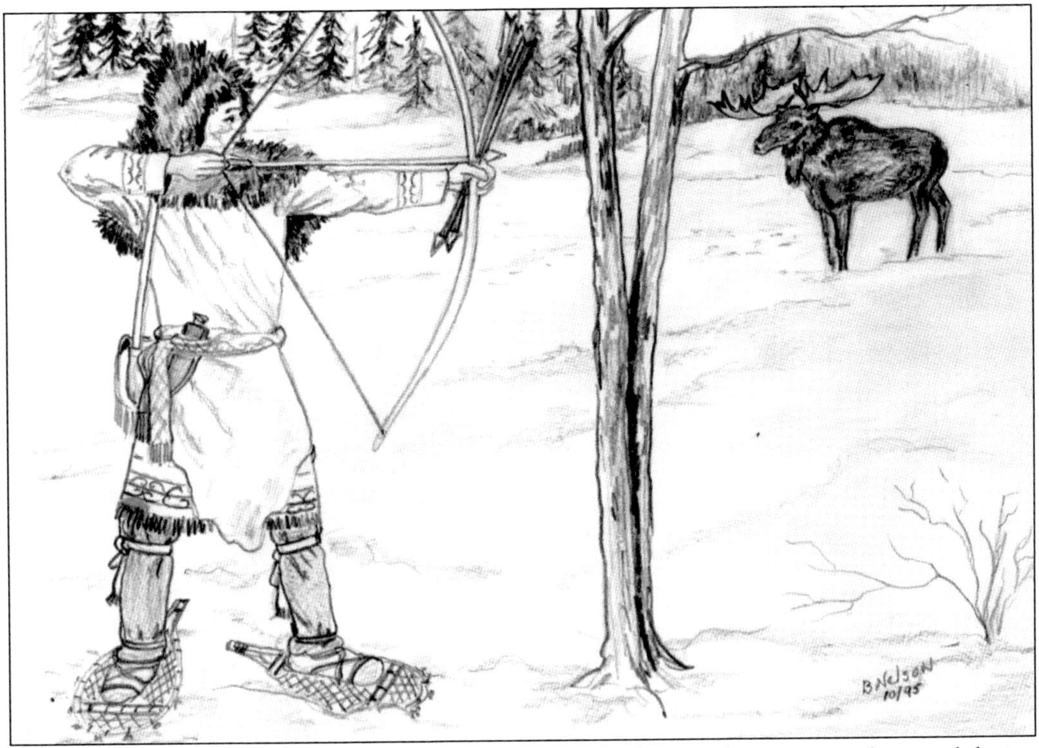

**INNOVATIONS.** Archaeological evidence suggests that the bow and arrow were first used during the Woodland period, and a variety of projectile points were specialized for different types of game. Besides the bow and arrow, snowshoes were a mode of winter travel. It is more than likely that this innovation was an invention of the more northern tribes of Canada and was adopted by Abenaki through contact. Early colonists learned to use and make snowshoes from the Native Americans.

**THE BIRCH BARK CANOE.** Also borrowed through contact from a more northern Native culture, the birch bark canoe was in common use by the Woodland period. Its lightweight and easily accessible materials made it more practical for long-distance travel and easier portage. The dugout was still utilized at permanent village sites, but the portable bark canoe gradually replaced it. The Orleans County Historical Society has examples of both, used on Lake Memphremagog, in their collections.

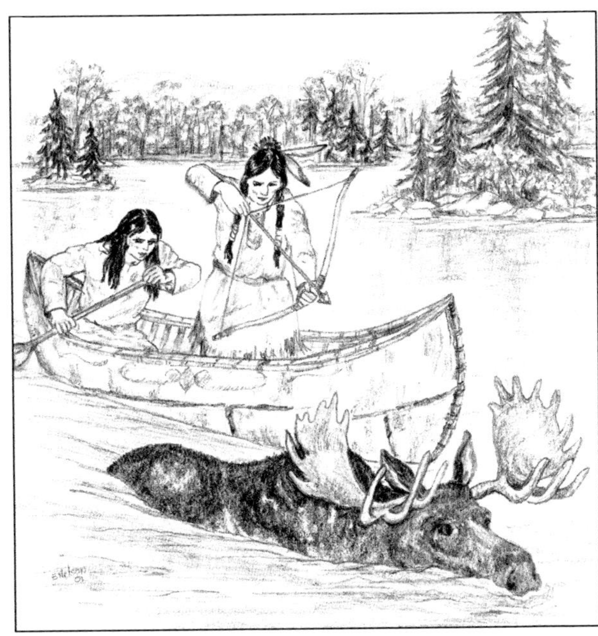

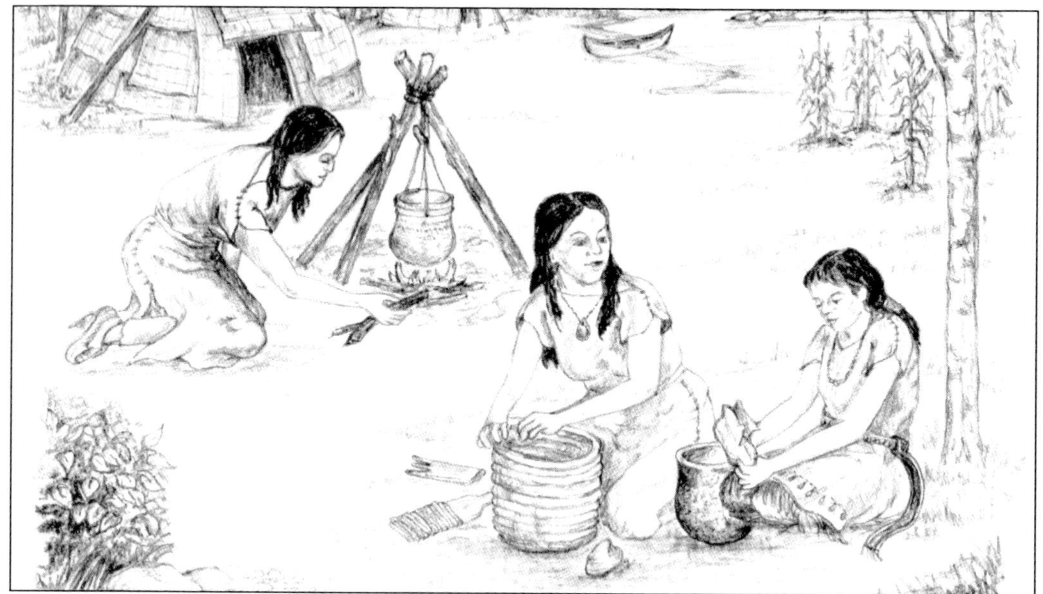

**Agriculture and Pottery.** Due to population growth and larger, more permanent villages, cultivation of maize, corn, beans, squash, and, in some areas, potatoes supplemented a family's seasonal round of hunting, fishing, and gathering. Because of this cultivation, ceramic cooking pots changed to rounded bottoms for easier stirring and added rims for hanging over the fires. Incised decorations on pottery sherds and food storage caches help archaeologists establish the dates of these innovations. One such village site is believed to be located on South Bay.

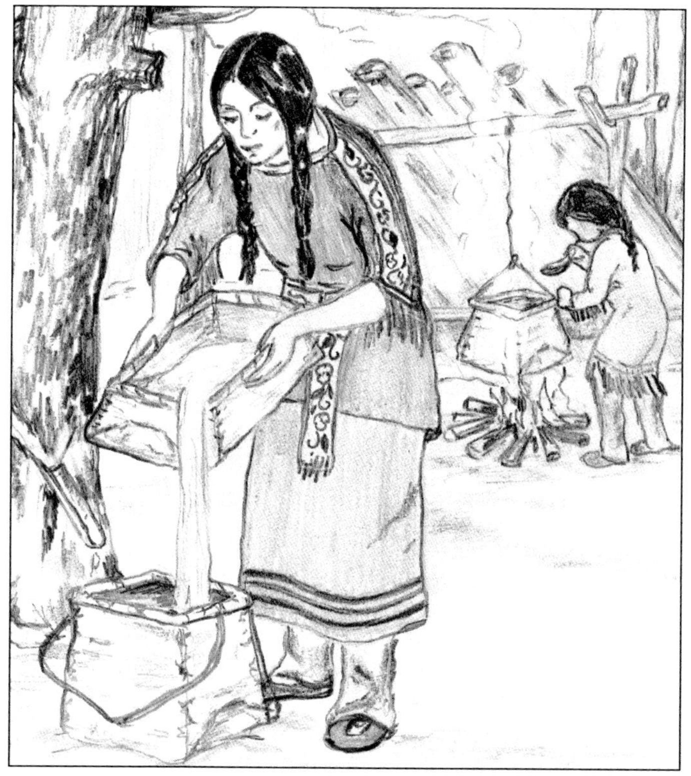

**Sugaring.** Sugar making from maple trees became a yearly activity well before colonists arrived in the New World. In early spring, Abenaki family bands would move into sugar camps within their hunting and gathering territories for the sweet water run. After boiling and stirring in wooden troughs, a family would pack enough sugar into birch bark cones to last a year. Besides corn, maple sugar was just one more gift of native tradition that helped the early colonists survive.

# *Two*

# The South Bay Headwaters

The South Bay of Lake Memphremagog is where the 32-mile-long international lake has its beginnings. The bay is two and a half miles long and was originally a portion of what was called the Coventry Leg until it was annexed to the town of Newport in 1816. In an unusual phenomenon, three rivers flow north into the bay. The Black and Barton form a diversified wetland, now a state wildlife refuge, before entering the lake. The third river, the Clyde, enters the bay on its eastern side. It became a main waterway route for the Abenaki, and later for the white man, to the Connecticut River, southern New England, and the Atlantic. The Barton also connected to the Connecticut via the Passumpsic and was an inland route. Samuel de Champlain was the first to travel through here *c.* 1608 with his Algonquian guides. The first white men to discover the bay and the lake were captives being carried to Canada by Wabanaki during the French and Indian Wars. John Stark was one of these; he later drew the first map of the lake and the surrounding area for the Continental Army. This is when documented history begins. As the town of Newport expanded and grew, businesses and homes sprang up along the bay close to town. And since that time, the South Bay of Lake Memphremagog has become a favored camp area for fishing by both Abenaki descendants and European Americans. It is an example of the interesting cross-cultural history typical of all the shore towns and points around Lake Memphremagog.

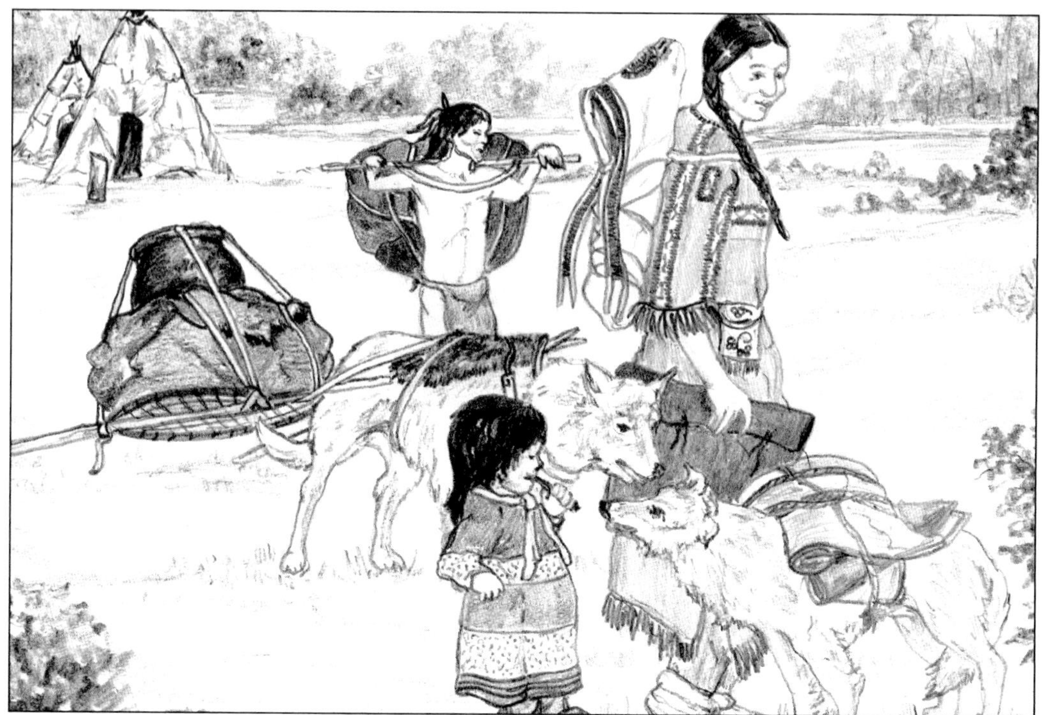

**Moving Camp.** During the Colonial period from 1600 to 1781, some contacts with the Wabanaki people had already been established, and a few cultural adjustments were in place. The Abenaki lived in large villages or base camps during the summer and winter seasons. One such village was located on South Bay. During spring and fall, they spread out in family bands for fishing, hunting, and gathering into territorial areas within watersheds, often to the same places that their ancestors had frequented for generations.

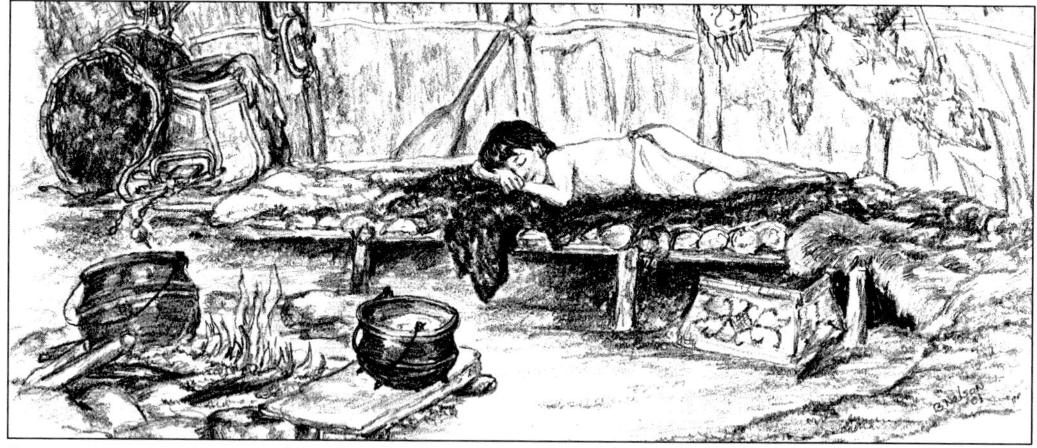

**Rapid Change.** Samuel de Champlain's arrival to the northeast in 1608 marks the beginning of the end of the cultural lifeways that had persisted for thousands of years. European colonists interrupted the environmental balance. Territories became settlements, and the introduction of trade goods, commercial fur trapping, and major diseases disrupted the Abenaki way of life. Cloth replaced leather for clothing, iron and brass cooking pots replaced pottery and bark vessels, and glass beads and ribbon replaced moose-hair and porcupine quill decorations. Europeans also introduced guns, whiskey, scalping, and metal traps.

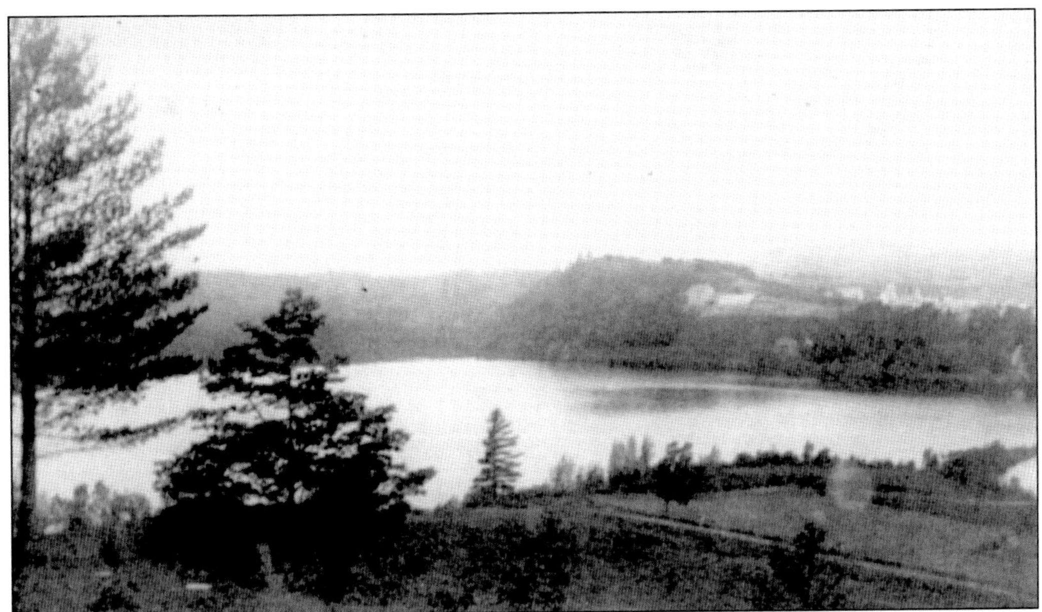

**The Bay.** South Bay is the two-and-a-half-mile-long headwaters for the 32-mile international Lake Memphremagog. The Black, Barton, and Clyde Rivers empty into it. South Bay was originally included in the Salem Grants in 1783, and what was not underwater was annexed to Derby on the east shore and Coventry on the western shore. Eventually, Newport expanded to include the northern portion of the bay.

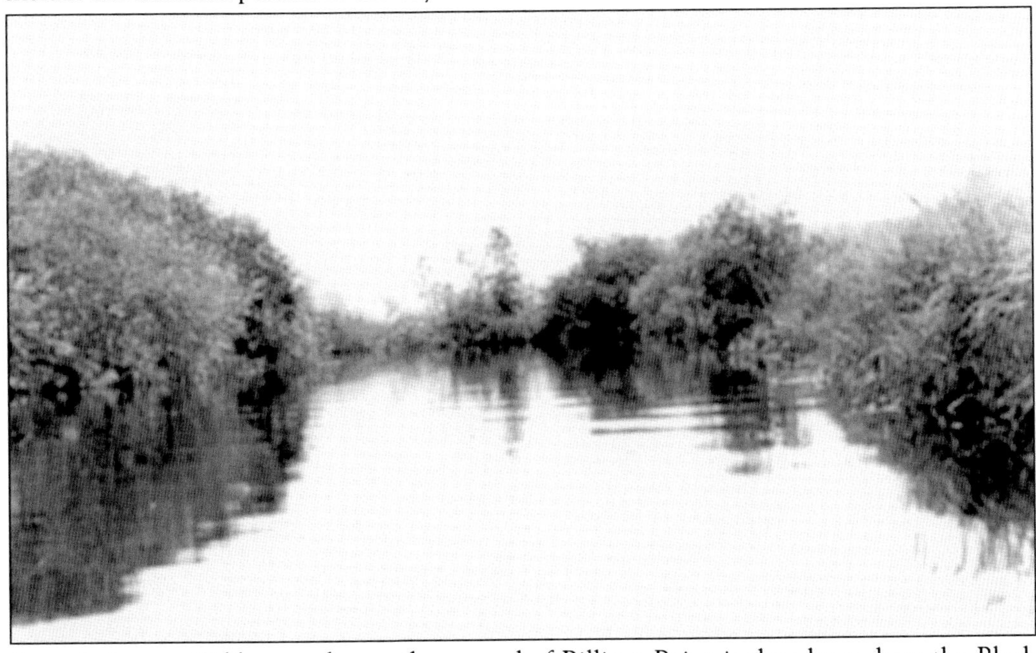

**Black's Inlet.** Hidden on the northwest end of Billings Point is the place where the Black River enters the lake into South Bay. Canoeing down this river, just five minutes from the city of Newport, one can go back in history and be in the wilderness between the cliffs of the Black River Swamp. Bird life abounds with herons, loons, and waterfowl swimming and wading in the shallows and hawks and ospreys soaring across the sky.

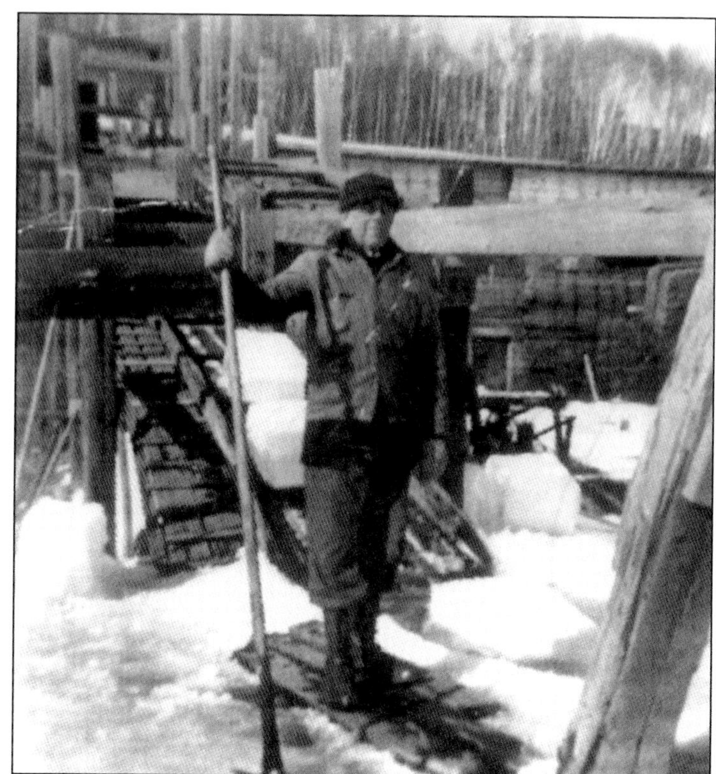

**The Ice King.** Peter Handy, known as "the Ice King of Northern Vermont," purchased the Newport Ice Company and its icehouses in 1912. Ice harvesting on South Bay began in December, when the ice was cut into 24-by-36-inch blocks. Horses used for hauling had to "toe the mark" as the grooves in the ice were cut. Jockmen, with long pike poles and sharp hooks, pushed the ice cakes through the channels and up the slip into the icehouses.

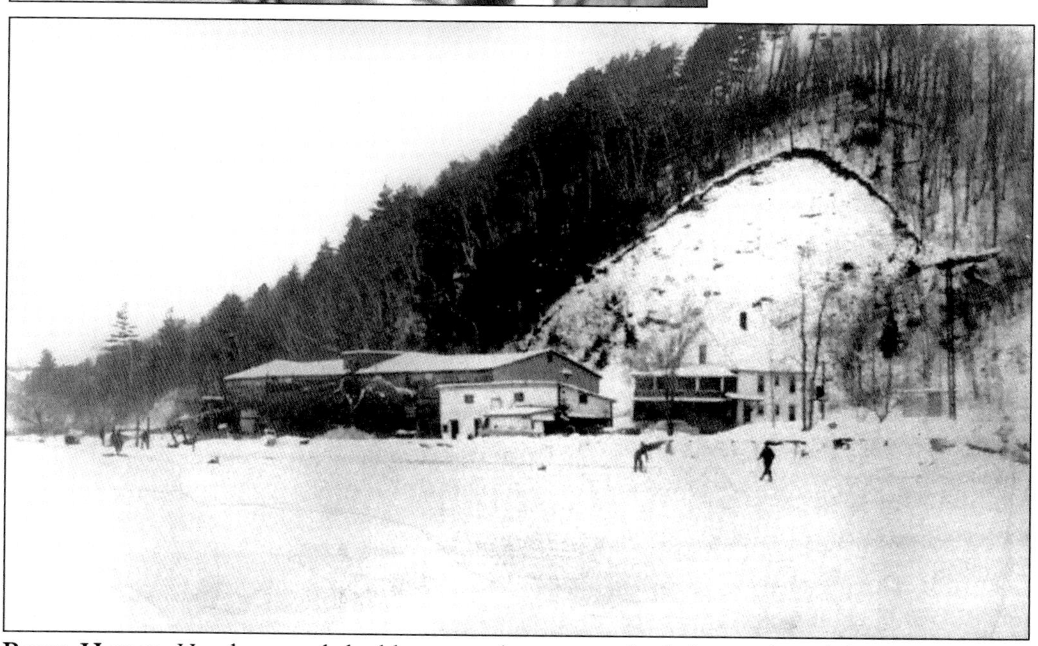

**Peter Handy.** Handy owned double-covered wagons, which he used to deliver ice all over Newport. A 50-pound cake of ice for an icebox cost 20¢. As the ice melted, the water ran into a dish underneath. During this time, when the woman of the house heard the dog lapping up the water, it was time to empty the pan. By the 1930s, mechanical refrigeration had replaced the icebox and doomed the harvesting of ice—a way of life on Lake Memphremagog.

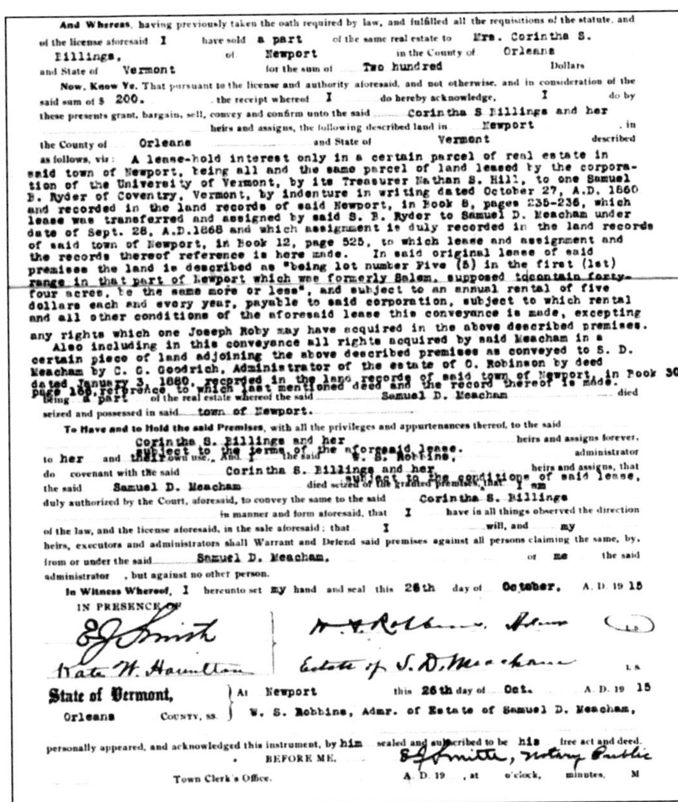

And Whereas, having previously taken the oath required by law, and fulfilled all the requisitions of the statute, and of the license aforesaid I have sold a part of the same real estate to Mrs. Corintha S. Billings, of Newport in the County of Orleans and State of Vermont for the sum of Two hundred Dollars

Now, Know Ye, That pursuant to the license and authority aforesaid, and not otherwise, and in consideration of the said sum of $ 200. the receipt whereof I do hereby acknowledge, I do by these presents grant, bargain, sell, convey and confirm unto the said Corintha S Billings and her heirs and assigns, the following described land in Newport, in the County of Orleans and State of Vermont described as follows, viz: A lease-hold interest only in a certain parcel of real estate in said town of Newport, being all and the same parcel of land leased by the corporation of the University of Vermont, by its Treasurer Nathan S. Hill, to one Samuel B. Ryder of Coventry, Vermont, by indenture in writing dated October 27, A.D. 1860 and recorded in the land records of said Newport, in Book 8, pages 235-236, which lease was transferred and assigned by said S. B. Ryder to Samuel D. Meacham under date of Sept. 28, A.D.1868 and which assignment is duly recorded in the land records of said town of Newport, in Book 12, page 525, to which lease and assignment and the records thereof reference is here made. In said original lease of said premises the land is described as "being lot number Five (5) in the first (1st) range in that part of Newport which was formerly Salem, supposed tdcontain forty-four acres, be the same more or less", and subject to an annual rental of five dollars each and every year, payable to said corporation, subject to which rental and all other conditions of the aforesaid lease this conveyance is made, excepting any rights which one Joseph Roby may have acquired in the above described premises.

Also including in this conveyance all rights acquired by said Meacham in a certain piece of land adjoining the above described premises as conveyed to S. D. Meacham by C. C. Goodrich, Administrator of the estate of O. Robinson by deed dated January 3, 1880, recorded in the land records of said town of Newport, in Book 30, page 169, reference to which last mentioned deed and the record thereof is made.

being a part of the real estate whereof the said Samuel D. Meacham died seized and possessed in said town of Newport.

To Have and to Hold the said Premises, with all the privileges and appurtenances thereof, to the said Corintha S. Billings and her heirs and assigns forever, subject to the terms of the aforesaid lease. to her and their own use. And I the said W. S. Robbins, administrator do covenant with the said Corintha S. Billings and her heirs and assigns, that subject to the conditions of said lease, the said Samuel D. Meacham died seized of the granted premises, that I am duly authorized by the Court, aforesaid, to convey the same to the said Corintha S. Billings in manner and form aforesaid, that I have in all things observed the direction of the law, and the license aforesaid, in the sale aforesaid; that I will, and my heirs, executors and administrators shall Warrant and Defend said premises against all persons claiming the same, by, from or under the said Samuel D. Meacham, or me the said administrator, but against no other person.

In Witness Whereof, I hereunto set my hand and seal this 26th day of October. A. D. 19 15

IN PRESENCE OF

E J Smith

Kate W. Hamilton

W. S. Robbins, Adm (L.S.)

Estate of S. D. Meacham L.S.

State of Vermont, Orleans County, ss. } At Newport this 26th day of Oct. A. D. 19 15 W. S. Robbins, Admr. of Estate of Samuel D. Meacham, personally appeared, and acknowledged this instrument, by him sealed and subscribed to be his free act and deed.

BEFORE ME, E J Smith, Notary Public

Town Clerk's Office. A. D. 19 , at o'clock, minutes, M

**THE UNIVERSITY OF VERMONT'S LEASE.** What is now Billings Point was first reserved for the University of Vermont for timber. It had previously been granted to Salem, but due to a mapping error became part of the Coventry Leg. In 1860, the land was leased to Samuel Ryder for $5 a year. After changing hands a couple of times, the lease was purchased by Herbert and Corintha Billings from Sutton, Quebec, for $200 in 1915. Winona Billings inherited the point and retained a camp there until the late 1960s.

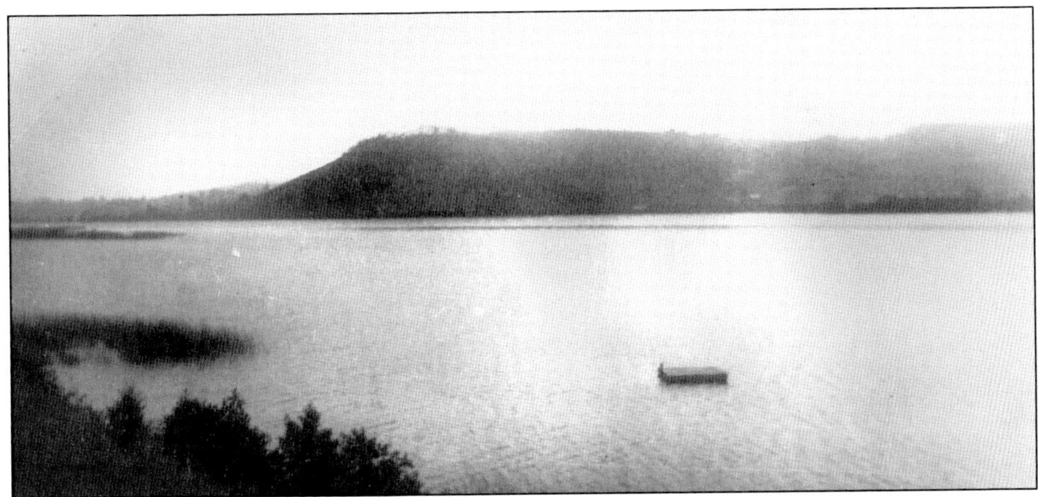

**A VIEW OF BACK BAY.** Originally called the Back Bay, Billings Point became the official name in the late 1950s in honor of Winona Billings and her family, who had lived there since 1904. During the summers, Winnie rented cottages and operated the Newport Youth Hostel for hikers and cyclists at her cottage property. She belonged to the Green Mountain Club and had covered 112 miles of the Long Trail footpath during the 1930s.

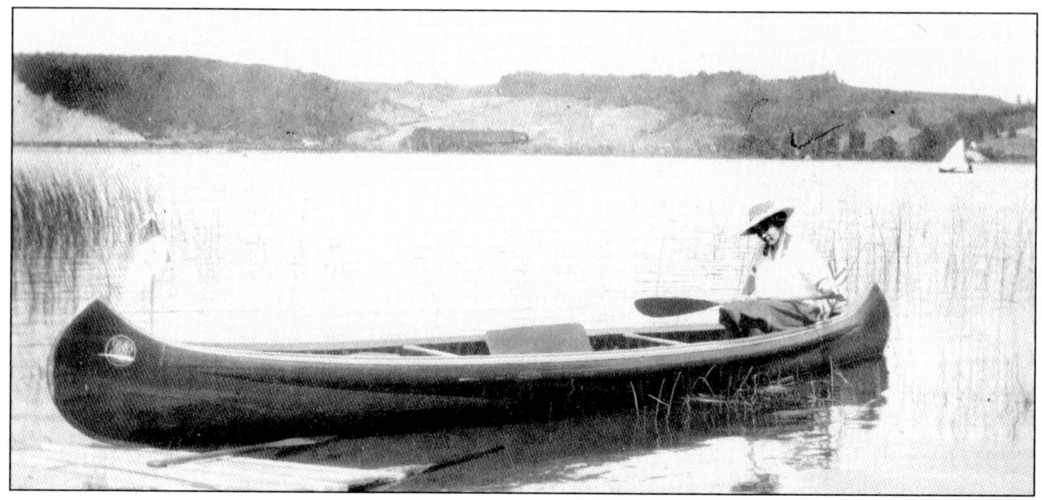

**WINONA BILLINGS.** Sitting in an Immigration and Naturalization Service canoe, Winnie Billings is about ready for a paddle around South Bay. She worked for the service for many years as a stenographer for hearings and as a member of the board with equal voting rights on all questions as to the admission or exclusion of aliens. This was an unusual position for a woman during the 1920s. After holding that position for 28 years, she retired in 1948 at 70 years old.

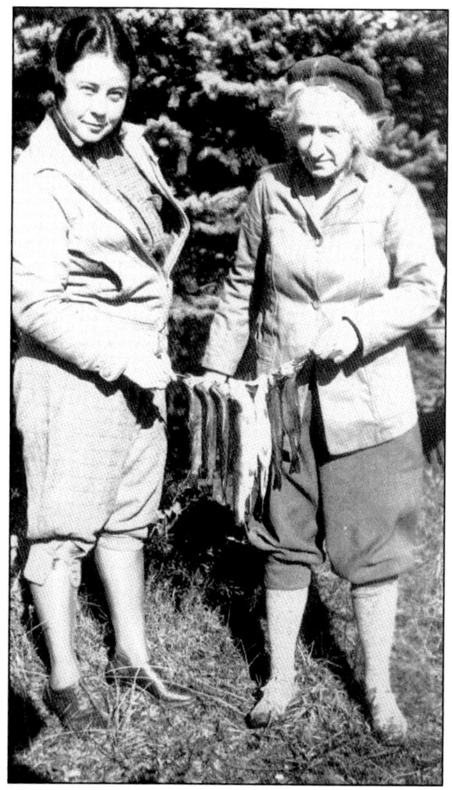

**HER FAVORITE HOBBY.** "My first full day after retirement from the US Immigration and Naturalization, I'm going to go fishing," Winona Billings remarked in May 1948, as she was about to complete 28 years of service with the federal government in Newport. Here, she is with a friend showing off the catch of the day. Billings is pictured on the right. She loved the nature, which honored her partial Abenaki heritage.

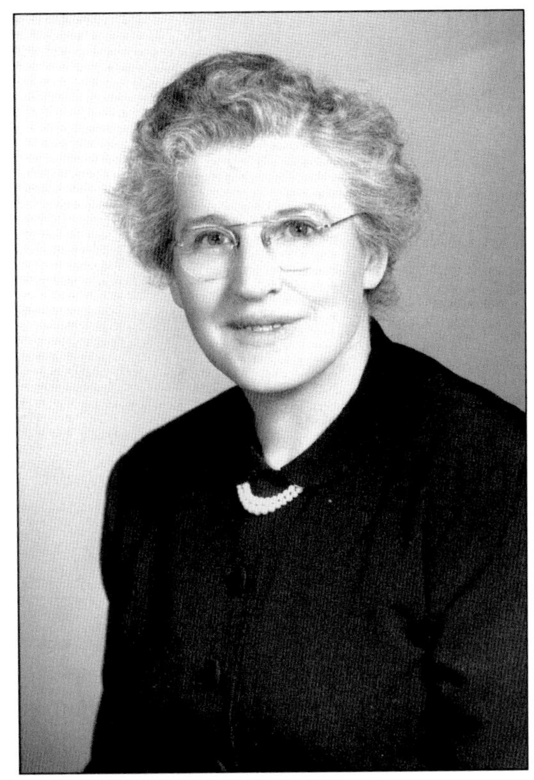

**Flora J. Coutts.** A longtime resident of Newport, Flora Coutts was the cofounder of the Coutts-Moriaty 4H Camp in 1936. She was the first woman to serve two consecutive terms in the Vermont Senate (1937–1939). During World War II, she served with the Red Cross in the China-Burma-India theater. She was the executive director of the Northern Development Association and, from 1961 until the mid-1970s, represented Newport in the Vermont House of Representatives. Flora Coutts died in 1983 at 85 years old and is remembered as a dedicated public servant.

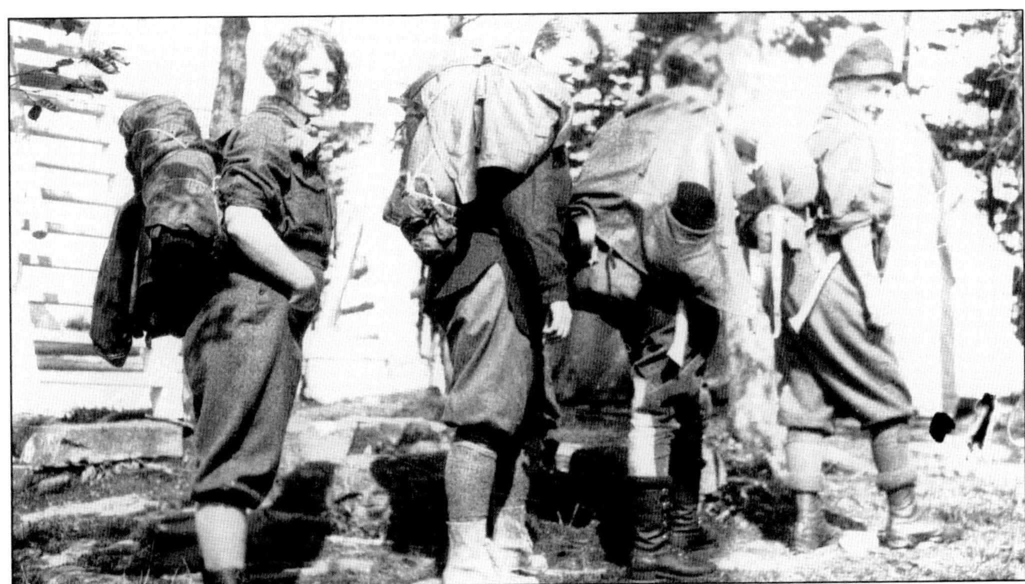

**Good Friends.** Flora Coutts also spent her summers at her South Bay camp on Billings Point; she was a neighbor and good friend of Winona Billings. Like Billings, Coutts was of Abenaki and Scotch descent, independent, and fond of hiking. She was also proud of the fact that she was an "end-to-ender," which meant she had hiked the full length of the Long Trail. In this photograph, Flora (left) and Winona (right) are heading out with friends.

# SOUTH BAY CAMP

## For Boys and Girls

## Lake Memphremagog, Newport, Vermont

South Bay Camp is ideally located in the northern part of the Green Mountain state, on the shore of the South Bay of beautiful Lake Memphremagog, an international body of water, two miles from the city of Newport and six miles from Canada. Well off the main highway, Route 5, yet easily accessible. It is an exceptionally fine summer vacation place for boys and girls from six to twelve years of age.

South Bay Camp is in charge of competent, thoroughly trained people. The spirit is always one of home and good fellowship. The program is planned to help the child in every way to be a well equipped citizen. Swimming is a major activity and instruction is given by recognized Red Cross instructors. Archery, Crafts, Hiking, Outdoor Cookery, Boating, Lawn Games, Long Trail trips and many other activities are included in the program. Tutoring extra.

South Bay Camp is operated by Mrs. Alfred Aldrich of Derby Line, for several years a teacher in Vermont schools and an experienced camp director. Councillors are personally selected for the contribution they will make to the camp program and benefits to the individual campers. Lasting friendships are formed.

The health of the child is carefully supervised. Food is well prepared and wholesome. Activities are all health and character building. Rest hour is regularly observed and welcomed by every camper. A camp nurse makes regular inspection. Parents and friends are requested not to visit during the week nor to bring or send candy, cookies and other articles of food.

The camp opens officially June          . Application for membership must be accompanied by references as to character from pastor or teacher.

Rates are modest. Boys and girls are welcomed by the week, month or season. Rates are $12.50 per week, $55.00 per month and $100.00 for season of nine weeks. A registration fee of $2.00 is asked, this must accompany the application. Rates are paid in advance. Season campers pay one-half down and the balance at the beginning of the second half period. There is no rebate for withdrawal. The following discount applies to the weekly rates when more than one boy or girl registers from the same family: 10 per cent from the total rate for two members from the same family. 15 per cent from the total rate for three members from the same family.

A deposit of $10.00 is requested for the use of the child at camp to cover boat ride into Canada, trips, laundry and incidentals. An itemized account will be kept.

Vacation clothes are worn, no special uniform required. The following list of essentials should be provided for: Vacation clothes, three or four changes of underclothes, plenty of socks, warm sweaters, raincoat or poncho, rubbers or boots, change or two of heavy pajamas, bathrobe and slippers, two swimming suits, towels, laundry bags, woolen blankets, sheets, pillow and pillow slips, sewing outfit, Bible, toilet articles (such as comb, brush, toothpaste and brush, soap, wash cloths.) In addition any equipment that suits the individual taste as flashlight, musical instruments, camera, games, Victrola records, cushions, books, sunburn and mosquito ointment. All articles must be plainly marked with the child's name and a list pasted in trunk cover.

Inquiries can be made to Mrs. A. L. Aldrich, Derby Line, Vt.; Miss Ruth Aldrich, Thayer Academy, South Braintree, Mass.; or Miss Lessel Coutts, 4540 Matilda Ave., Bronx, N. Y.

**SOUTH BAY CAMP.** During the late 1930s and early 1940s, South Bay Camp was attended by both local and visiting campers. This is a camp advertising flyer.

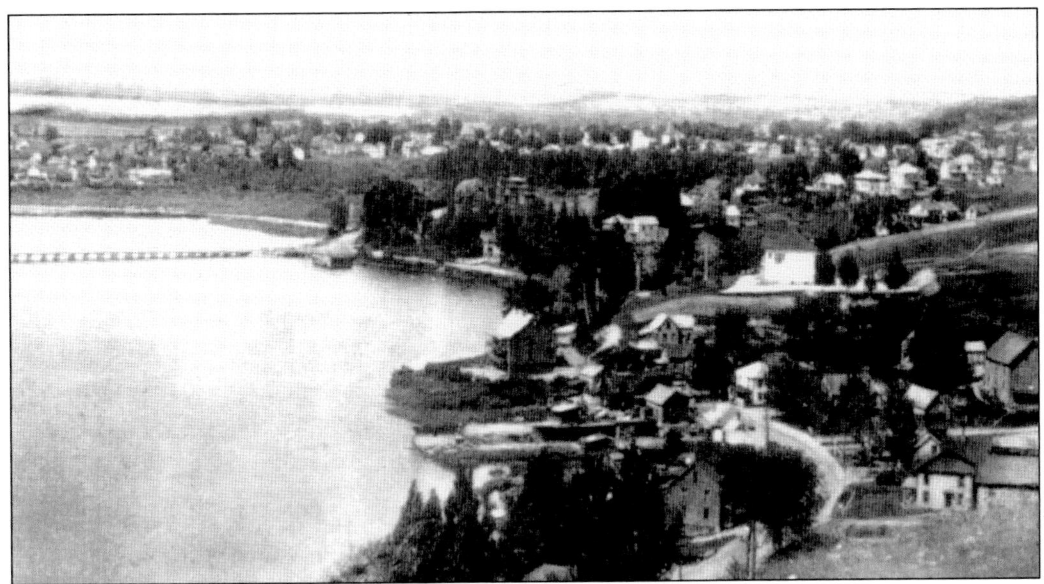

**Glen Road.** On the northeast shore of South Bay quite a settlement grew up around the end of Long Bridge and gradually expanded to include much of the eastern shoreline. At certain times the area was called Stove Pipe City and Glenside but is now known as Glen Road.

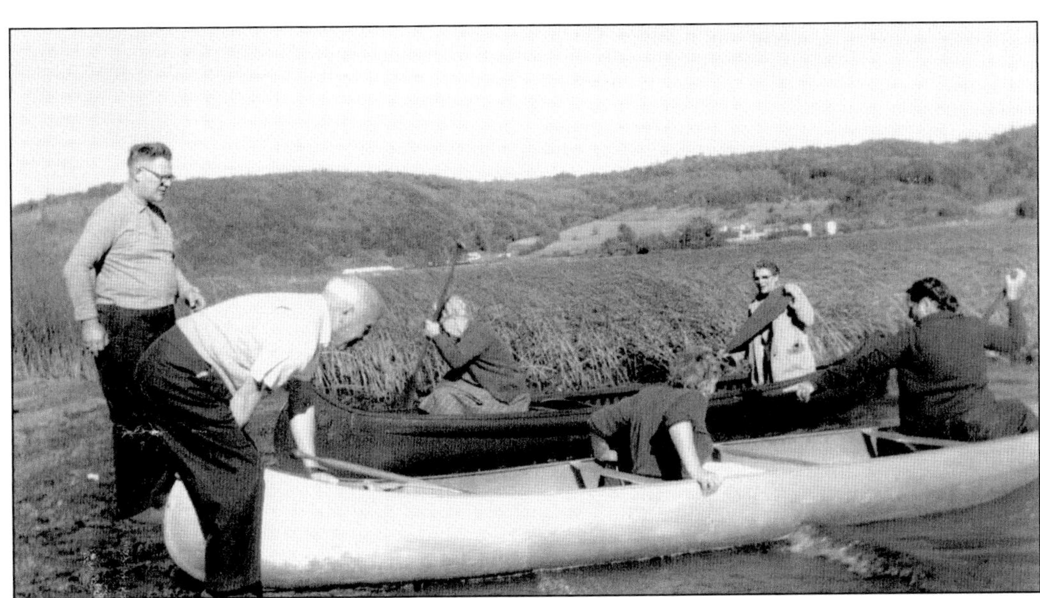

**Young at Heart.** A group of elders relives the "good ole days" with a canoe ride around South Bay. At least three of them are in their 70s. Pictured are, from left to right, Alfred Aldrich, Mr. A. Foster, Alice (Coutts) Aldrich, Flora Coutts, Ann (Coutts) Aldrich, and Mrs. A. Foster.

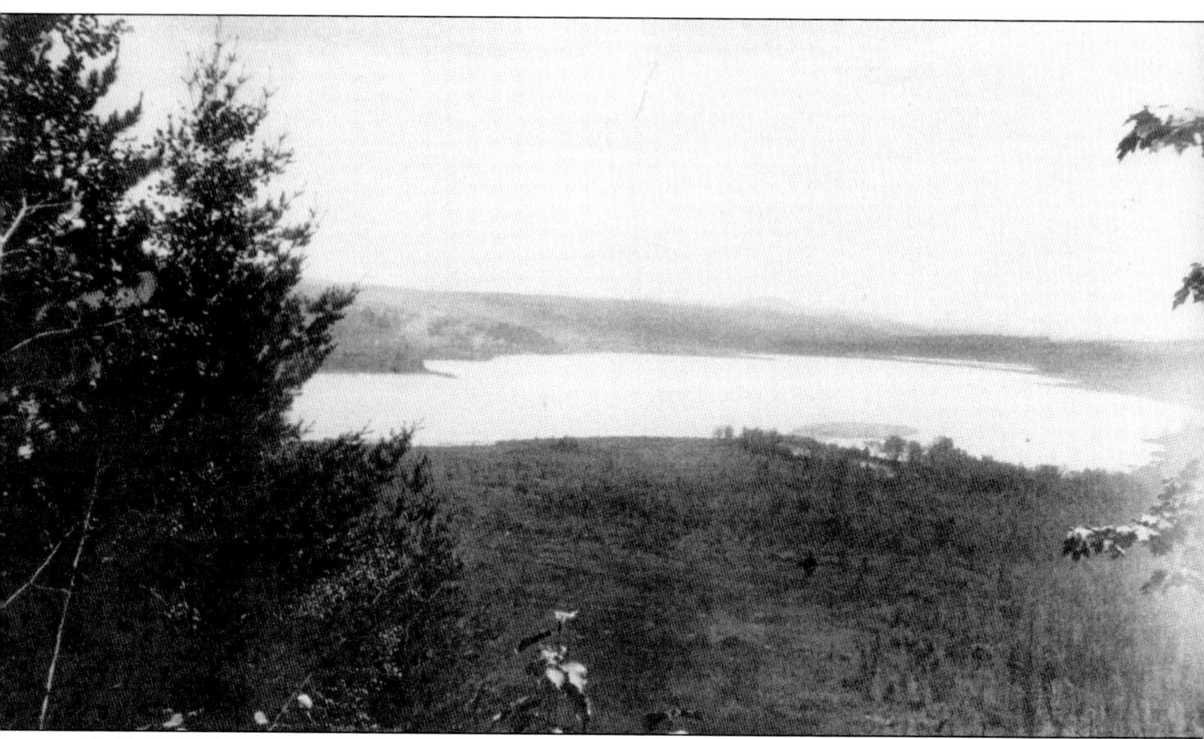

**A View of South Bay.** This wonderful view of the southern end of South Bay shows, with a bit of imagination, the refuge area and wetlands where Lake Memphremagog has its beginnings. One can imagine the view of wilderness thousands of years ago, when the Native Americans first ventured into this area.

# *Three*

# DUNCANSBORO

In 1781, the Vermont General Assembly granted a peninsula of dense wilderness at the head of Lake Mamlabegwok, or Memphremagog, to Nathan Fiske, George Duncan, and associates. The charter states the following:

> The General Assembly of the State of Vermont do hereby give and grant to Nathan Fiske and George Duncan and associates the tract of land situate in the county of Orleans, and known on the Surveyor General's map of the state by the name of Duncansboro. The inhabitants of said township shall plant and cultivate five acres of land, and build a house at least 18 feet square on the floor, on penalty of forfeiture if not so settled and cultivated. Given and granted by the Act of the General Assembly bearing the date the 26th day of October one thousand seven hundred and eighty-one.

The first dwelling was built in 1793 by Dea. Martin Adams. In 1800, there were 11 families. It is said that these first families came upriver from Barton and decided to settle because the frosts had not destroyed the crops around the lake. In 1802, the paperwork was in progress at Montpelier, and the township was officially chartered in September 1803. In October 1816, West Derby and a portion of Coventry were annexed, and the town of Duncansboro's name was changed to Newport.

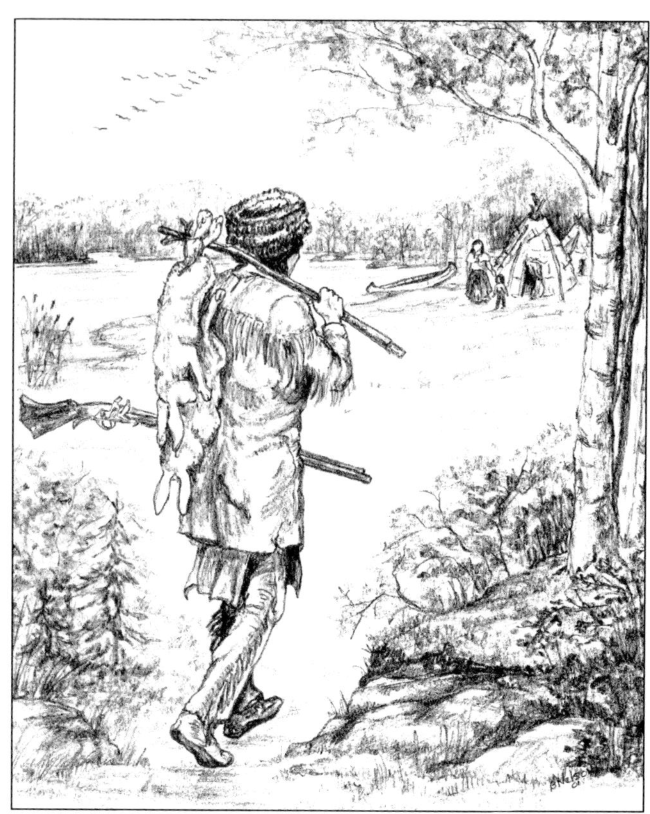

**ONLY RABBITS.** During the postcolonial period (1781–1945), settlement activities caused game animals to become nearly extinct, and the rapid growth of pasture and farmland caused deforestation along the shores of Lake Memphremagog. The fur trade collapsed, and traditional hunting and fishing territories were taken over or lost to progress. Many small enclaves of local Abenaki tried to cling to their lifeways and retain traditional seasonal activities at temporary camps for sugar making, hunting, and fishing.

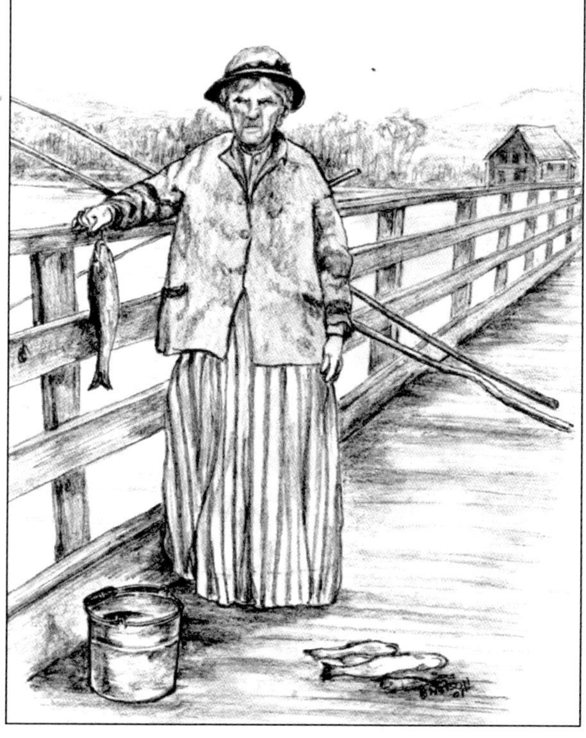

**AUNT SALLY.** At age 78, Sarah Horton, or "Aunt Sally," as she was called, made her living by selling the fish she caught from Long Bridge. During the 1800s, many Abenakis adapted to town and rural life, surviving as laborers, guides, housekeepers, and farmers. Being Indian was unsafe, so in order to hide in plain site, intermarriage with whites was commonplace. Some retained their cultural identity, while others hid their heritage even from their own kin. Many Abenaki were assimilated into European families.

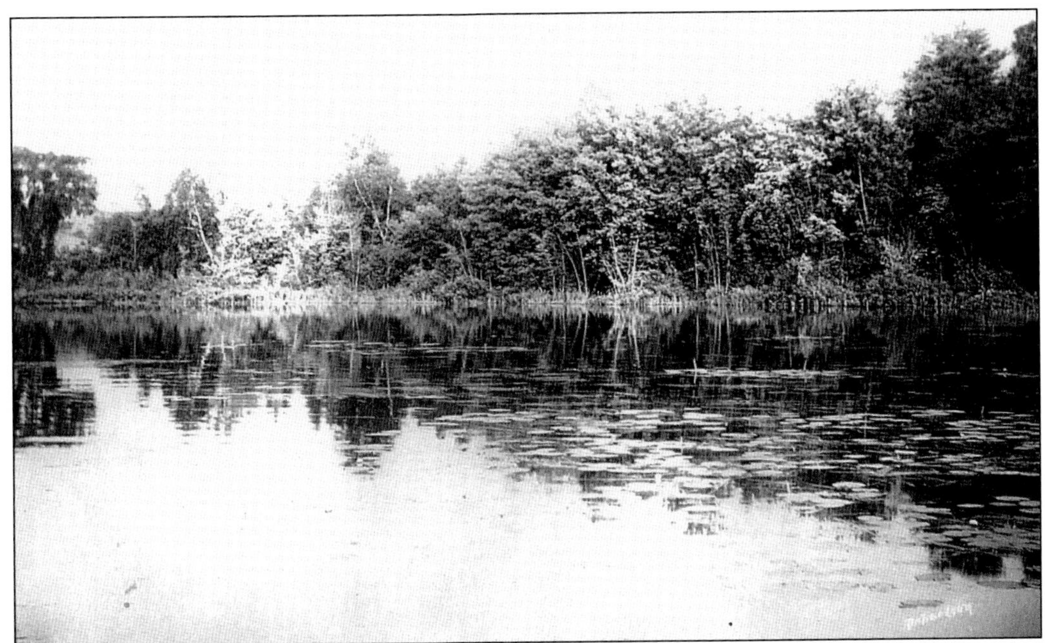

**The Horse Ferry.** In 1814, Judediah Richardson lived on a farm near Pendar's Cove on Indian Point. He applied for and obtained a charter to run a horse ferry from the bluffs, then called Derby Landing, to a landing in Duncansboro, now Whipple Point. Richardson's horse ferry ran for 10 years, and the landing became known as Richardson's Landing. That portion of West Derby became annexed to Newport in 1917.

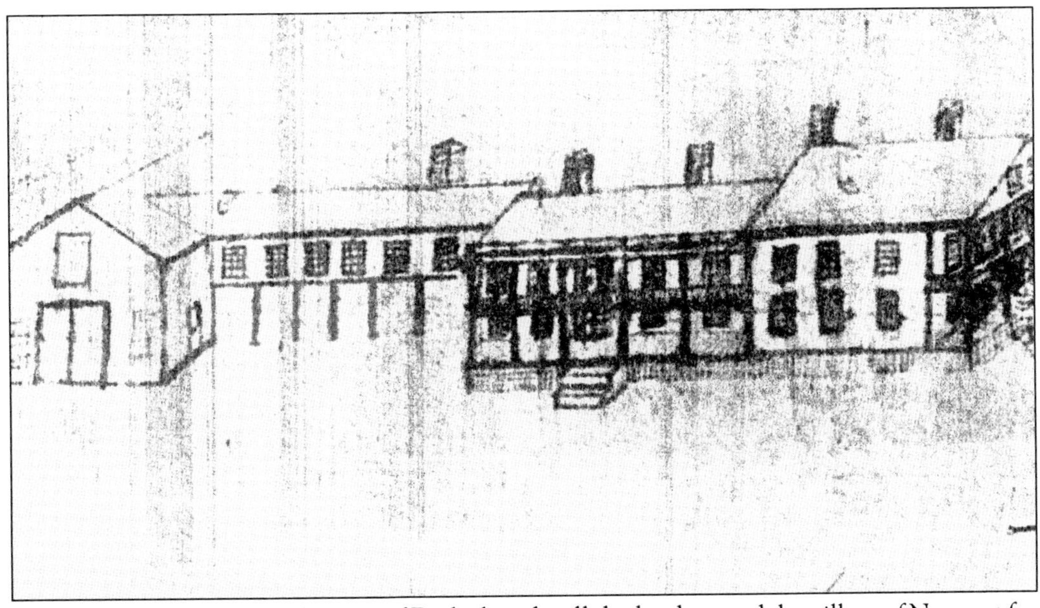

**George Smith.** In 1820, John Sias of Derby bought all the land around the village of Newport for $250. In 1828, he sold the same land to George Smith, who married Sias's daughter Sally. Smith built a log cabin for a lumberman's camp to clear the land for future homes and businesses. This log cabin was moved across the street and used to build the first stages of the Memphremagog House in 1838.

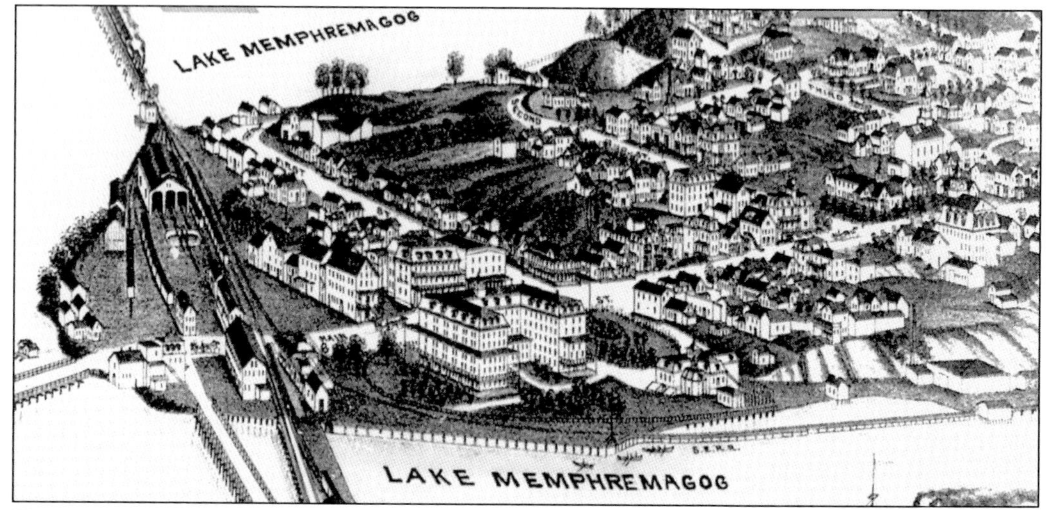


**THE MEMPHREMAGOG HOUSE.** George Smith sold the Memphremagog House, which he had begun constructing in 1838, to Phineas Page in 1845. Page began building the second stage, which was a two-story addition. This hotel was the first structure on Main Street in Newport. In 1858, Phineas Page sold the Memphremagog Hotel to Simon and Samuel Pendar for $3,000. The Pendar brothers added the fourth story and piazzas, a third phase of the hotel's construction. Again, in 1861, the hotel changed hands and was purchased by the Passumpsic Railroad, resulting in the addition of a train station and a passenger ticket office in the basement.

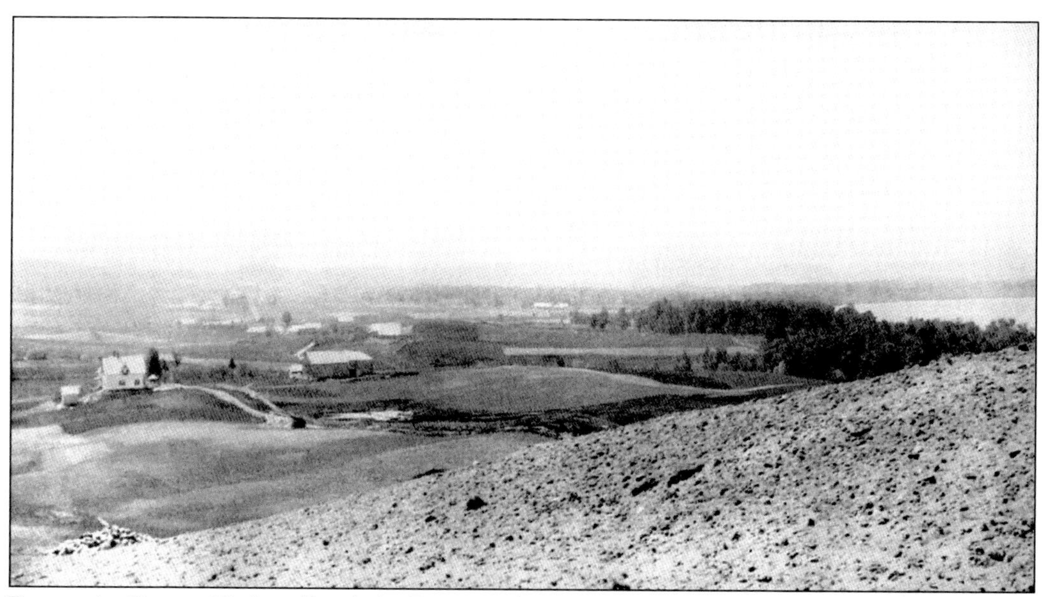

**PENDAR'S FARM.** Today, Pendar's Farm is known as the Prouty Beach and recreation campgrounds, bordering Pendar's Cove, Lake Memphremagog, and Scott's Farm and Cove. Here, the Pendar brothers farmed the land, raising a large variety of fruits and vegetables to serve in their Memphremagog Hotel dining room. The Pendars owned the hotel from 1858 to 1861, when they sold it to the Passumpsic Railroad.

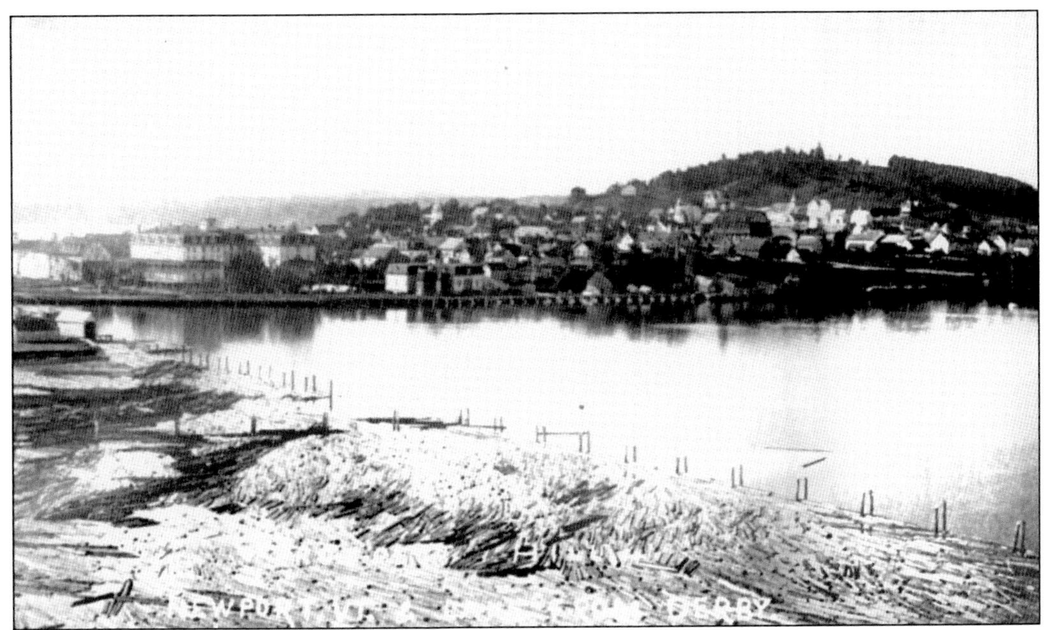

**The Last Stage.** The final proprietor of the Memphremagog Hotel was George Goode, who purchased it c. 1890. In 1891, Goode felt that more sleeping rooms were needed, so he added the French roof. In this photograph, the hotel with the French roof is shown in the middle left. Also visible is Prospect Hill, before St. Mary's Catholic Church was built. The massive number of logs floating in the foreground illustrates the lumber industry's importance to the Memphremagog region. On May 7, 1907, a fire burned the Memphremagog Hotel and destroyed another one of the Newport and lake landmarks.

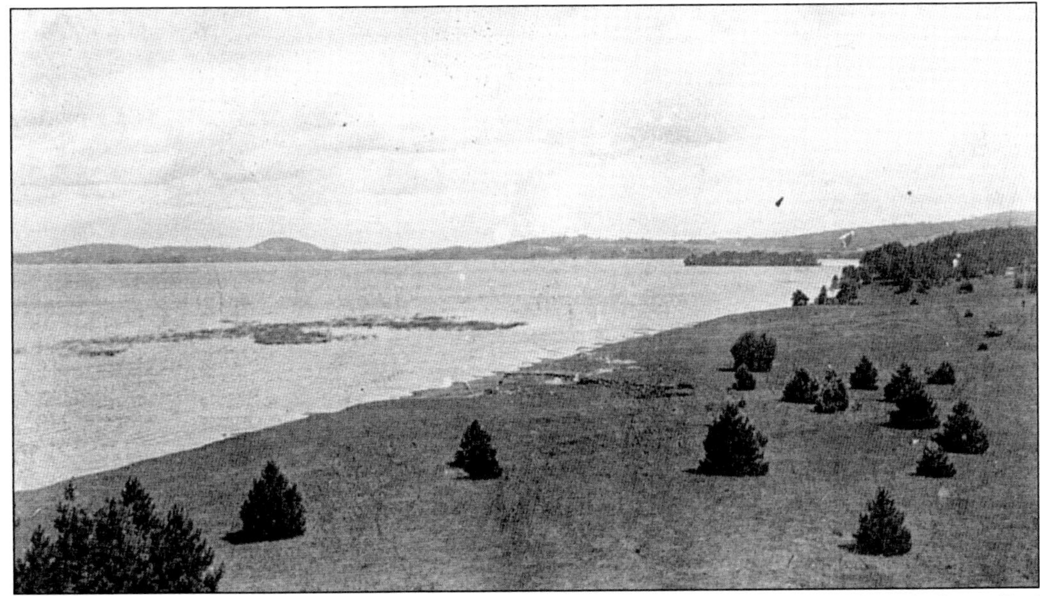

**The Bluff's Legacy.** In 1868, Nathaniel Ball purchased 75 acres of farmland, including all of the land to the end of Indian Point. He eventually sold the land to Charles F. Bigelow, including what was known as Knowlton's Bluff, located on the north side of Indian Point and in view of Horseneck Island.

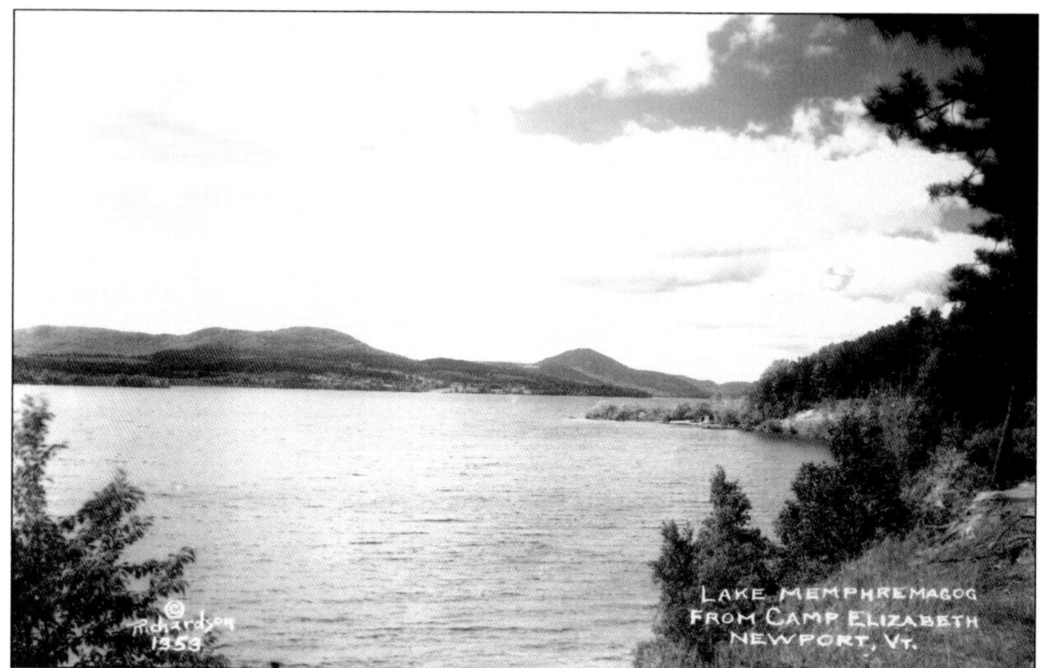


**THE BLUFFS.** In October 1906, William George Scott of Compton, Quebec, bought Ball's old farmland from Charles Bigelow. It was on the south side of the bluffs, which he named Bluffside Farms. This farm still remains in the Scott family generations later and is the only working farm left in the city of Newport.

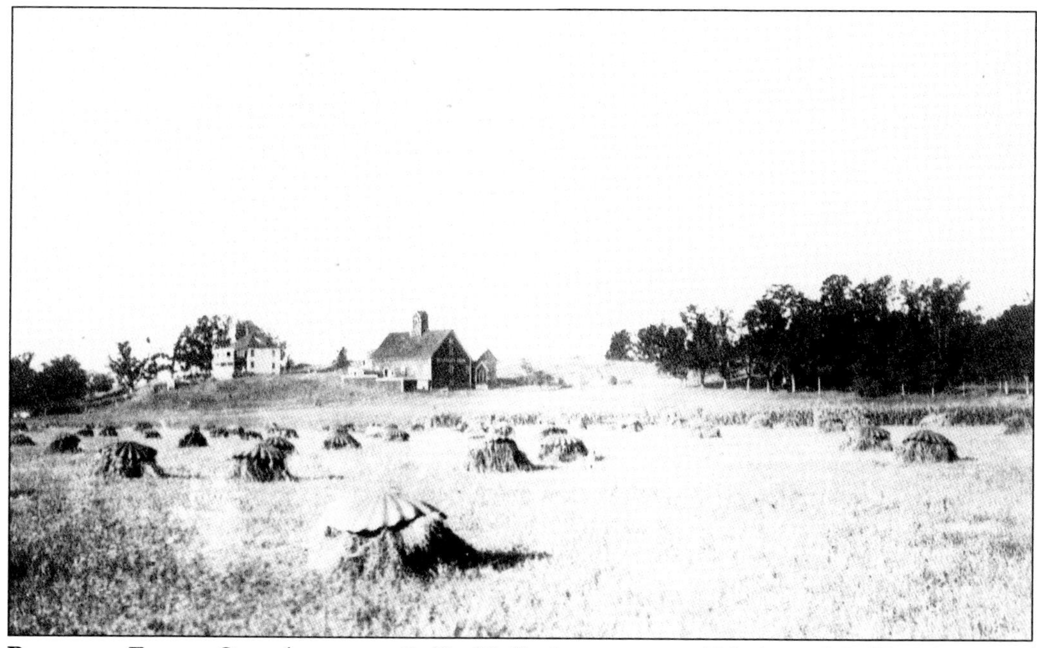

**BLUFFSIDE FARMS.** Once known as Ball's Bluff, this portion of Nathaniel Ball's 75 acres of farmland was leased out into lakefront lots for summer cottages. Today, this scenic farm is known as Bluffside Farms and has been passed on from generation to generation since William James Scott purchased it in 1906.

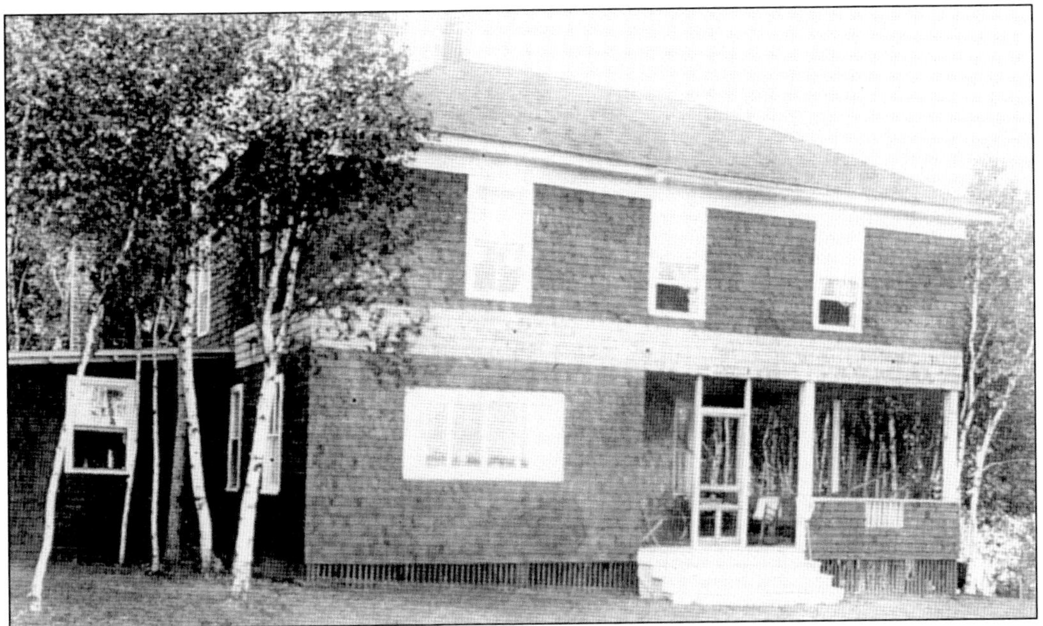

**BIRCHMERE.** A two-story summer cottage with a broad veranda and all of the modern conveniences was built by Charles F. Bigelow between 1902 and 1903. On July 18, 1903, his daughter Beatrice Amy's ninth birthday, the family moved into their summer home on the bluffs overlooking Lake Memphremagog and the mountains of Vermont and Canada.

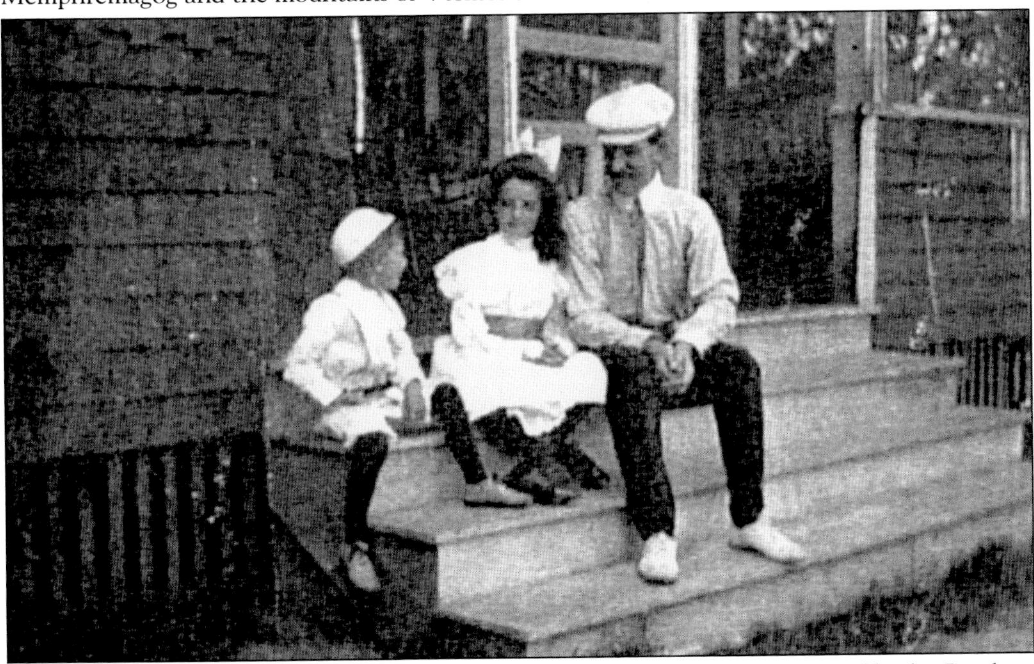

**THE CHARLES BIGELOW FAMILY.** Sitting on the steps of Birchmere Cottage are Charles Bigelow, his son Rudolph, and his daughter Beatrice Amy. Other cottages nearby were owned by the Roots of Second Street, Ralph Hamlett of Main Street, Dr. Harry Hamilton, George Frost of the Frost Veneer Seating Company, Judge Alfred of School Street, Dr. O.B. Gould, and Edgar J. Prouty of the Prouty & Miller Lumber Company.

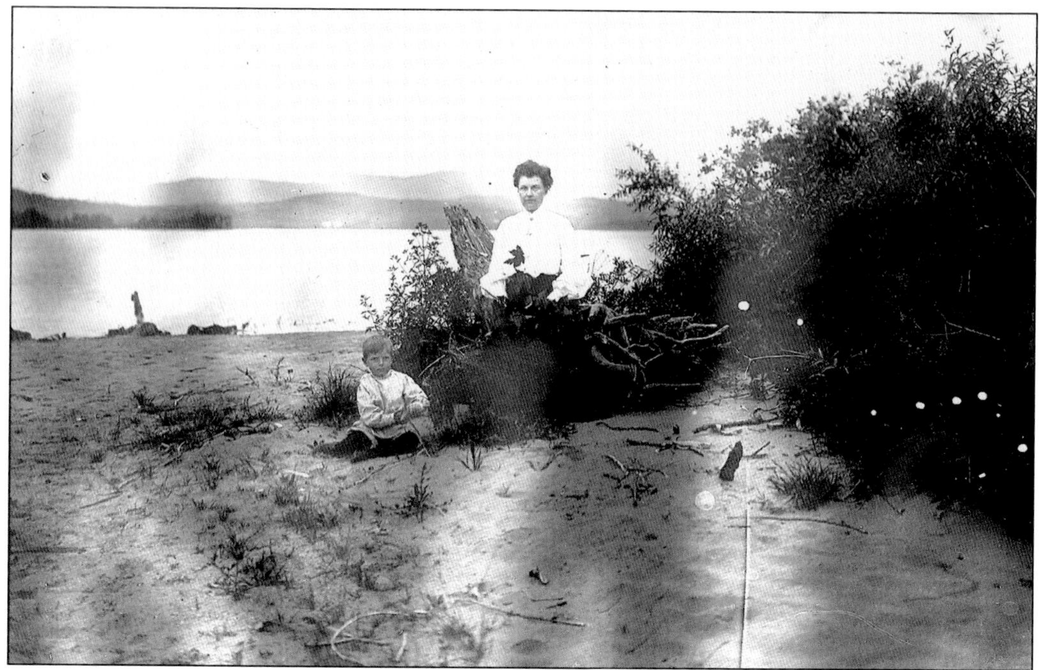

**BIRCHMERE BEACH.** Mabel Hall married Charles Bigelow in 1893. He was born in Georgeville, Quebec, the son of Ezra and Mary (Bullock) Bigelow. Here, Mabel is on the beach at Birchmere Cottage with her son Rudolph. Rudolph married Helen Savage, and they had two sons, Charles and Robert.

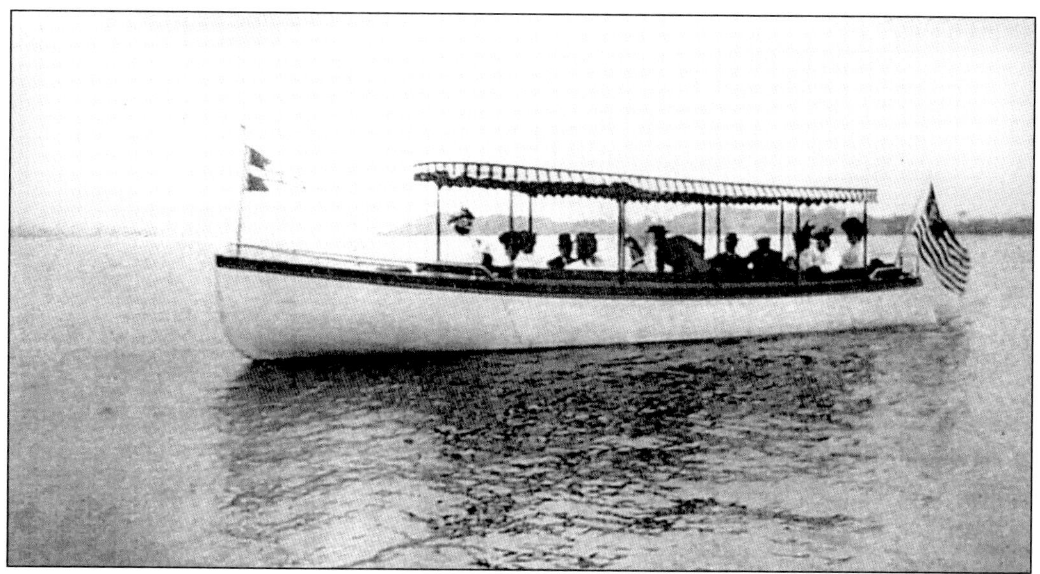

**THE QUEEN MAB.** Charles Bigelow named his steam launch after his wife, Mable. It is seen here on the lake in 1904. Today, the *Queen Mab*'s boat bell can still be heard on the bluffs coming from the family's summer cottage, where several more generations of Bigelows still enjoy summers. Once, stagecoaches crossed the lake here by horse ferry to the Old Ferry Road, way before the arrival of the Balls, Bigelows, and Scotts.

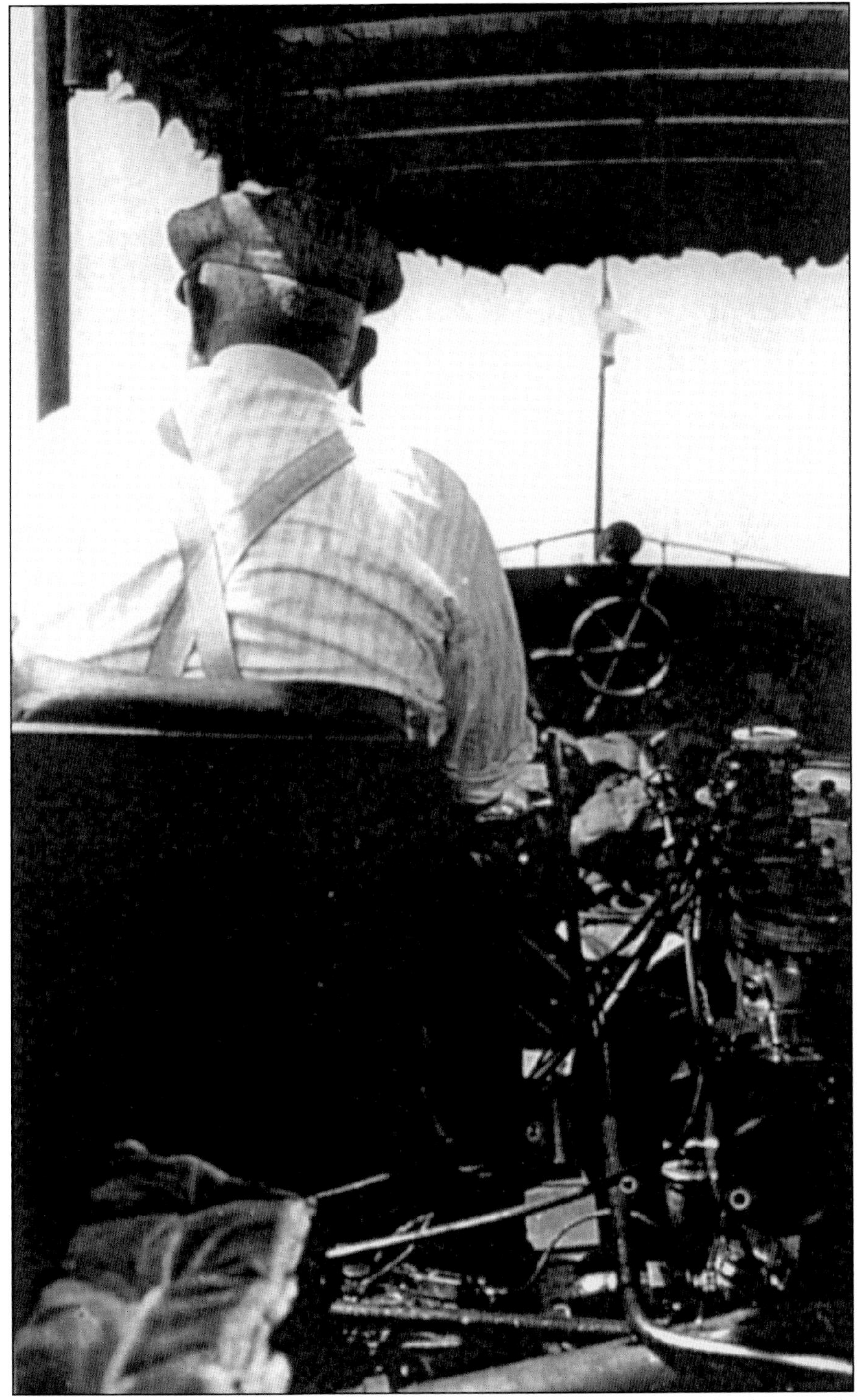

**CHARLES R. MOORE.** The engineer Charles Moore (1863–1933) invented the first combination storm and screen door here in Newport in 1893. In the early 1900s, he bought Bigelow's *Mab* steam launch and renamed it the *Mountain Maid*.

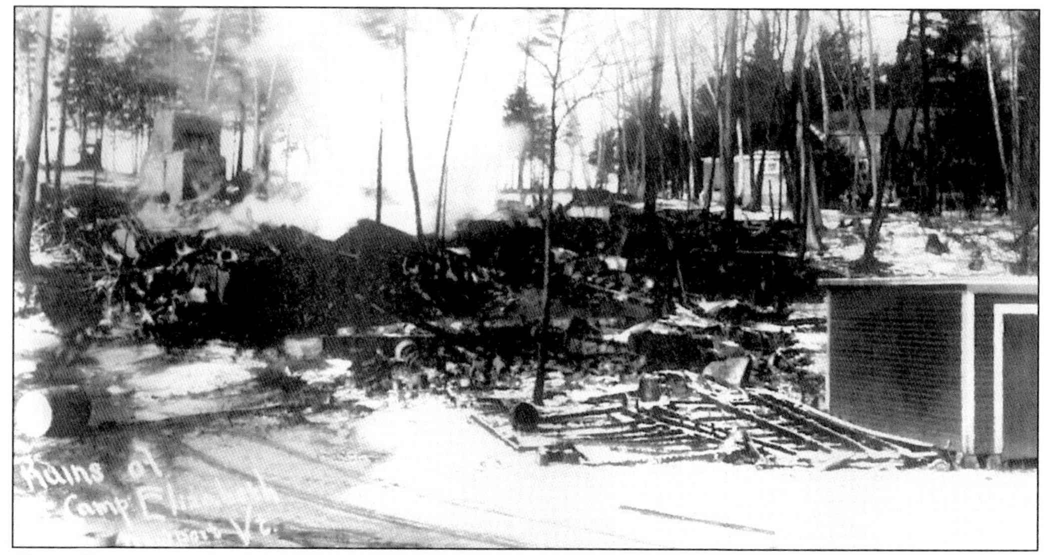


**CAMP ELIZABETH.** In the early 1900s, Frank Flint owned a cottage on the bluffs called Sunnyside nearby his popular summer resort. In 1933, the three-story, 40-room hotel burned to the ground and was later rebuilt as a resort on a smaller scale. In 1938, Kenneth Roberts, the author of the novel *Northwest Passage*, drove from Maine to Camp Elizabeth to see the beauty of Lake Memphremagog and Indian Point, which was a turning point in his book.

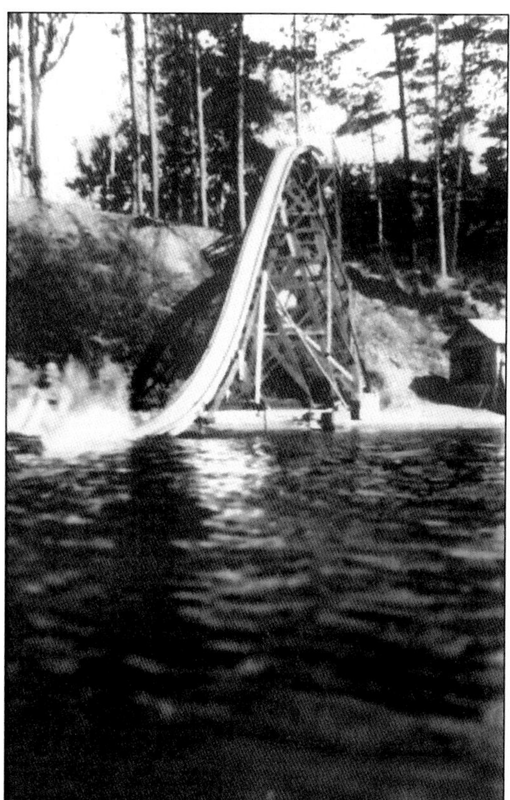

**THE TOBOGGAN SLIDE AND CHUTE.** Camp Elizabeth, on the bluffs of Indian Point, was frequented by summer residents and resort guests. One of the feature attractions was the resort's toboggan slide, which was also used for winter sports. George Frost, an industrialist of the Frost Veneer Seating Company at Prouty Bay, helped build the chute. Frost owned two cottages near Camp Elizabeth and was very proud of "his lake."

*Four*

# THE INTERNATIONAL BORDER

The Memphremagog region is divided by the boundary line that separates two great countries: the United States and Canada. Along this imaginary line, except where it cuts through the forests, there are columnar markers on land and island to indicate its position. But that is where the division ceases. Americans and Canadians share identical interests and cultural heritage. The first survey of the area was conducted in 1767 in order to mark a division between Canada and the Province of New York. In 1772, a line was again drawn incorrectly. It had been decided to use the 45-degree north parallel of latitude, which marked the midpoint between the equator and the North Pole, even though it was uncertain where the exact location was into the 1800s. A survey taken as late as 1908 still showed the existence of minor errors. The demarcation crosses the lake at Province Island, but the shore towns of both countries are unanimous in their love of their Great Lake.

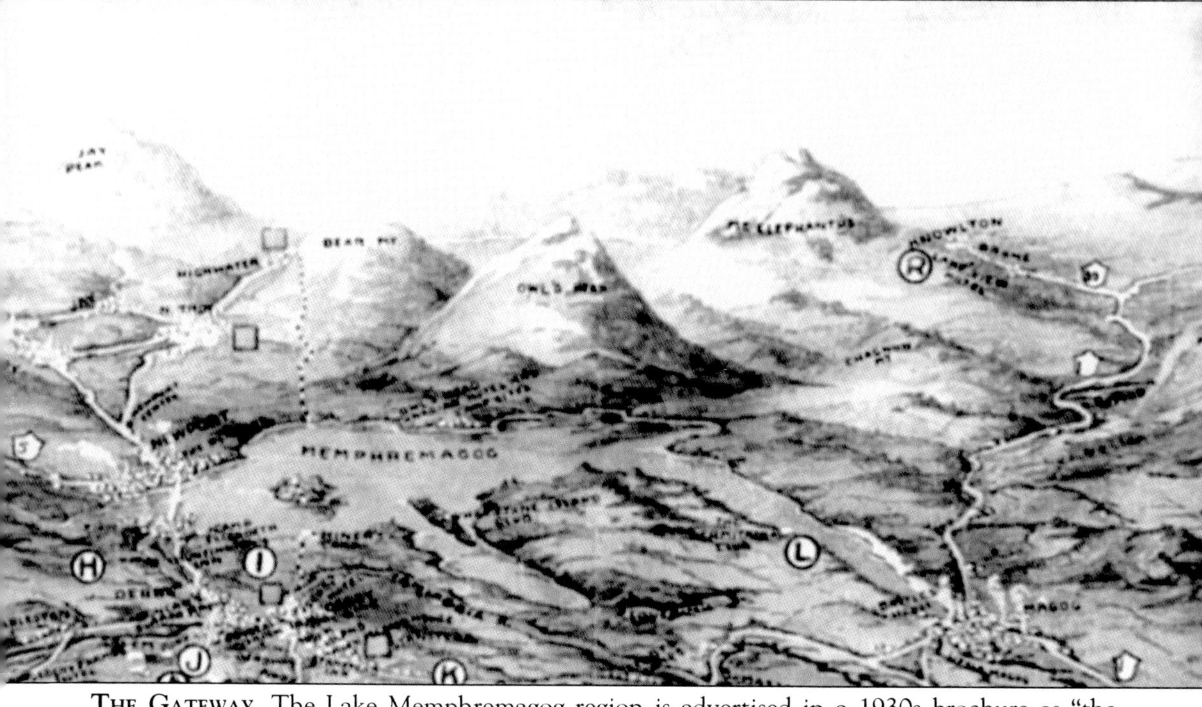


**The Gateway.** The Lake Memphremagog region is advertised in a 1930s brochure as "the Canadian Gateway to Northeastern Vermont—The New Arcadia." Those on the American side would call it "the American Gateway to the Eastern Townships of Quebec." This is a portion of the brochure's map.

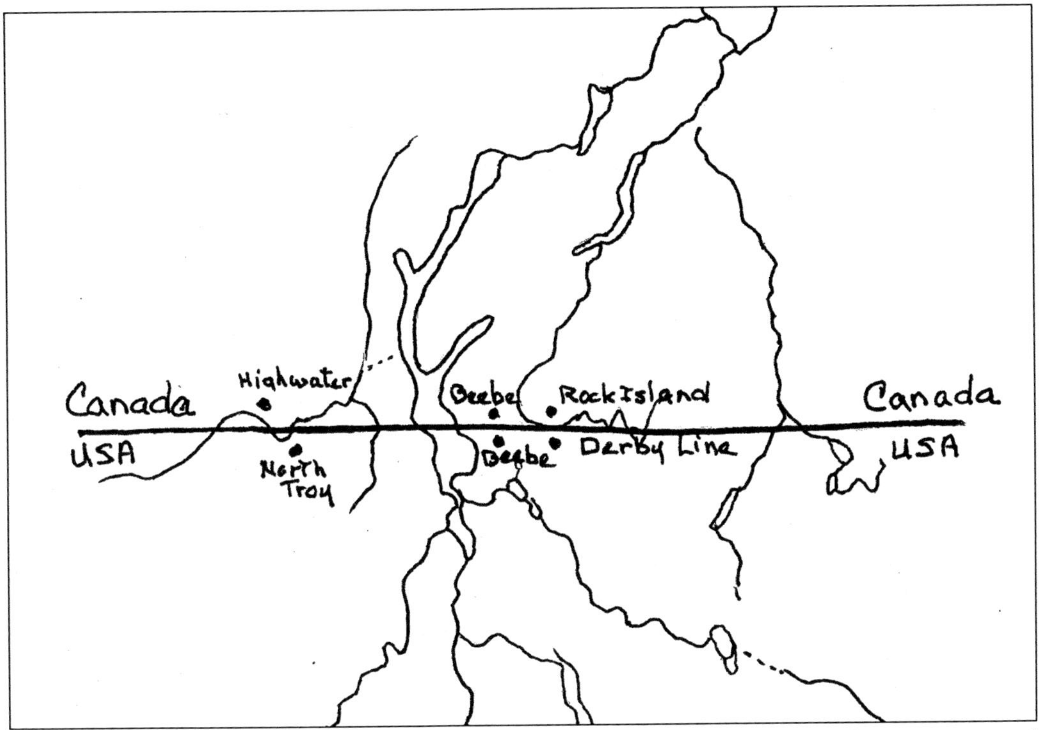

A MAP OF THE BORDER. Shown here are the border towns and their locations around Lake Memphremagog.

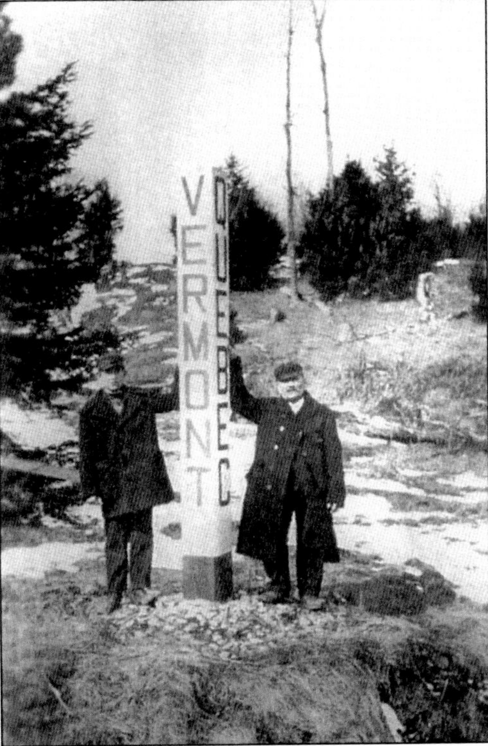


MARKERS. The international border between Vermont and Canada was established along the 45th parallel. In 1772, a surveyor's mistake had this line passing through Province Island one thousand feet too far south. On August 8, 1842, the error was corrected, and a boundary marking post was installed on the east shore of Memphremagog, where it still stands today. To mark the position of the instruments, a survey station rock can be found on a ledge near the lake. It reads, "Captain Robinson, Astronomical Station 422 feet north of the boundary line and 595 feet south. August 1845."

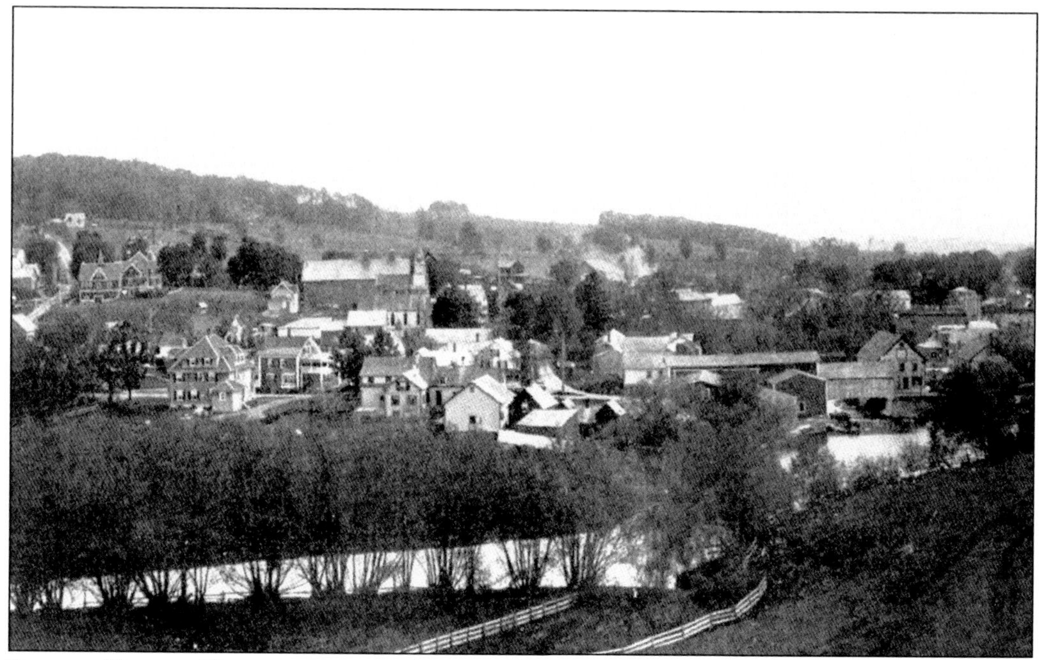

**Border Towns.** The communities that straddle the Vermont-Canada border are called the three villages or the border towns. Derby Line, Vermont; Rock Island, Quebec; and Beebe, Vermont and Quebec, are the border towns whose economies and culture are shaped by their residents living in harmony.

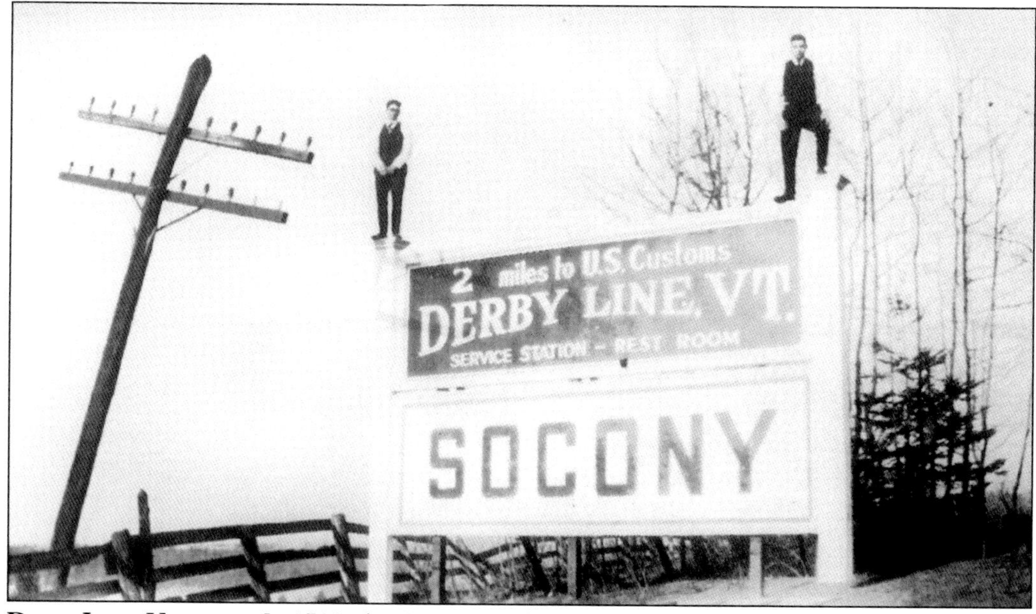


**Derby Line, Vermont.** In 1798, the Continental Congress mandated that revenues be collected in order to raise money for the new independent government. The first customs office was located in a wooden building between Derby Line and Rock Island, which at that time was on one of the very few roads through northern Vermont. In this photograph, the Willey brothers show-off atop a border advertising sign.

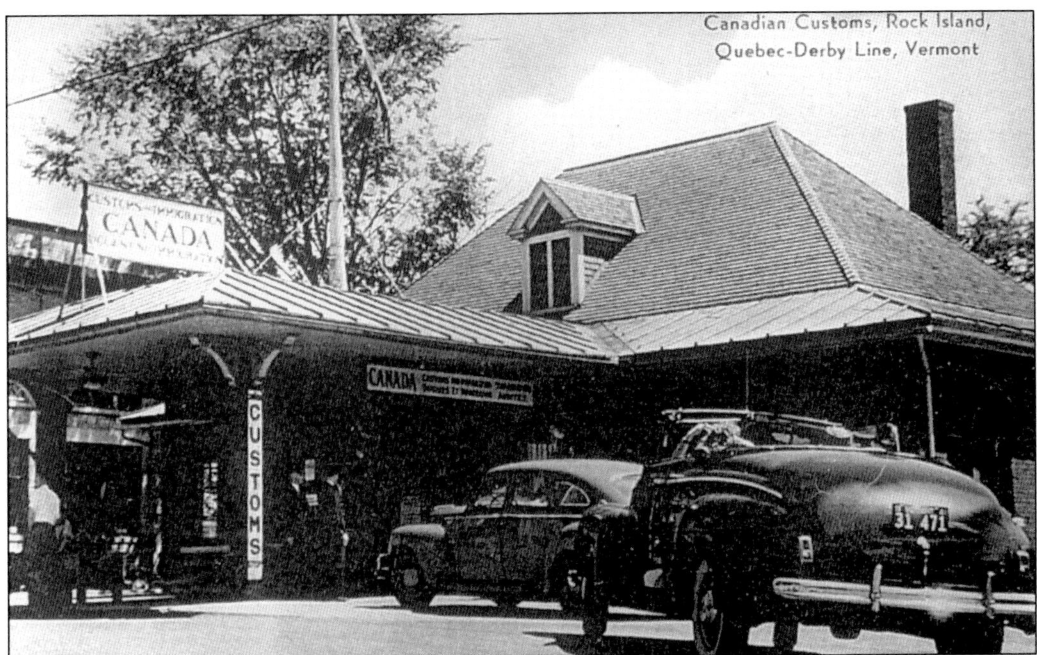


ROCK ISLAND, QUEBEC. The Rock Island customs and immigration building is in downtown Rock Island and handles most of the local people who frequently shop, bank, and socialize in both communities. In the early 1900s, several businesses and factories were located on or very near the border. Butterfield Tap & Die had shops on both the Canadian and American sides. There was also the temptation to carry across ready-made illegal goods such as alcohol and tobacco.

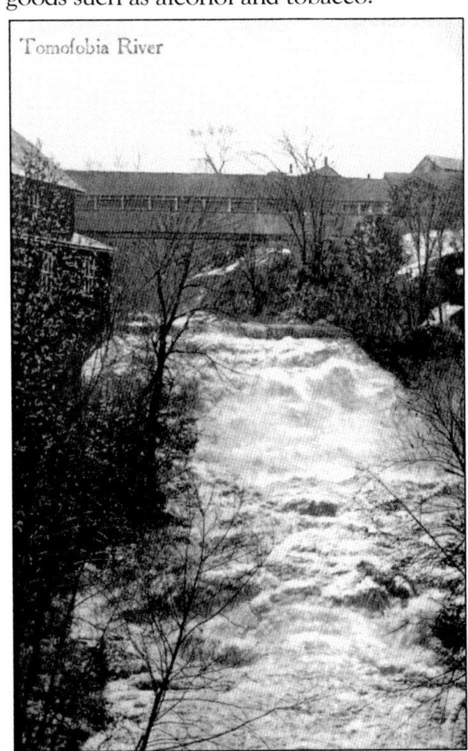


THE TOMIFOBIA RIVER BRIDGE. The swift-running Tomifobia River flows between Canada and the United States at the Derby Line-Rock Island border crossing. It was once spanned by the long covered bridge pictured above. As one entered Canada from Derby Line, he traveled down the steep hill, through the bridge at the bottom, and on to the Rock Island customs house before climbing another hill into Stanstead.

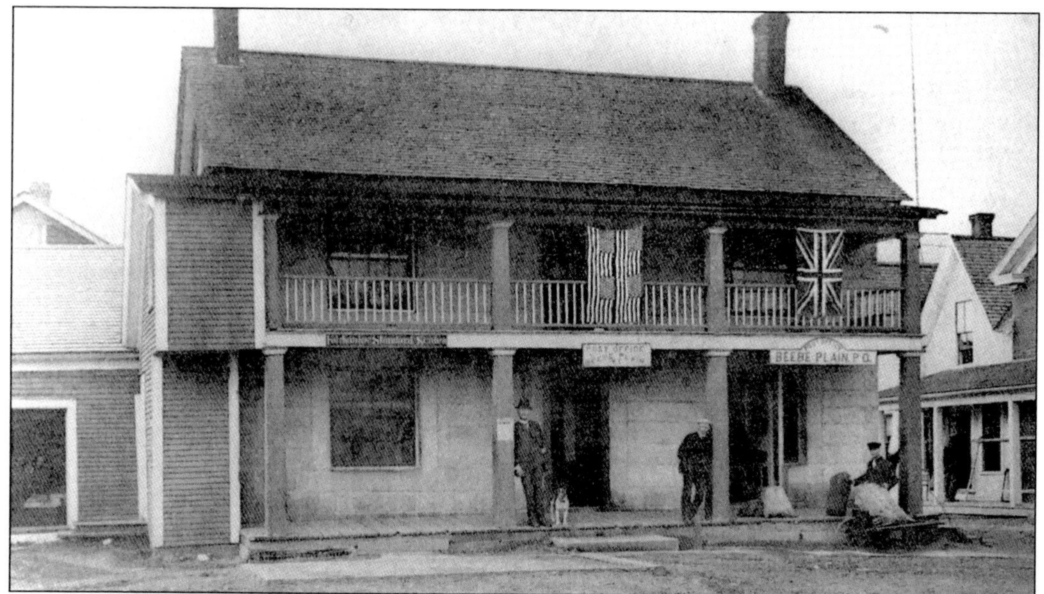


**THE POST OFFICES.** When the boundary was drawn and surveyed, it was discovered that the village of Beebe, part of the Derby Township, was no longer a single village but instead two separate towns in two different countries. One of the adjustments that had to be made was the establishment of separate post offices. The solution was to build a wall and cut out a space to hang another door. The population still considered itself one community.

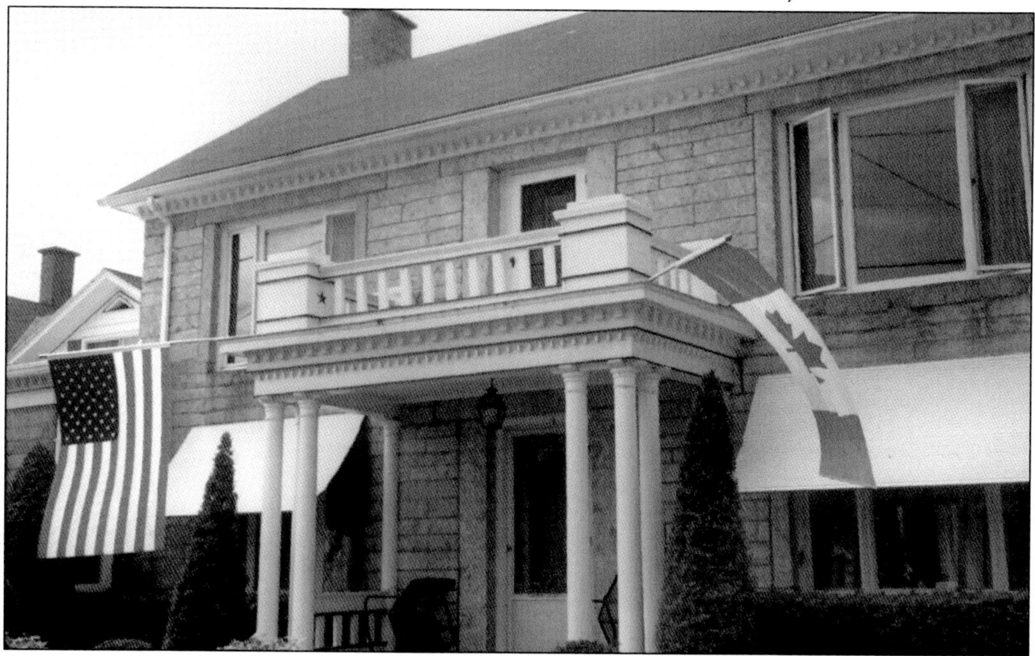

**BEEBE, VERMONT, AND BEEBE, QUEBEC.** In an unusual situation, the international border runs down the center of a residential street in Beebe. The street runs west toward Rock Island; the houses on the north are in Canada, and those across the street are in the United States. The street was named Canusa more than 50 years ago to illustrate the situation. This house is on the corner of Canusa Street, the friendliest unguarded border in the world.

**People Without Borders.** Mamlabegwok at the big waters was at the heart of the Abenaki homeland and served as a crossroads for travel and trade. The Abenaki, or the St. Francis Indians, did not acknowledge kings or governments and were caught between English and French claims of possession, religious fervor, and agendas. The international border disrupted their way of travel and separated the Alnobak's traditional homelands into allied fronts, even though they were left out of the treaties.

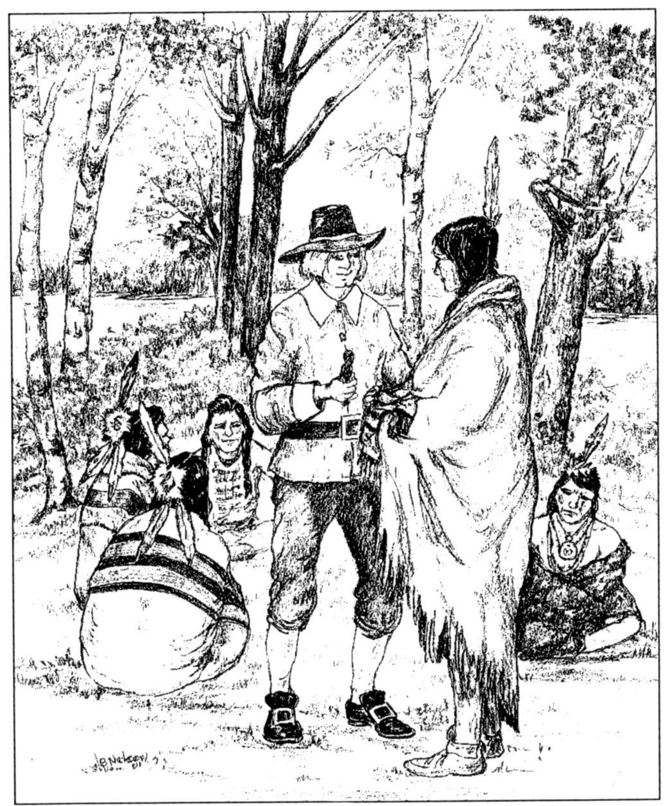

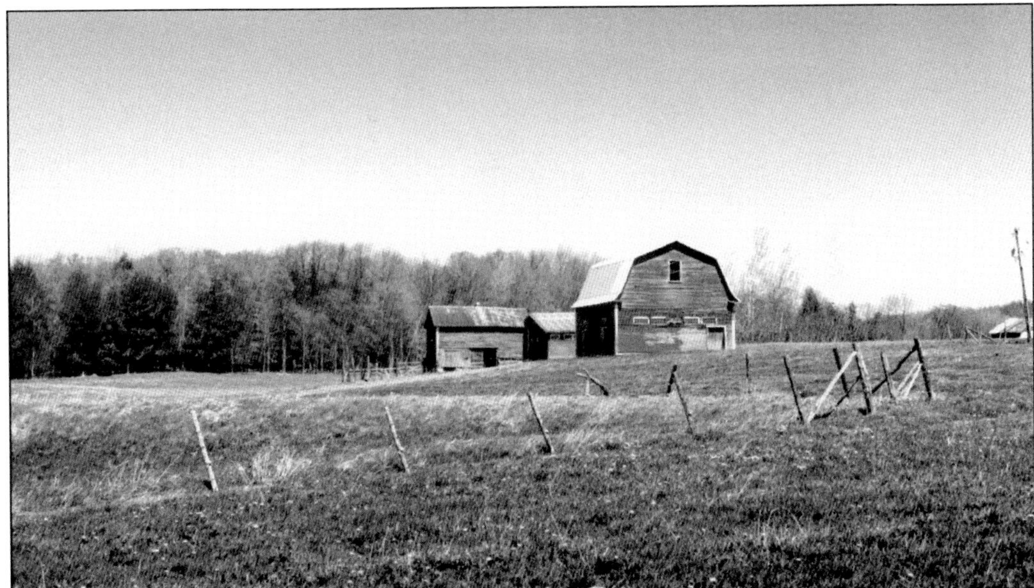

**North Derby.** The most northern portion of the township of Derby includes Eagle Point, which borders the international boundary. The Eagle Point Farm was originally the Parker Farm, located on what was set aside in the earliest days for the support of the minister of the gospel. It was called "Minister Land," and the arrangement was that the land would be taxed at 5¢ an acre.

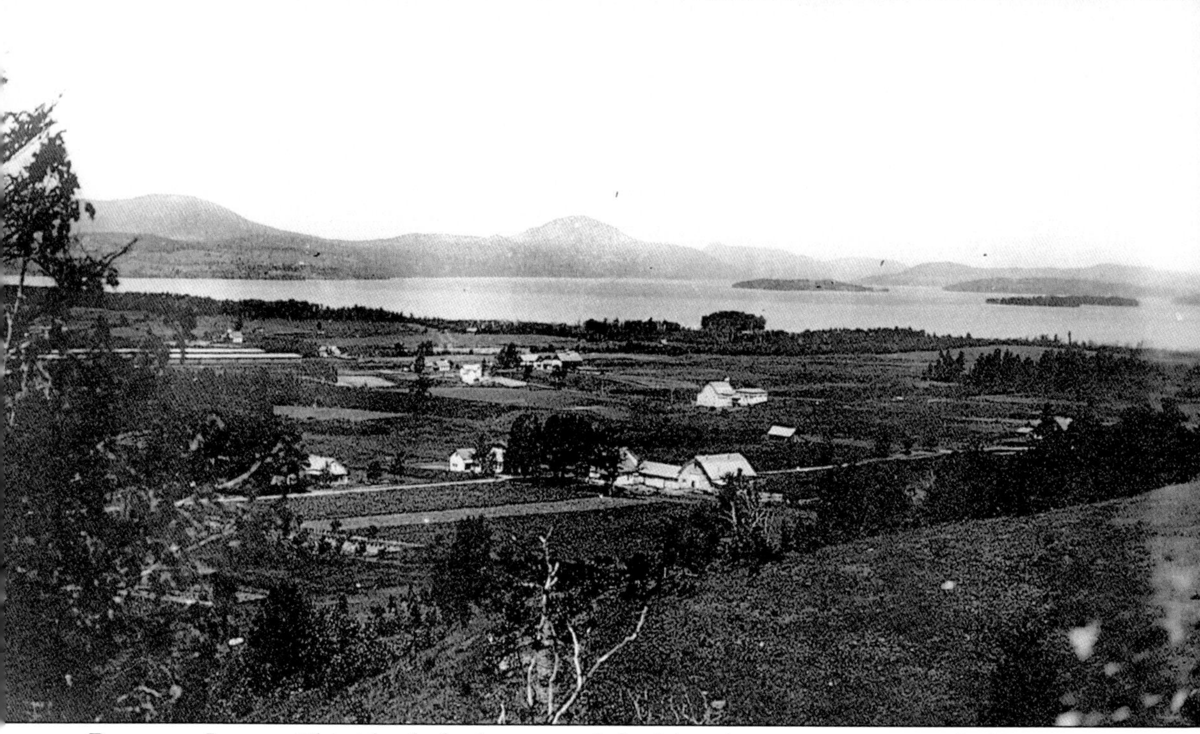

**Province Island.** This island, the largest on Lake Memphremagog, consists of 100 acres cut by the 45th parallel, the international border between Canada and the United States. One-third of the island lies in U.S. waters and is located six miles north of the city of Newport. In the background is Mount Elephantis, named for its resemblance to a sleeping mastodon with an outstretched trunk, to the left of Owl's Head Mountain. In the front of Province Island are Belle and Black Islands.

**An Inventor in a Border Town.** Henry Seth Taylor was born in 1833 in Stanstead, Quebec. He was a jeweler and the inventor of a horseless carriage known as the Steam Buggy. It was a self-propelled, two-seating, wood-burning steam boiler that predated the motorcar by 25 years. Taylor exhibited his Steam Buggy in New England and eastern Canada, where it often frightened horses, children, and old ladies. In 1875, Taylor lost control on a hill because his invention was not designed with brakes. (Courtesy of Stanstead Historical Society, Canada.)

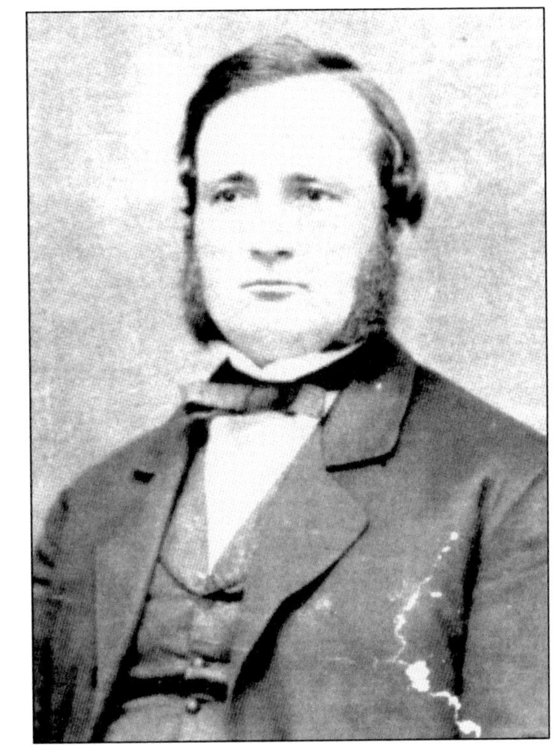

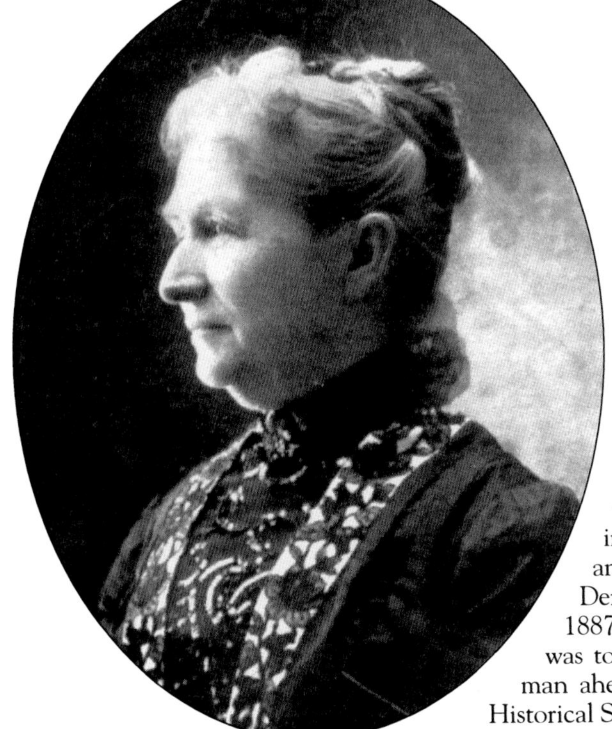

**Jeanette Taylor.** The second wife of inventor H.S. Taylor was Jeanette (Clark) Taylor. They had three children: Harriet (born in 1865 in Canada), Charles (born in 1869 in Vermont), and Grace (born in 1879 in Canada). In 1879, Henry purchased land in Stanstead, Quebec, and moved his wife and family back across the border from Derby Line, Vermont. Henry Taylor died in 1887 on the verge of the motorcar era that was to revolutionize transportation. He was a man ahead of his time. (Courtesy of Stanstead Historical Society, Canada.)

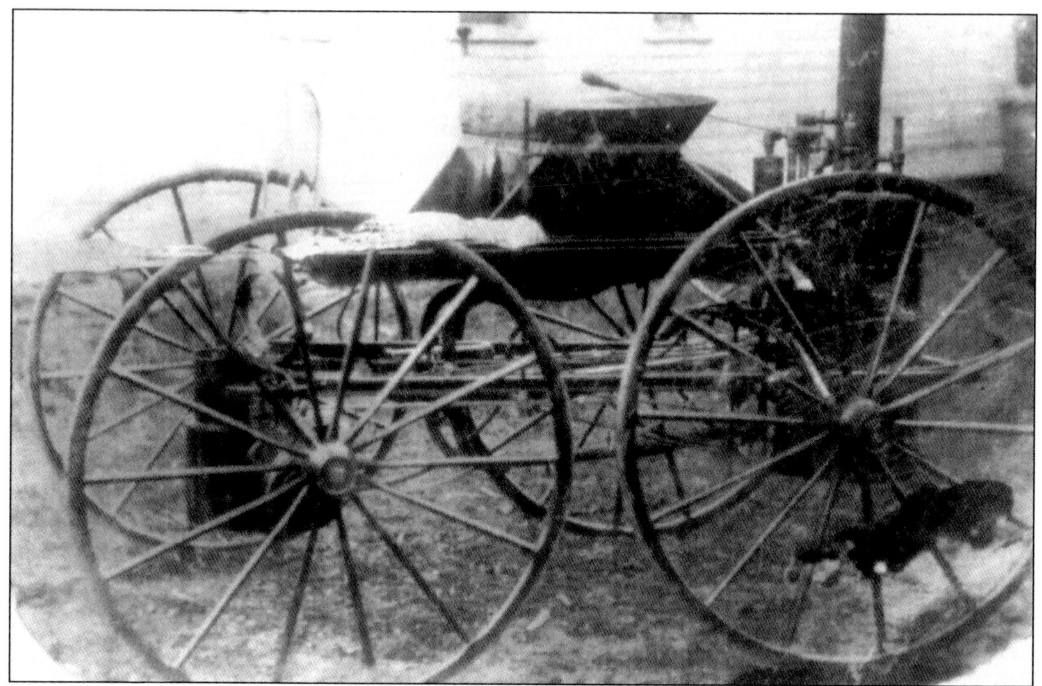

**The Horseless Carriage.** Canada's Steam Buggy was exhibited at the Stanstead Fairgrounds in 1867 and was met with more scoffers than admirers. When steam clouds enveloped both Taylor and the buggy, crowds drew around to view this "magician's trick." After his accident in 1875 resulting from the lack of brakes on the vehicle, Taylor took the shattered buggy back to his barn and hoisted it into the loft to be forgotten. In 1965, Canada's oldest horseless carriage was restored and sent to the Ontario Center of Science and Technology in Toronto. (Courtesy of Stanstead Historical Society, Canada.)

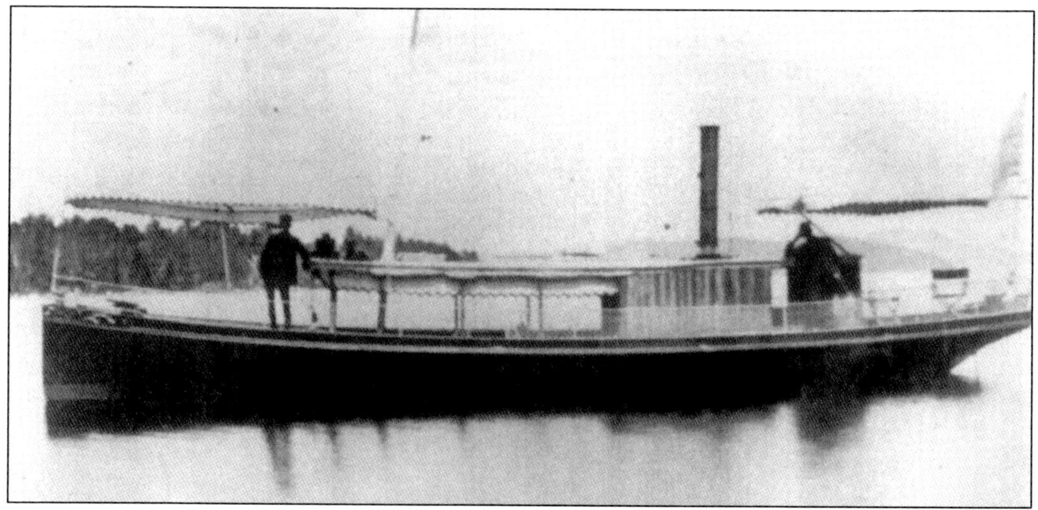

**The Gracie.** In 1877, Taylor used the boiler from the Steam Buggy stored in his barn to create an elegant steamer yacht that could accommodate 25 to 36 people. He named it the *Gracie*. It was 50 feet long and 10 feet wide, with deck chairs and a scalloped awning. After use on Lake Memphremagog for 11 years, it was sold in 1888 and placed on Lake Winnipesaukee, New Hampshire, to be used as an excursion yacht. (Courtesy of Stanstead Historical Society, Canada.)

# *Five*

# THE EAST SHORE

The earliest east-shore settlers and their neighbors on the Canadian side had a hard time of it. There were no gristmills or sawmills nearer than West Derby and the nearest blacksmith was in Brownington. When they first built their homes and made their pitches, neither boards nor nails were available. The settlers had to adz the logs for floors and cover their cabins with bark or fasten shingles with wooden pins. Glass windows were a rarity. In order to grist their grain, they had to row to Duncansboro, shoulder their bags, and carry them a couple of miles to the mill in West Derby. The lands on the northeastern shore were not yet chartered in 1800. The settlers who made improvements, supposing they would be allowed to retain them, were surprised when the authorities in Quebec made grants of these lands to Sir Robert Milnes and others. Not until 20 years later were the claims finally settled at $1 to $4 an acre, the supposed value of the land in the wild state. Eventually, settlements and villages sprang up all along the east shore and on the west shore of the long arm of Fitch Bay, Lake Park-North Derby, Cedarville, Magoon Point, MacPhearson Bay, Jewett's Point, Georgeville, Hermitage, and up to Magog at the outlet.

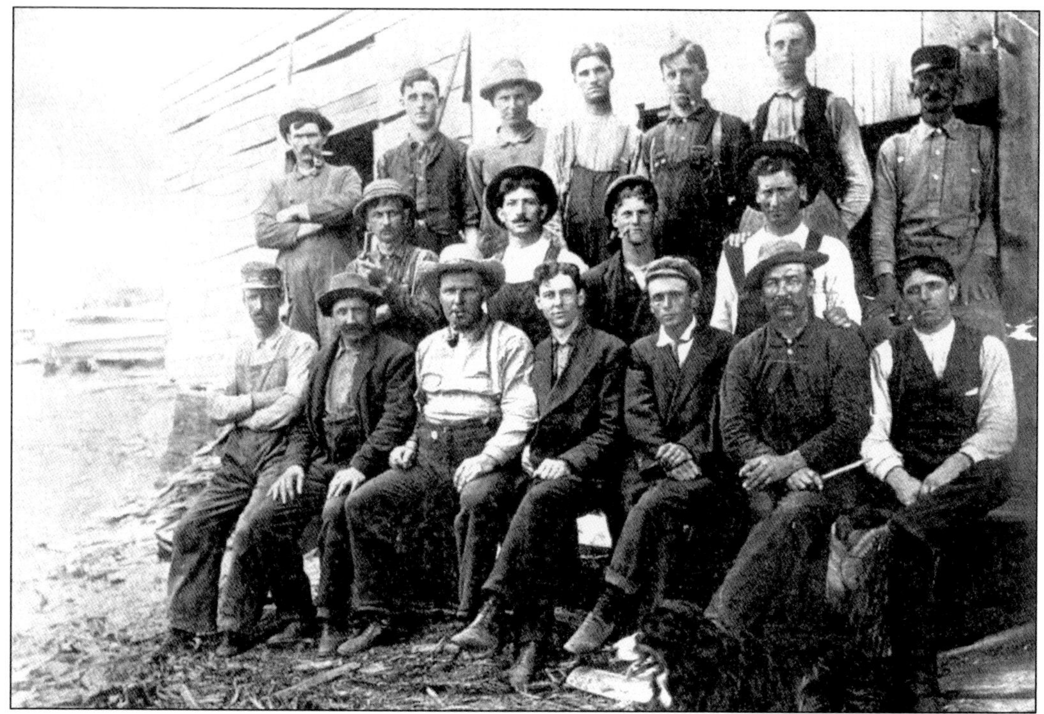

**The Beach's Mill Crew.** Beach's Sawmill in North Derby was owned and operated by Nathan A. Beach of Magoon Point. In 1906, his logs were boomed from Magoon Point to North Derby. This mill crew photograph was taken in 1907. Pictured, from left to right, are the following: (front row) ? Mosher, Sam Wheeler, ? Belknap, ? Bean, ? Renihan, John Wheeler, and ? Gardine; (middle row) ? Haskell, Joe Pete, Clarence Blanchard (with pipe), and ? Barnes; (back row) ? Huce, ? Reinehand, C. Copp, Henry Saule, ? Molton, ? Bern, and ? Renihan.

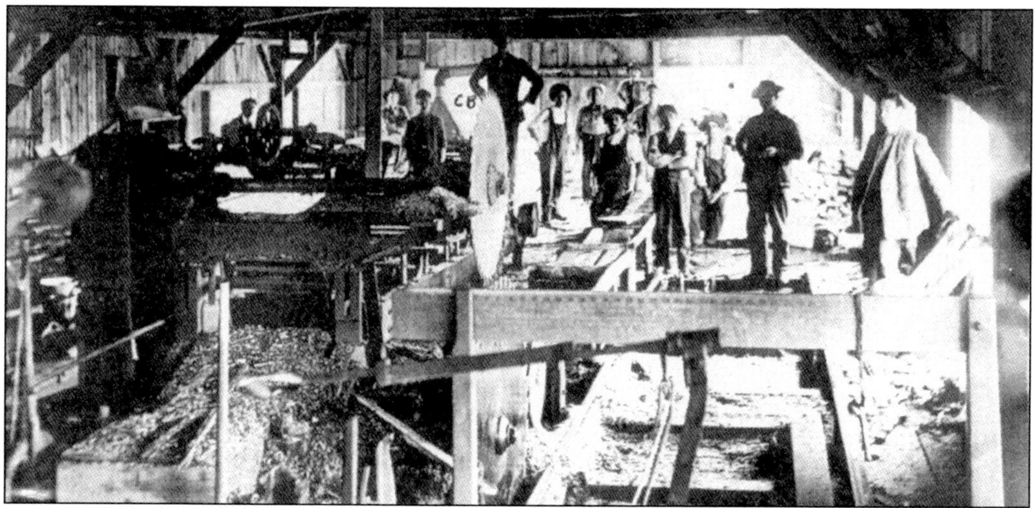

**Beach's Sawmill.** C.C. Blanchard stands behind the saw blade of the mill in North Derby. On July 7, 1910, the mill, with a large quantity of lumber, burned. The watchman reported that he had gone through at 11:00 p.m., but by morning, the mill, valued at $10,000, was a total loss and nothing but a heap of ashes. Beach's daughter Ruth Illingworth said that the fire was started by sparks from the Boston & Maine train.

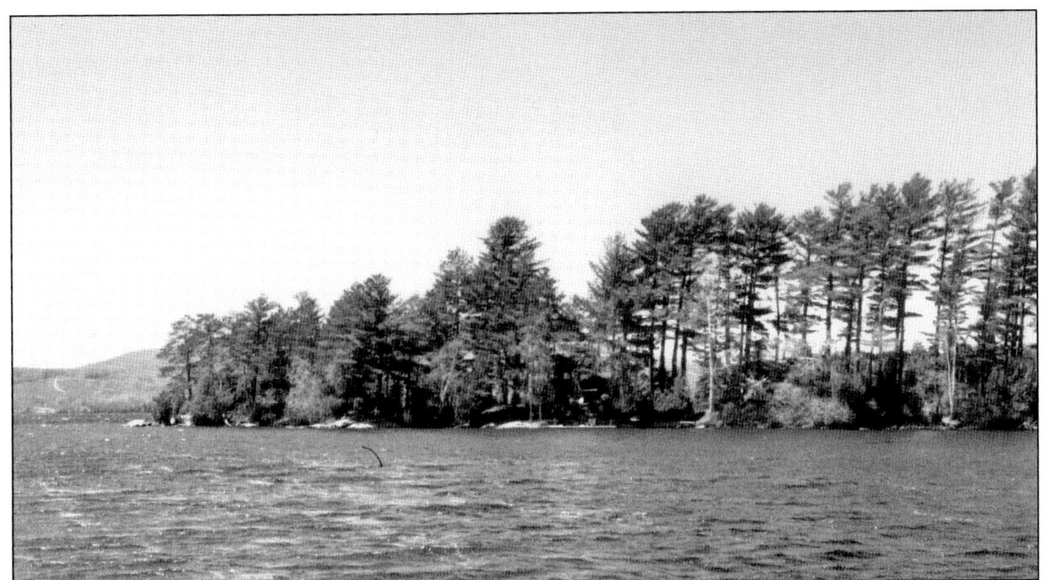

**Island Point.** In 1886, Frank M. Hawes purchased land just north of Jackson Creek on Eagle Point. Hawes named it Island Point because the far end was near Cove Island. Frank Hawes married Harriet Foster in 1877; she was the daughter of Austin T. and Sarah (Gilman) Foster. Hawes, a schoolteacher in Massachusetts, spent summers at Island Point with his family.

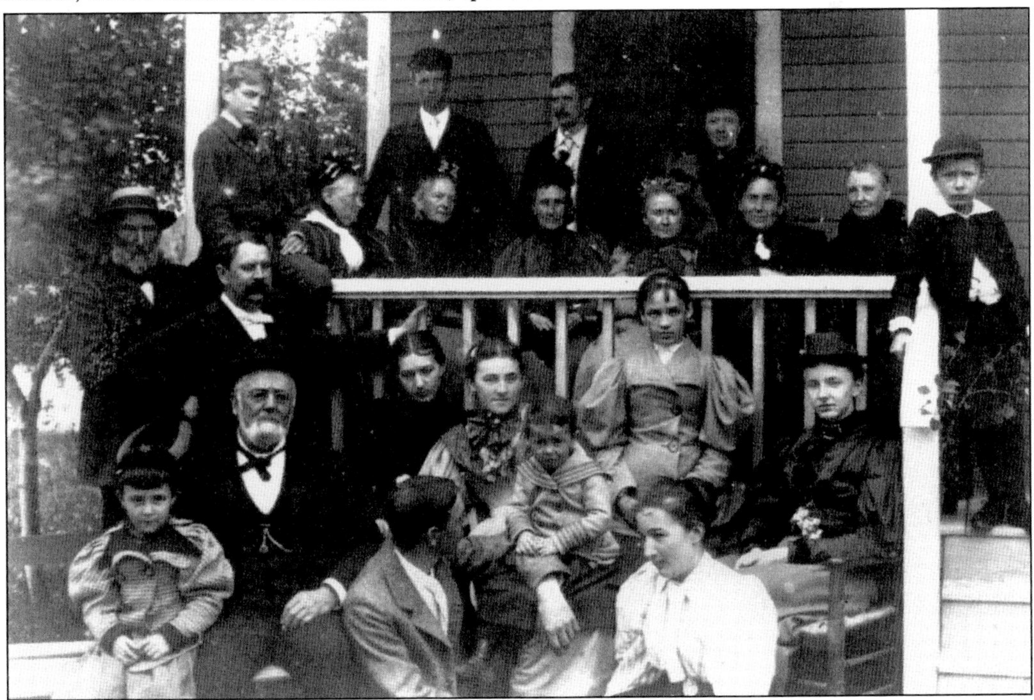

**A Family Gathering.** The Hawes, Fosters, and Knights gather for a family photograph at Island Point. Second from the left is the white-bearded Austin Foster (1822–1900). Other family members in attendance were Austin's wife, Harriet (Foster) Hawes (1854–1940); Sarah (Gilman) Foster (1830–1910); Ben Knight and his wife, Ruth; and the Knights' daughter, Lydia (Knight) Earle (1867–1934).

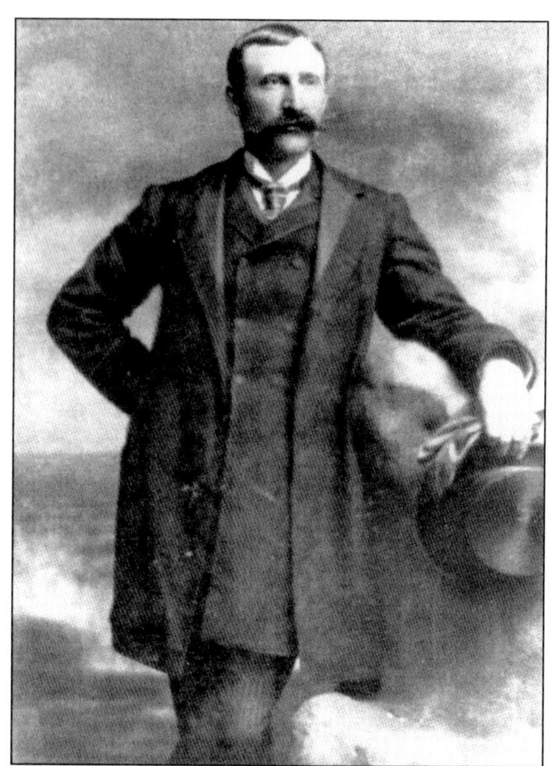

**Garvin Magoon.** In 1889, Garvin Reynolds Magoon purchased one of the cottages from Frank Hawes. Magoon was born on December 3, 1859, in Stanstead County, Quebec, the son of Stewart and Caroline (Miller) Magoon and one of six siblings. After college in 1884, he went to work for the Alonzo Lyman Bailey Piano Company in New Hampshire. Garvin married Ella Amy Mayo in June 1888 and raised three children: Ethel, Ellen, and Mayo McKinley. Garvin Magoon retired in 1926 and died in Lancaster, New Hampshire, in 1938.

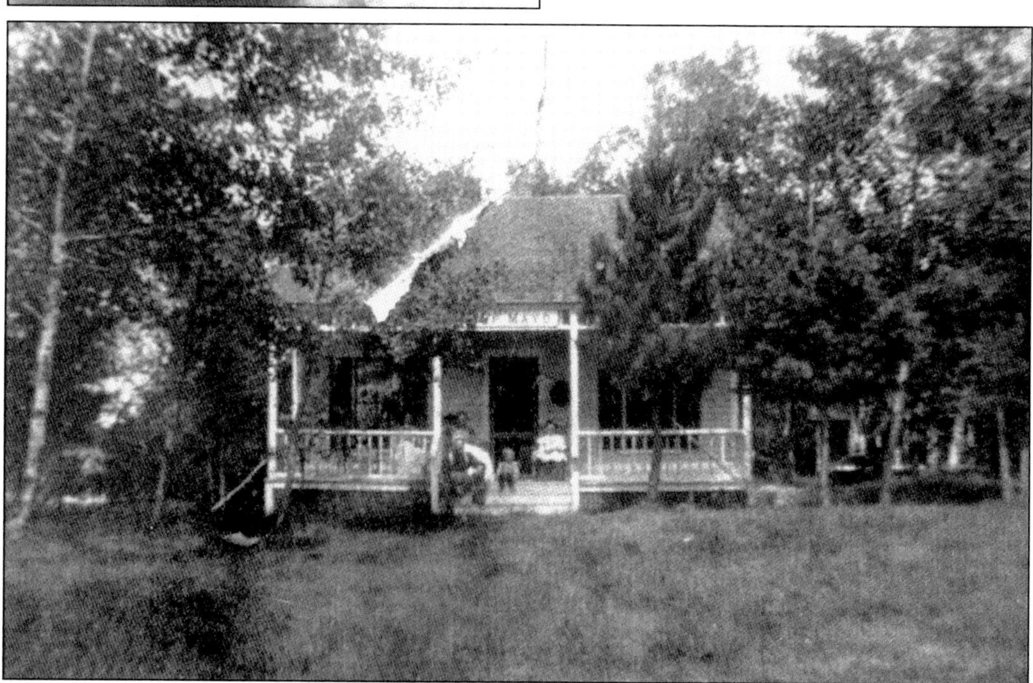

**Mayo's Cottage.** Mayo McKinley Magoon, born in 1896, is seen here as a young boy with his father on the front steps of their summer cottage at Lake Park, very close to the international boundary between Vermont and Quebec. Mayo married Katherine Underwood and raised three children: Thomas, Bruce, and Jean Francis. He passed away in 1963.

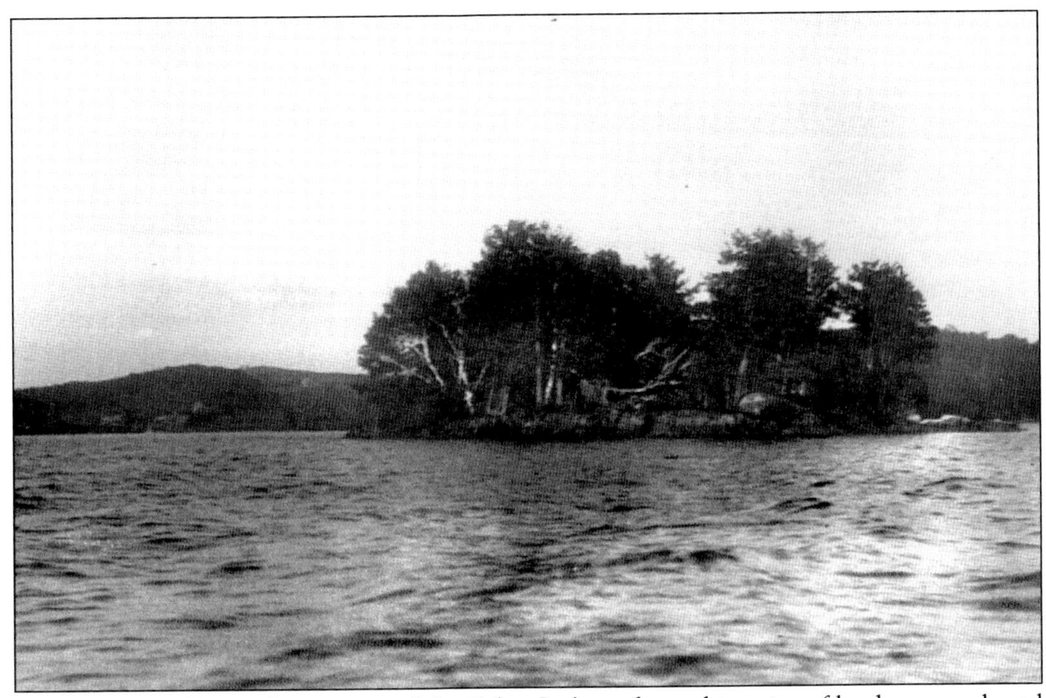

**St. Johnsbury Park.** Once a part of the Selon Jackson farm, this point of land was purchased by a group of men from St. Johnsbury, Vermont, in the 1880s. These men formed the St. Johnsbury Boat Club. The name was changed from St. Johnsbury Park to Eagle Point because a pair of eagles once nested in a tree by the shore not far from the border. The name is still used today.

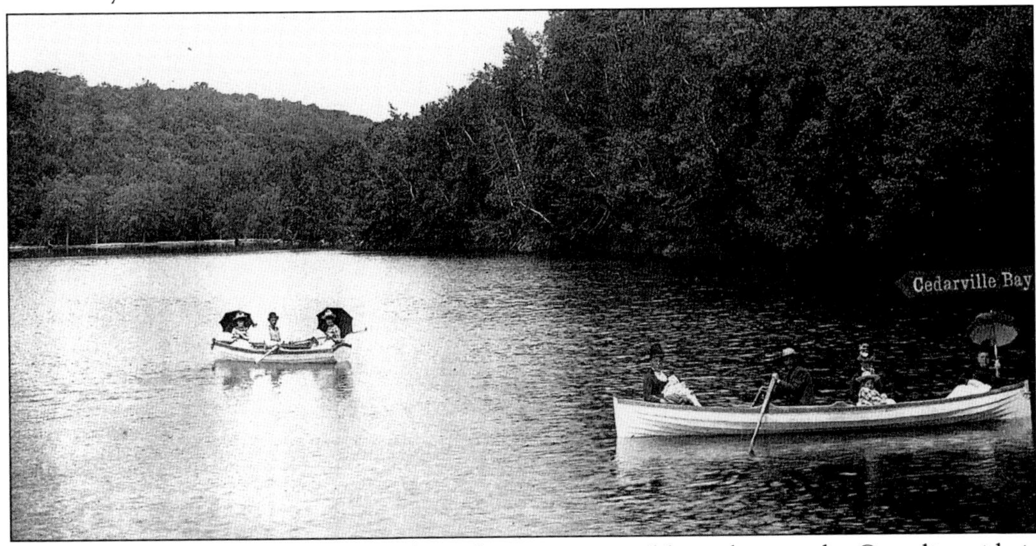


**Cedarville Bay.** A short distance from the international boundary on the Canadian side is Cedarville Bay, Quebec. It was named such because of the groves of cedar trees growing along the Memphremagog shoreline in that location. The cottages were close together, the first of which was owned by the Honorable R. Stanley Weir of the recorder's court in Montreal. After passing about 20 cottages, one could step across the line into the United States without noticing it.

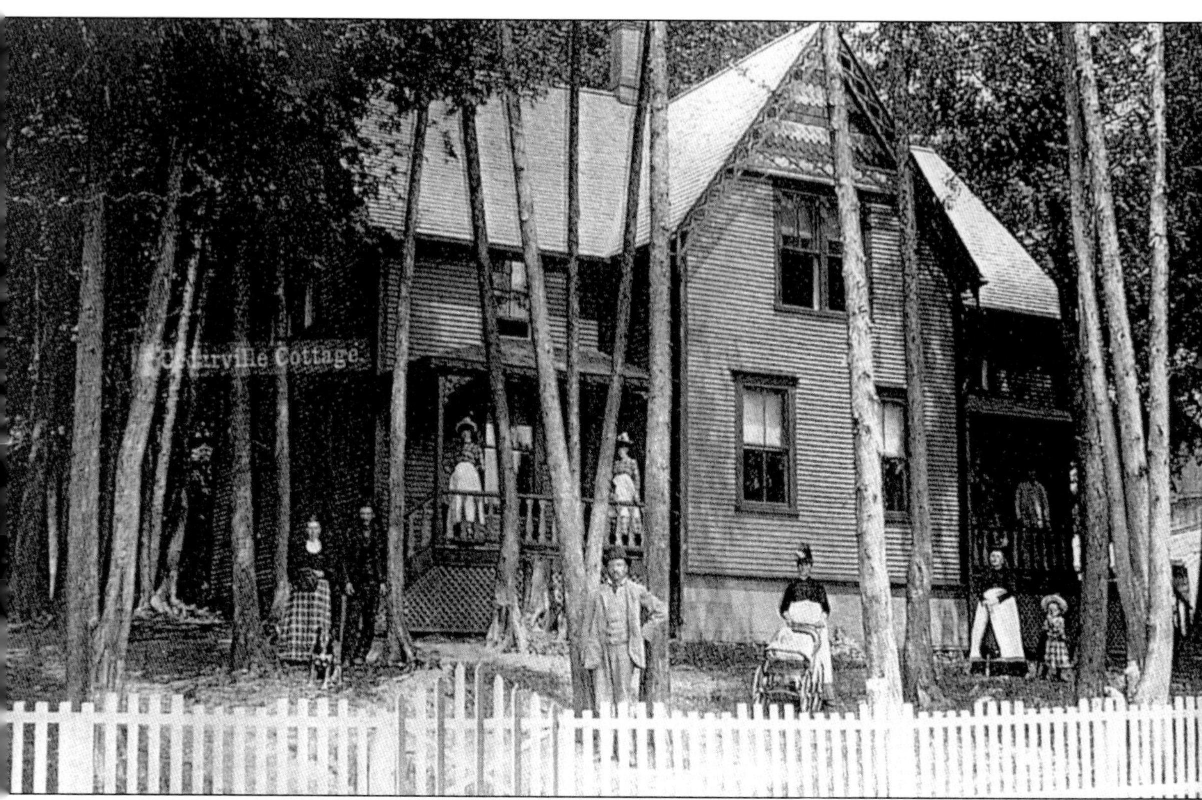


**CEDARHURST.** The Honorable Robert Stanley Weir, born in 1856 in Ontario, Canada, was also a musician. At his summer cottage in Cedarville, he wrote the words of "Oh Canada," first published in 1908. These words were set to a melody composed by Calixa Lavallee, with the French version written by Adolphe Barile Routhier. On July 1, 1980, the country proclaimed "Oh Canada" its national anthem, and that same year a 17¢ stamp was issued picturing these three gentlemen. The Weirs' summer residence was a large, sprawling house with verandas and a music room that opened into a large room for dances. Margaret Weir tended vegetable gardens, orchards, and flower beds. A boathouse on the lake held a canoe, a sailboat, and rowboats, as well as the *Cedarhurst*, a 20-foot-long craft with an inboard motor and seating along the sides. In 1940, this summer home was torn down, and the lumber from it was used in the building of the Independent Order of Odd Fellows hall at Rock Island.

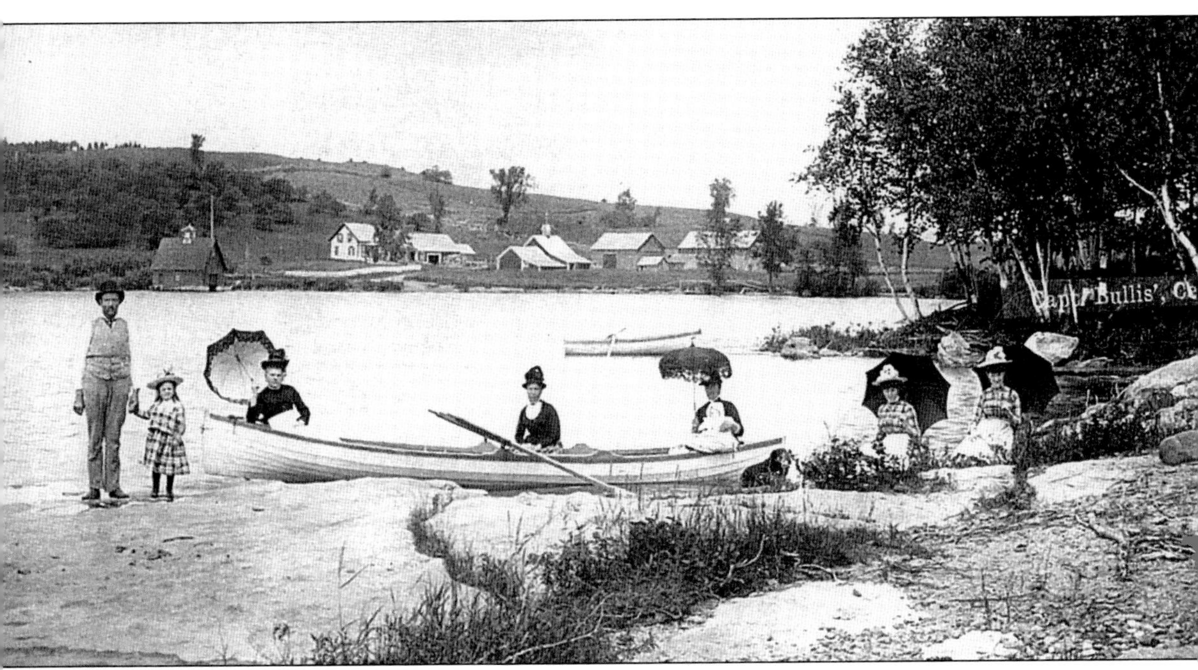


**WEIR PARK.** In Cedarville, Quebec, not far from his summer home, Judge Weir is on an outing. He is standing by the canoe with a child. Weir Park, given by the judge's children as a memorial, is as popular a place for families to enjoy today as it was during his time. Judge Weir and his wife, Margaret (Douglas), had six children. The boys gave their lives for their country. Douglas died in World War I, and Roland, a pilot in the Royal Canadian Air Force, was killed in World War II. Judge Weir died at Cedarhurst in August 1926, at the place where his dreams for a Canadian national anthem were realized.

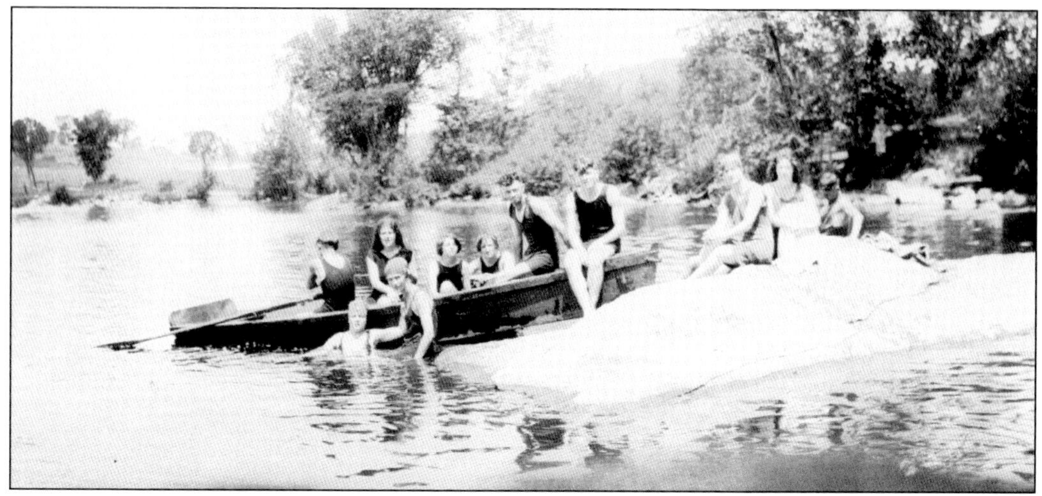

**Auntie's Camp.** Family and friends enjoy a day of swimming and fun at their aunt Rosella (Cole) Toleman's camp in Cedarville, Quebec, in 1924. Toleman lived in North Derby but spent summers nearby on her beloved Lake Memphremagog. The camp was a favorite gathering place for the younger generation of Abenaki descendants.

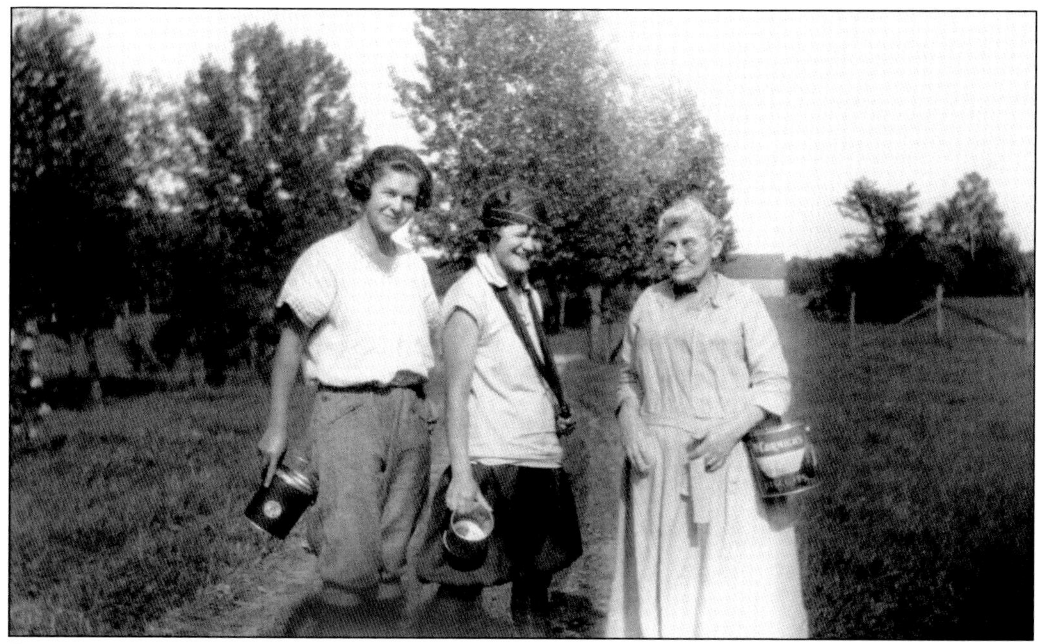

**Berrying.** Passing on an Abenaki lifeway tradition, great-grandmother Edla Aretta (Cole) Longeway takes the younger generation to her favorite berry patch at her sister's camp in Cedarville. Tin pails have replaced the traditional cedar bark berry baskets.

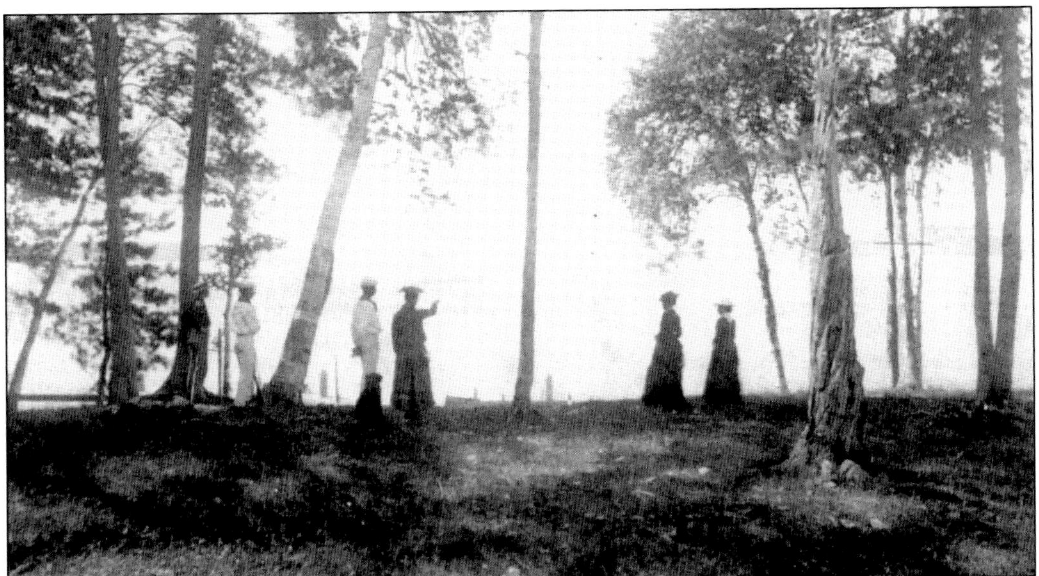

**Bay View Park and Beach.** This park and beach are located on Magoon's Point, where the long arm of Fitch Bay reaches out of the east shore of Lake Memphremagog. Bay View Park was once owned by the Boston & Maine Railroad. Here, the *Lady of the Lake* boating excursions stopped at constructed docking facilities. In 1879, the railroad built a pavilion to hold concerts and light operas. When the *Lady of the Lake* excursions were discontinued, the pavilion was moved across the lake to the Mountain House Hotel and Resort at Owl's Head Mountain on the west shore.

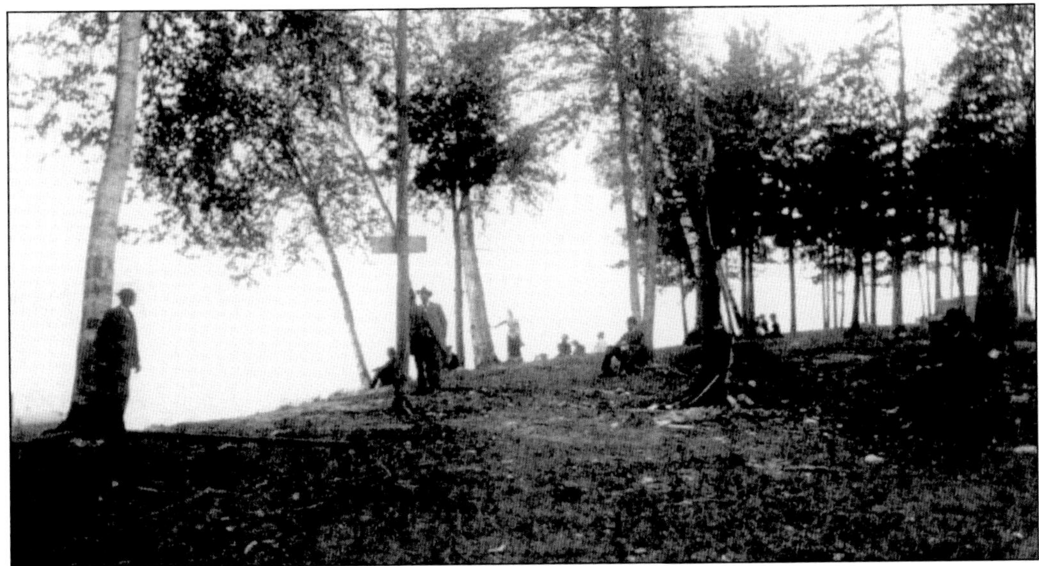

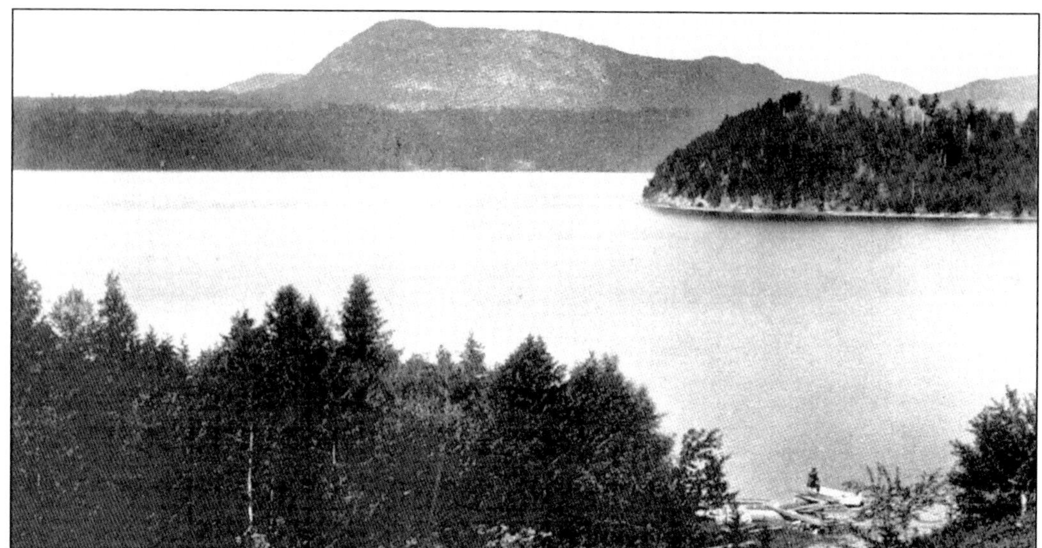

**The Belmere Point Estate.** Sir Hugh Allan chose one of the most picturesque shores of Lake Memphremagog for his summer home. His view across the lake took in Molson Island and the majestic profile of Elephantis Mountain. Sir Hugh Allan was a senior partner in Allan Brothers Steamships, which held a fleet of ocean steamers and was the founder of Dominion Commerce. In July 1871, the queen of England presented him the honor of knighthood, using his chosen name of Sir Hugh Allan of Ravenscrag. (Courtesy of Stanstead Historical Society, Belmere Bequest.)

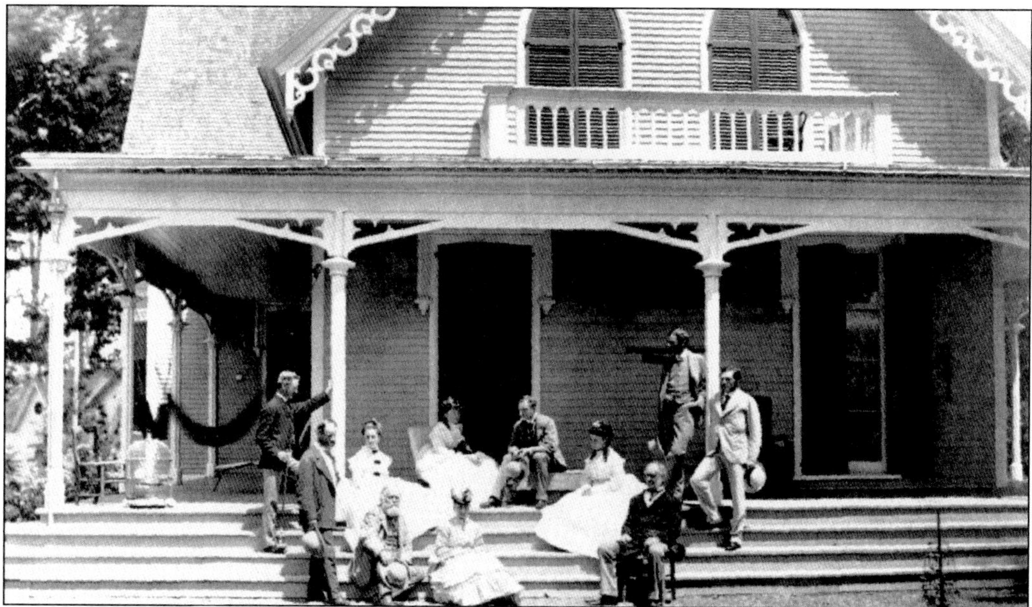

**Sir Allan.** Born in Scotland in 1810, Sir Hugh Allan married Matilda Smith in 1844 and together they raised eight children, four of them sons. In the summer, the family took the train from Ravenscrag, their home in Montreal, to the Belmere estate. Ravenscrag was built in 1863 and was named after a Scottish castle. A bearded Allan is seen here sitting on the stairs. He was the first president of the Lake Navigation Company of Memphremagog, a company chartered by the Canadian government. (Courtesy of Stanstead Historical Society, Belmere Bequest.)

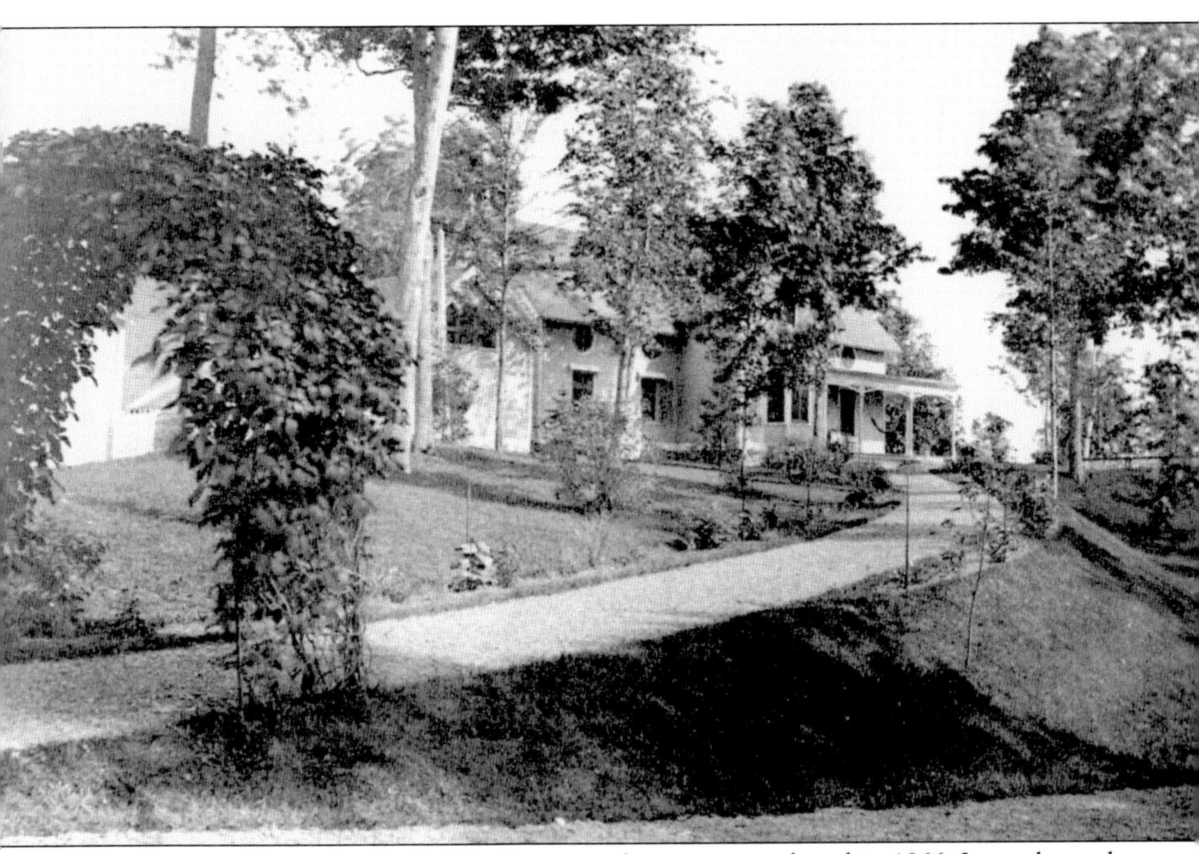

**The Belmere Villa.** Sir Hugh Allan's summer home was purchased in 1866. It was located on a peninsula between MacPhearson Bay and Molson's Island. The estate consisted of 1,000 acres, and a mile-long driveway was protected by an iron gate set on fieldstone posts. Nearby the entrance was the gatekeeper's cottage. The Union Jack could most always be seen here snapping in the breeze. (Courtesy of Stanstead Historical Society, Belmere Bequest.)

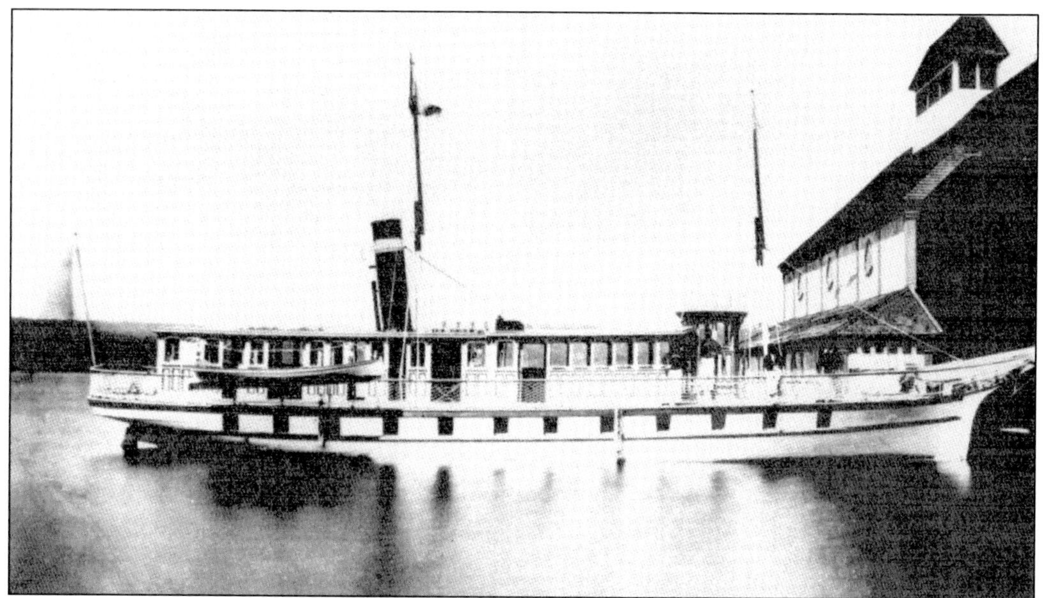

**THE ORFORD.** This 85-foot-long private yacht was built in 1867 and was owned by Sir Hugh Allan at Belmere. In 1869, the *Orford* carried Sir John Young, governor general of Canada, and Prince Arthur William Patrick (born in 1850 at Buckingham Palace, the third son of Queen Victoria) to Newport, Vermont, where they registered as Memphremagog Hotel guests. (Courtesy of Stanstead Historical Society, Belmere Bequest.)

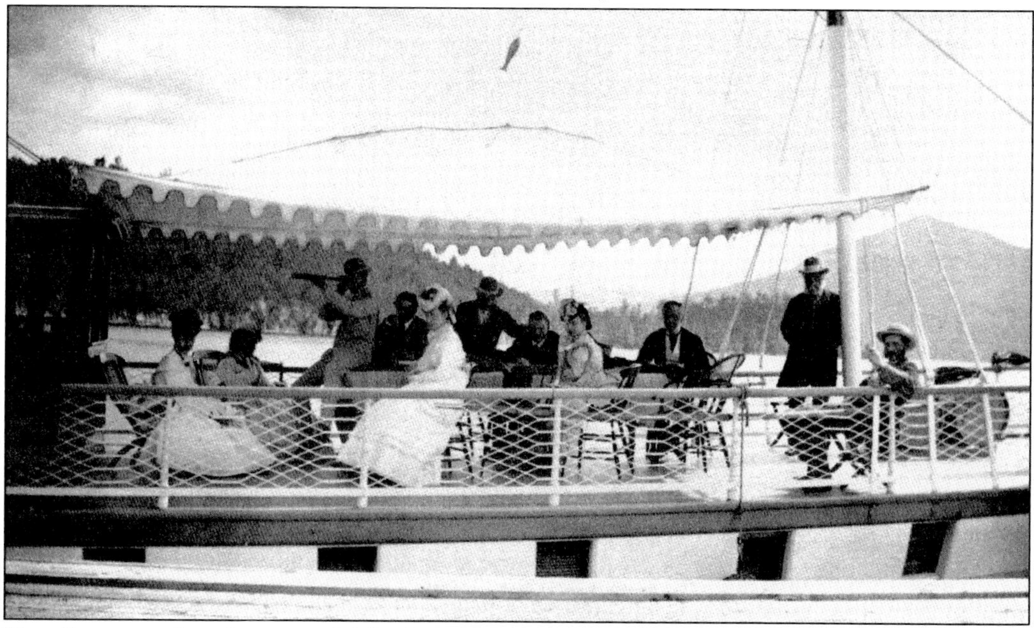

**THE ORMOND.** Another one of Allan's private yachts was the *Ormond*. Sir Allan, bearded and wearing a hat, stands near the pole as the boat glides away from the Belmere estate boathouse. Under the awning in comfortable basket chairs, guests look forward to a pleasure cruise. After Sir Hugh Allan's death in 1882, the H & A Allan Ship Line in Montreal was passed on to his brother Andrew. After Andrew's death, Andrew's son Hugh took over until 1931, when the company dissolved. (Courtesy of Stanstead Historical Society, Belmere Bequest.)

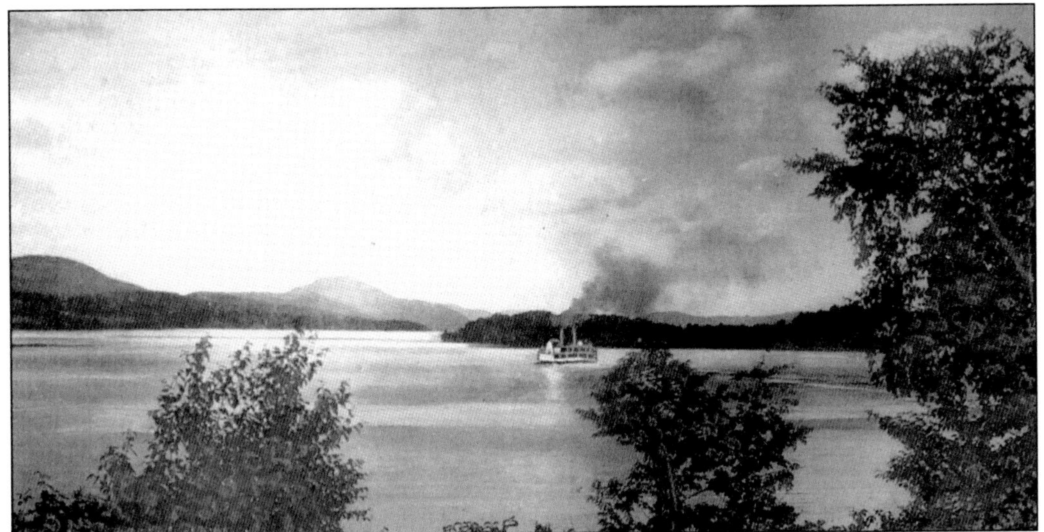

**RIAH JEWETT.** On Lake Memphremagog's steamer the *Mountain Maid*, the prominent character "Riah" Jewett (1795–1868) told his spellbinding stories. He moved to the area from New Hampshire with his family when he was five, and they settled on Jewett's Point, north of MacPhearson Bay. Riah and his stories, especially those of Lake Memphremagog's sea serpent, earned him notoriety. No amount of reasoning could change his mind about the serpent; indeed, he could give the date and time of all his encounters with the sea serpent, known today as Memphre.

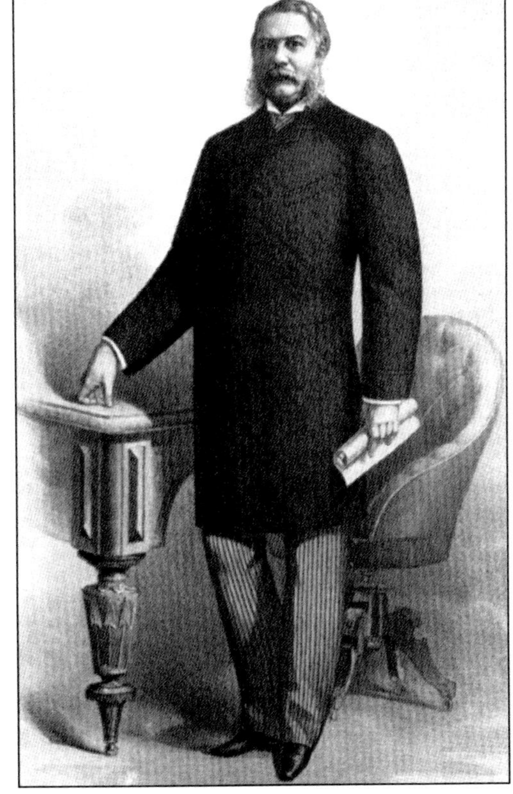

**THE TWENTY-FIRST PRESIDENT.** Chester A. Arthur (1829–1886) had ancestral roots in the Memphremagog region. Uriah Jewett's mother, Sally (Stone) Jewett, was the sister of George W. Stone. George's daughter Malvina married Rev. William Arthur at Dunham, Quebec, in 1821. Born in Fairfield, Vermont, in 1829, Chester A. Arthur was their first son and the fifth child of nine. He later became the 21st president of the United States.

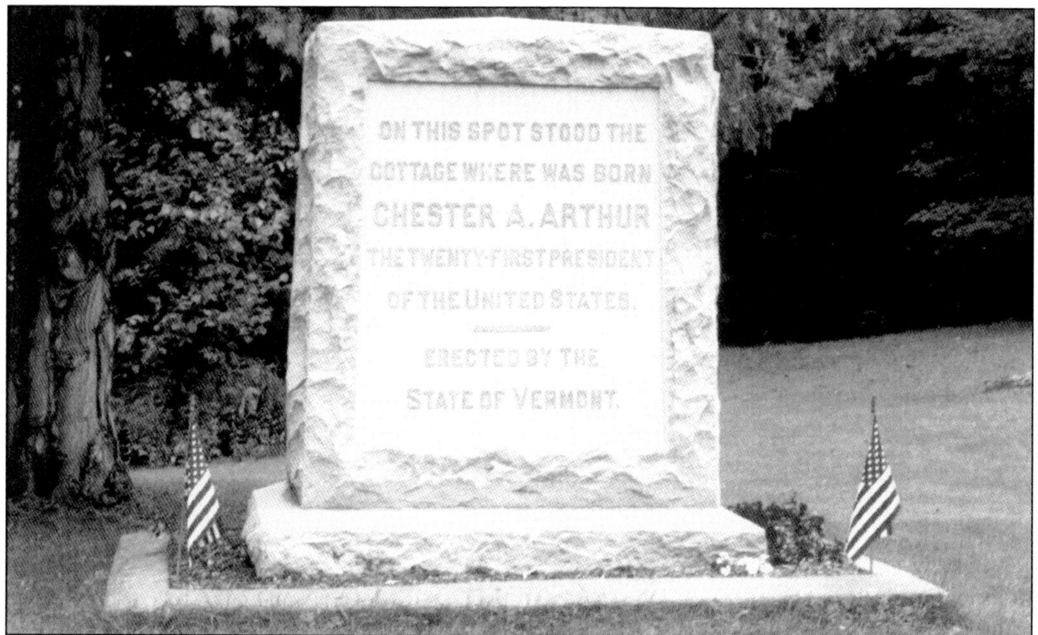


**The President's Memorial.** The Chester A. Arthur Memorial in Fairfield, Vermont, marks the spot of the log cabin where Arthur was born on October 5, 1829. The Fairfield Baptist Church is where his father preached at the time. The church still stands today on a hill overlooking rural Vermont.

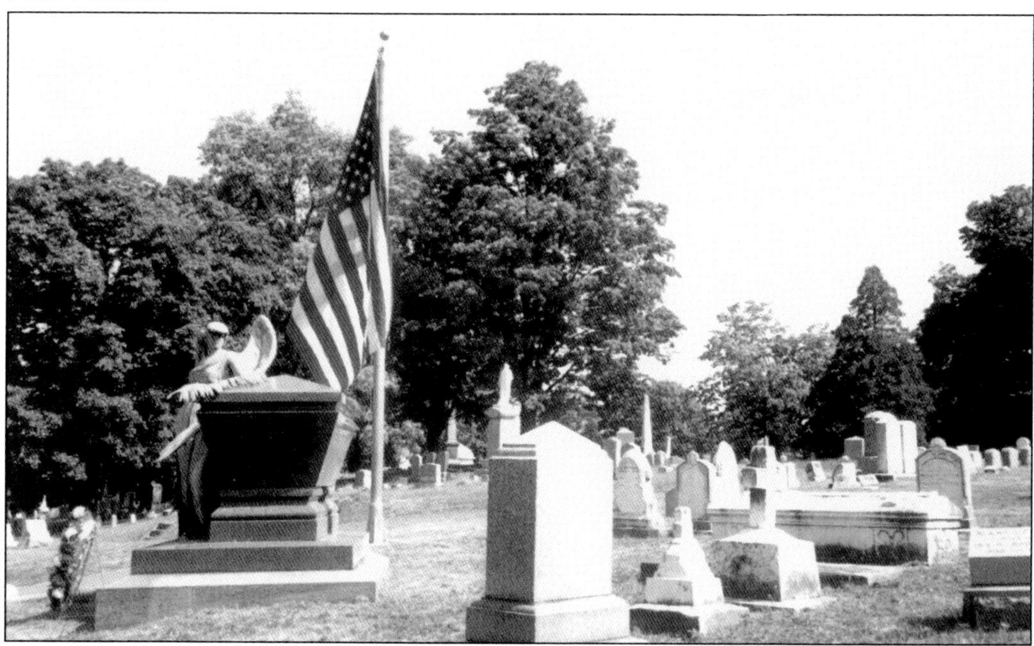

**The Cemetery Monument.** The *Angel of Sorrow* statue was erected at the Albany Rural Cemetery in New York three years after President Arthur's death in 1886. The cost was $10,000. The cemetery plots were purchased in 1864 by Rev. William Arthur, an Irish immigrant, and his wife, Malvina (Stone) Arthur, long before Chester Arthur became the 21st president of the United States in 1881.

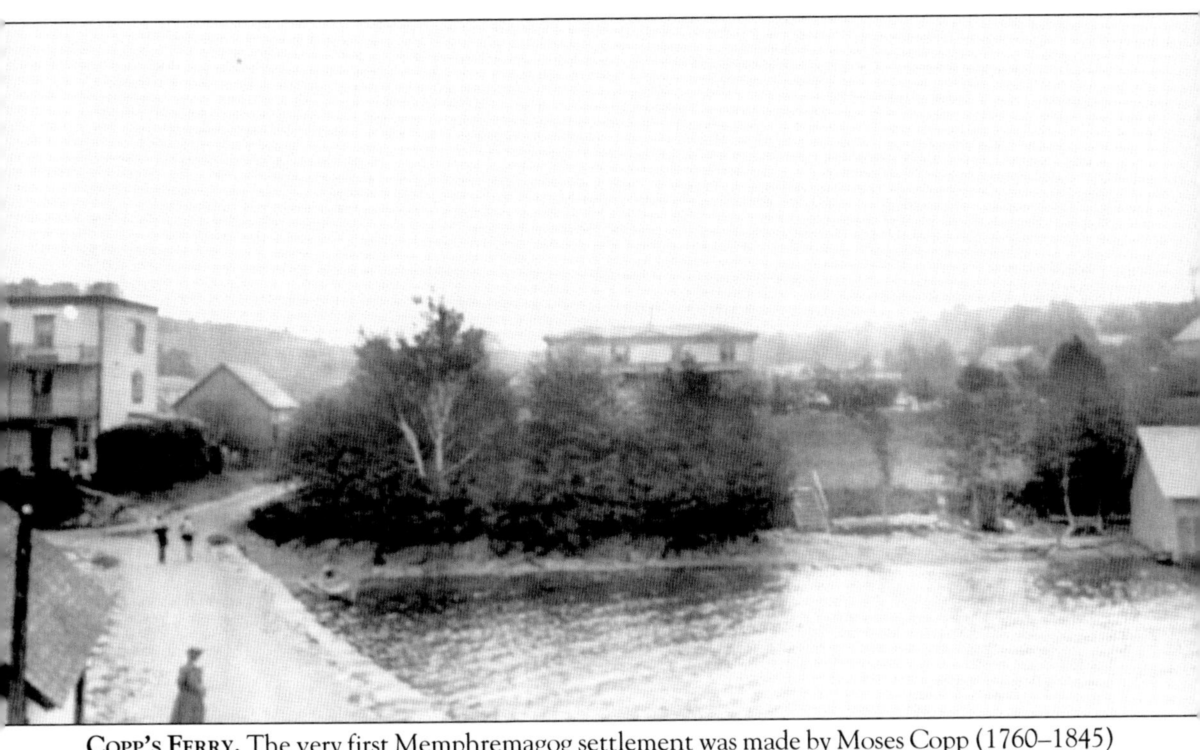

**Copp's Ferry.** The very first Memphremagog settlement was made by Moses Copp (1760–1845) c. 1792. He and three other men—Amasa Merriman and Joseph and Joel Ives—passed up the lake in a dugout canoe made in Newport and camped on the spot now known as Bedroom Point. In 1797, Moses Copp, his wife Anna (Miles) Copp, and their children moved across the lake from Sargent's Bay and ran one of the first ferries at Copp's Ferry. In 1822, the name was changed to Georgeville after Copp's first-born son. By 1829, he had replaced his scow with a horse-powered ferry, which he named the *Ho-Boy*, to transport stagecoach passengers and freight up and down the lake.

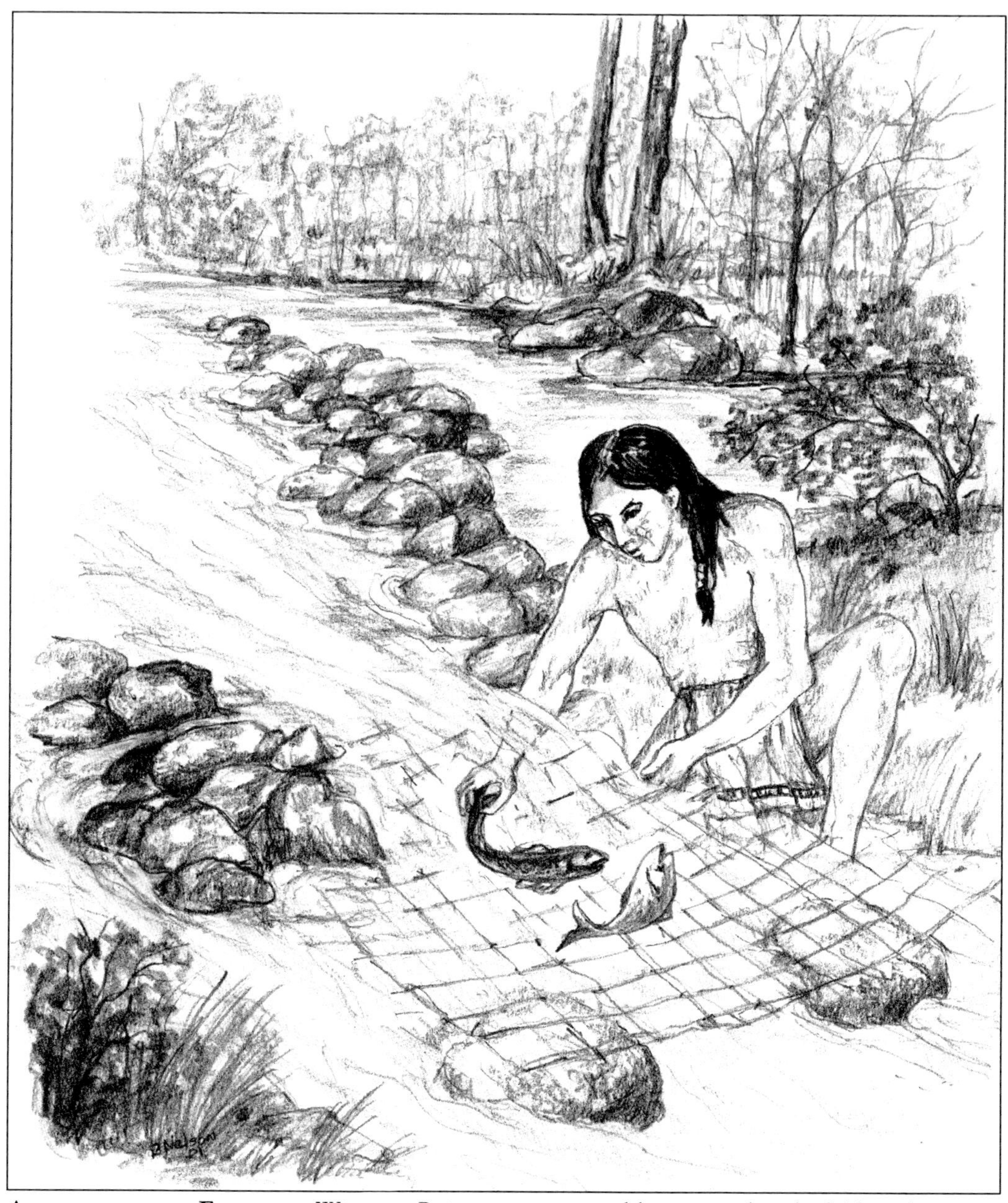

**Archaeological Evidence.** Wigwam Point was so named because a band of Abenaki, or St. Francis, Indians had an encampment of wigwams here, even after settlement. Among them was an Abenaki woman named Minnehaha, probably the daughter of a band leader, not an Indian princess. Archaeological evidence of fishing weirs has been found around the shores of Lake Memphremagog near small streams and favorite encampment sites. Some weirs were temporary, like this one at Wigwam Point, made with stones laid along the streambed in a V-shape with a cordage catching net at the narrowest point. Sometimes, inserted wooden stakes were used in place of stones. For the price of a keg of whiskey, the first house was moved to the point from its place on Channel Street in Georgeville in 1864. One of Georgeville's earliest industrial sites, a factory, was once located here.

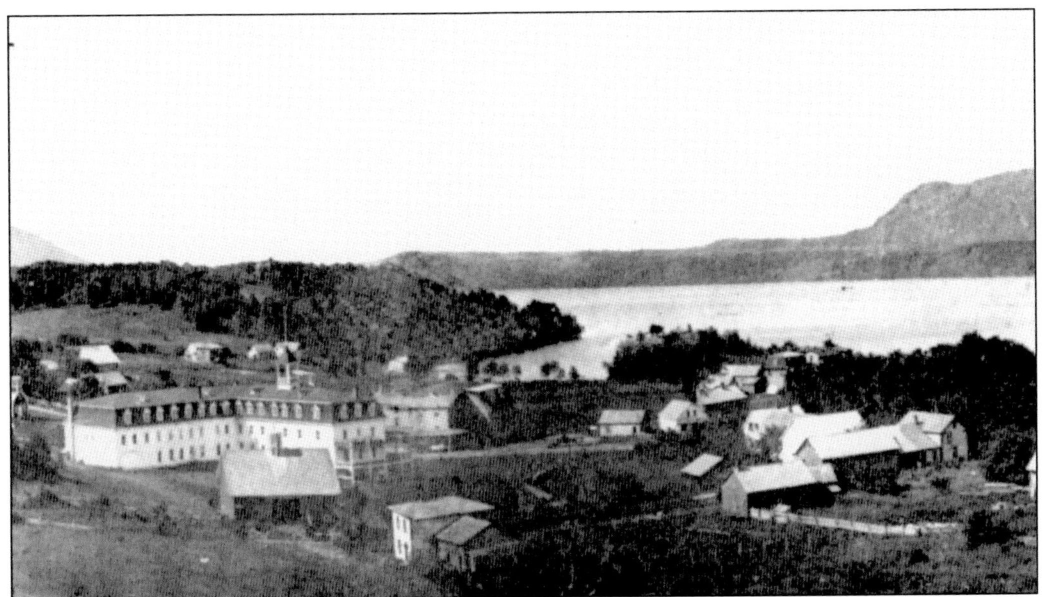

**The Camperdown Hotel.** The first public house around Lake Memphremagog was the Camperdown Hotel built in Georgeville, Quebec, at the center of the village. Richard Holland, originally from Massachusetts, constructed it in 1810. Stagecoaches passed by in large numbers, and teams waited in line to be ferried across the lake. This popular summer hotel was destroyed by fire on July 18, 1898.

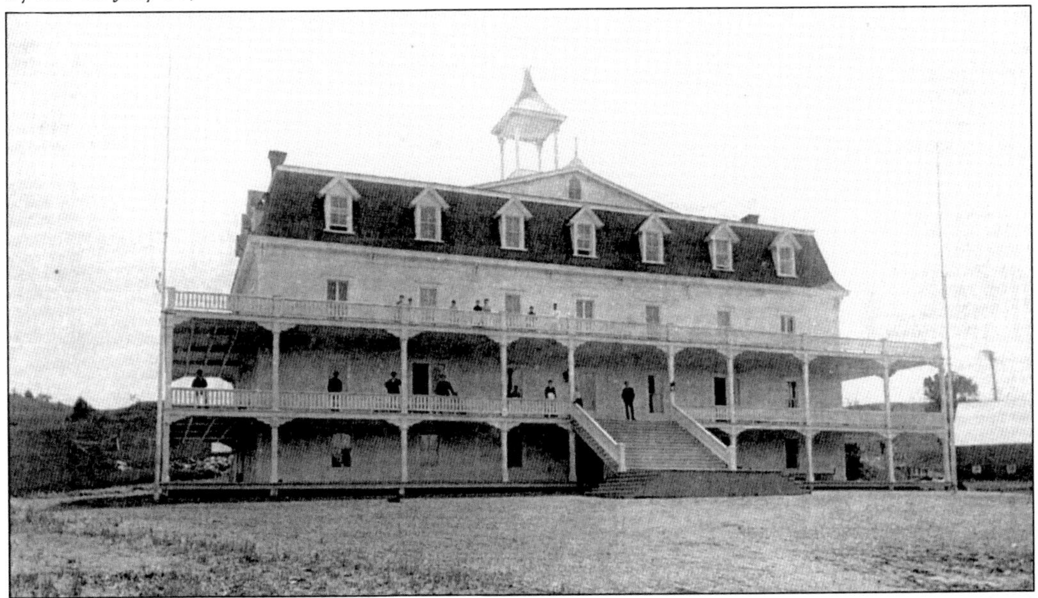

**Abraham FitzJohn Channell.** In 1814, the Camperdown Hotel was purchased from Richard Holland by Abraham F. Channell (1748–1858). Channell, born in London, England, was an apprentice to a tailor before joining the British service. His vessel was captured and taken to Boston Harbor. Channell came to Georgeville in 1810, bought the hotel in 1814, and remained innkeeper until 1854. Channell's vigor was noted on his 75th birthday. It is said that he ran across his barroom, jumped, and planted his heels against the door as high as his shoulders. He died at the age of 110.

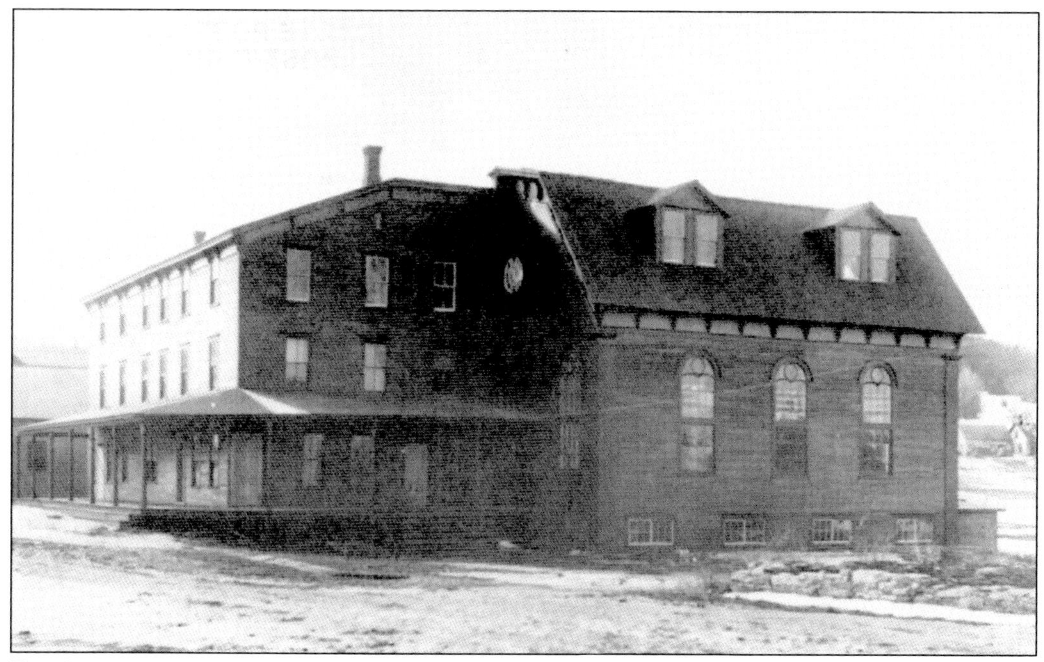

**The Elephantis Hotel.** This hotel in Georgeville, Quebec, was built by Nathan Beech in 1893 between Channell and Bullock Hill Roads. The Elephantis Hotel was moved and attached to the old Methodist church, converting part of the church into a dance hall. On July 18, 1898, Elsie Beech, Nathan's wife, dropped her kerosene lantern and set the hotel on fire. Nine other buildings also burned that night, including the Camperdown Hotel.

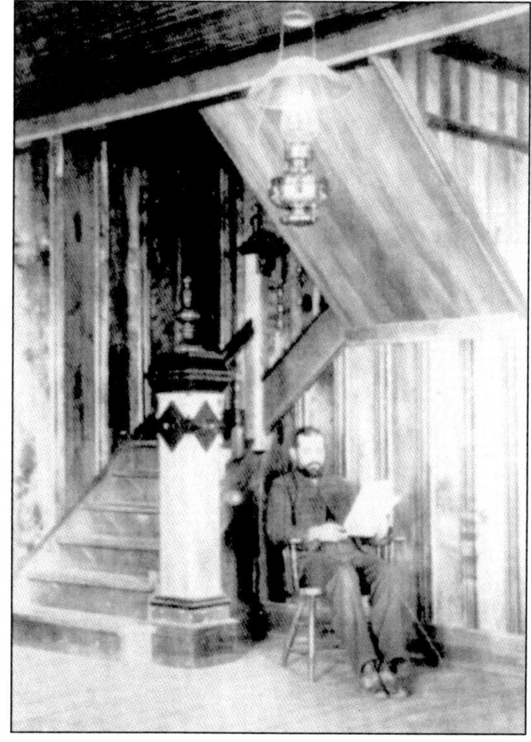

**Charles Sewell Copp.** The great-grandson of Capt. Moses Copp sits in the lobby of the Elephantis Hotel. Charles Sewell Copp was postmaster from 1888 to 1895. He married Gertrude Ella Beech, the daughter of Nathan and Elsie, the proprietors of the hotel. (Courtesy of Georgeville Historical Society, Canada.)

**CAPT. GEORGE W. FOGG.** One of the four children of Josiah and Polly Fogg, George Washington Fogg was born *c.* 1819. Orphaned at the age of 13, he came to Georgeville and entered the household of Asa and Hannah (Thayer) Lilly on Bullock's Hill, where he soon began his navigational career. Fogg operated a houseboat for a ferrying service across the lake from Georgeville to Knowlton's Landing. After that, he launched the first steamer on the lake in 1850—the *Mountain Maid*.

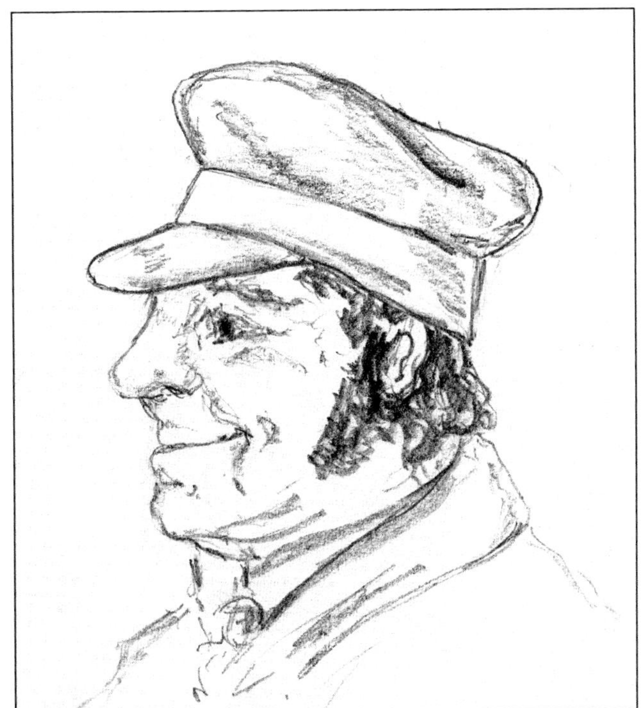

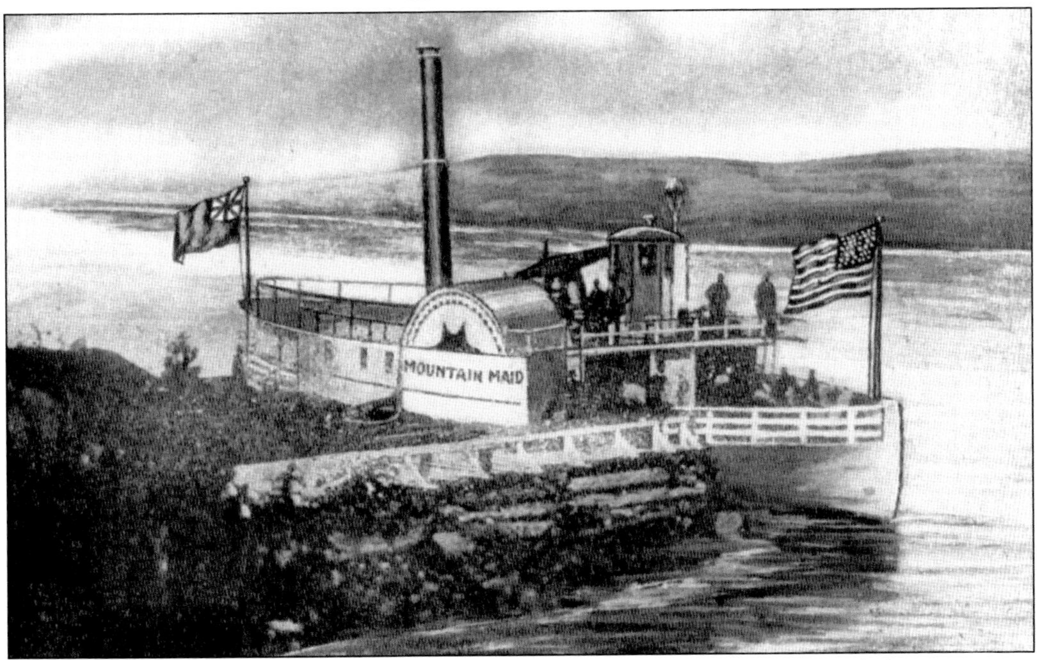


**THE LAUNCHING OF THE *MOUNTAIN MAID*.** As the Georgeville Brass Band played, the ceremonies began on June 27, 1850, for the launching of the *Mountain Maid*. Toasts, speeches, and honors were given to Capt. George Fogg and Orson Spear, of Burlington, Vermont, for the idea of the steamer. Spear, a shipwright, supervised the building of the steamer as it was fitted up in the finest style with a saloon, staterooms, and offices. Captain Fogg stood at the helm from 1850 until 1868. (Courtesy of Georgeville Historical Society, Canada.)

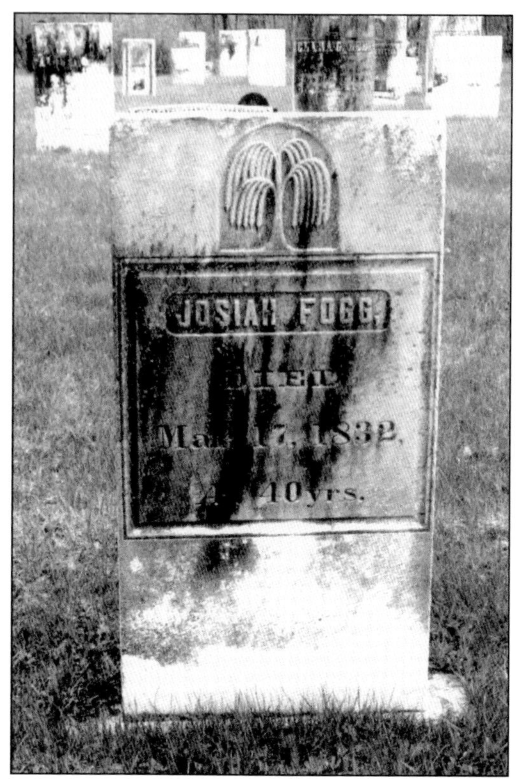


**THE MOULTON BURYING GROUNDS.** In Stanstead, Quebec, the Moulton Cemetery is named after the Moultons, who settled here in 1798 and raised a family of 12 children. The ancestors of many well-known families are buried here, including Capt. George Fogg's parents. The graves of Josiah Fogg (1793–1832), a farmer from Stanstead, and his wife, Polly (1792–1826), are in this cemetery. Josiah and Polly had four children: John in 1817, George in 1819, Charles in 1821, and Mary Ann in 1822. Capt. George Fogg and his siblings were orphaned at a young age. George went to live with brickmaker Asa Lilly in Georgeville, where he was one of the first to run a ferry on the lake.

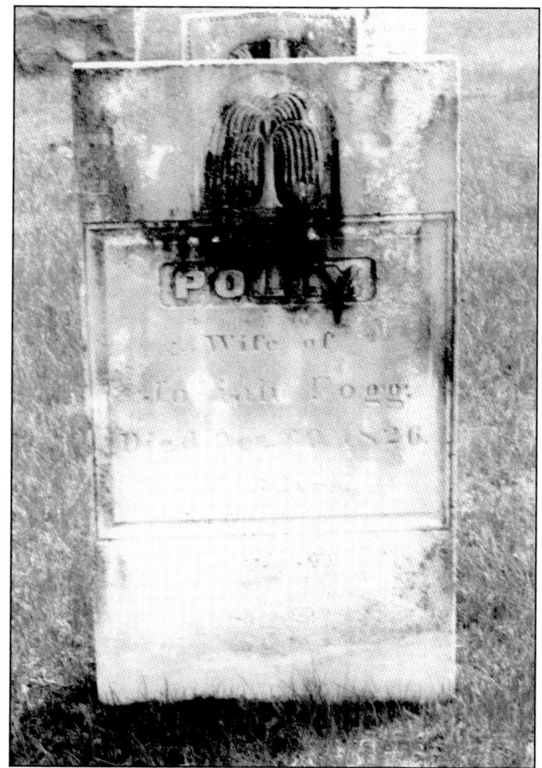

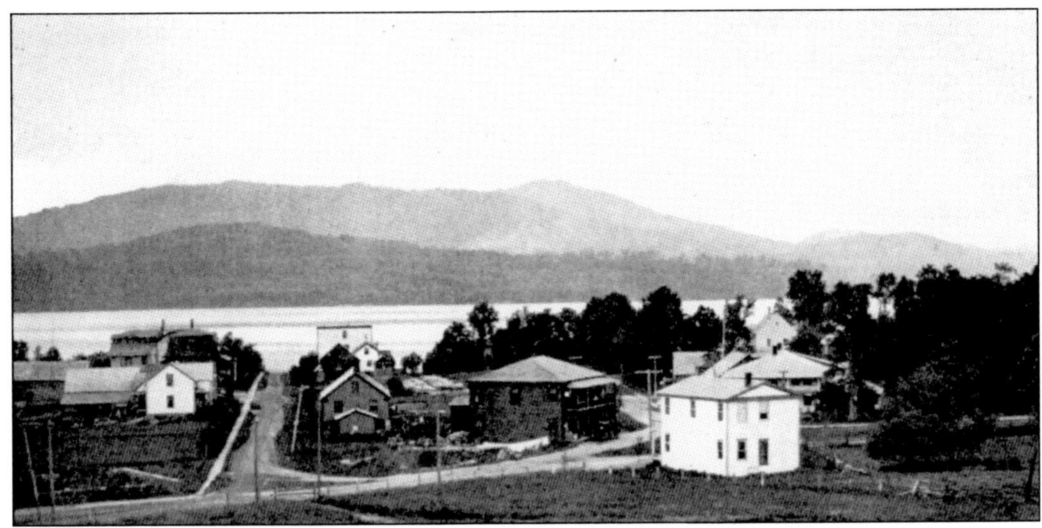

**A Celebration.** On June 27, 1850, a celebration took place in the vacant field between the two lake streets to christen the steamer the *Mountain Maid*. A bottle of wine was broken over the bow by Captain Fogg's wife, Sophronia (Lilly) Fogg. The steamer took to the water before being towed back to her mooring for the completion of construction.

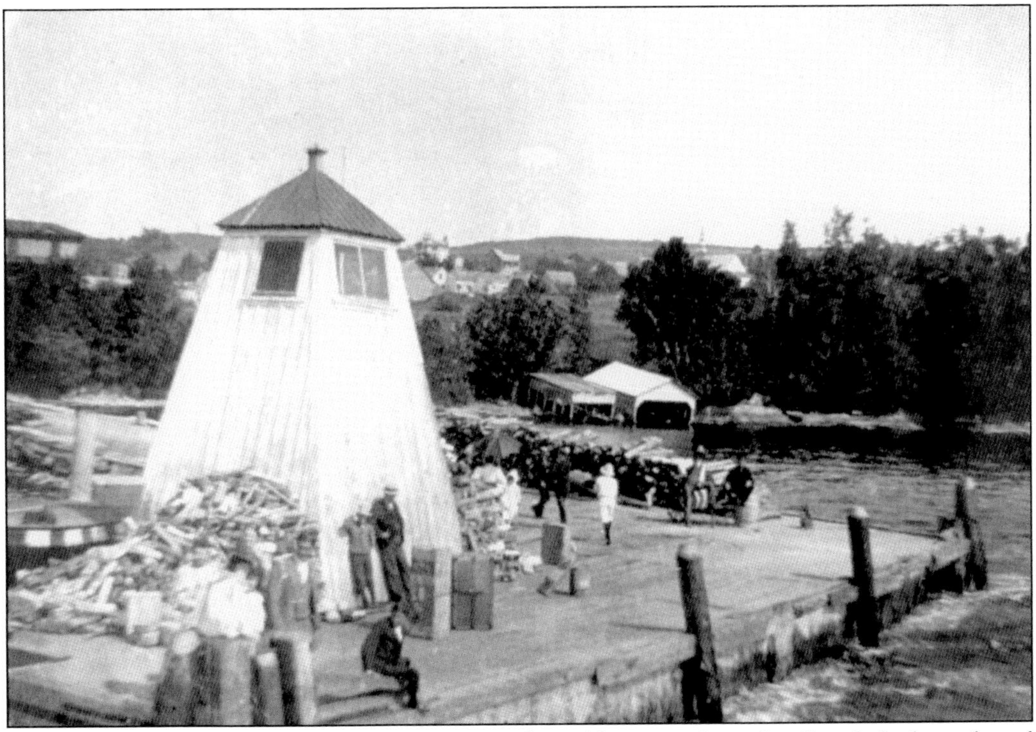

**The Georgeville Wharf.** The *Mountain Maid* would stop to "wood-up" with fuel purchased from local farmers. With specially designed wheelbarrows, enough wood could be hauled onto the lower deck for a day's run. For 40 years, the *Mountain Maid* played a significant role on the lake between Newport, Vermont; Georgeville; and Magog, Quebec. In 1892, it was towed to the Magog Wharf to be dismantled.

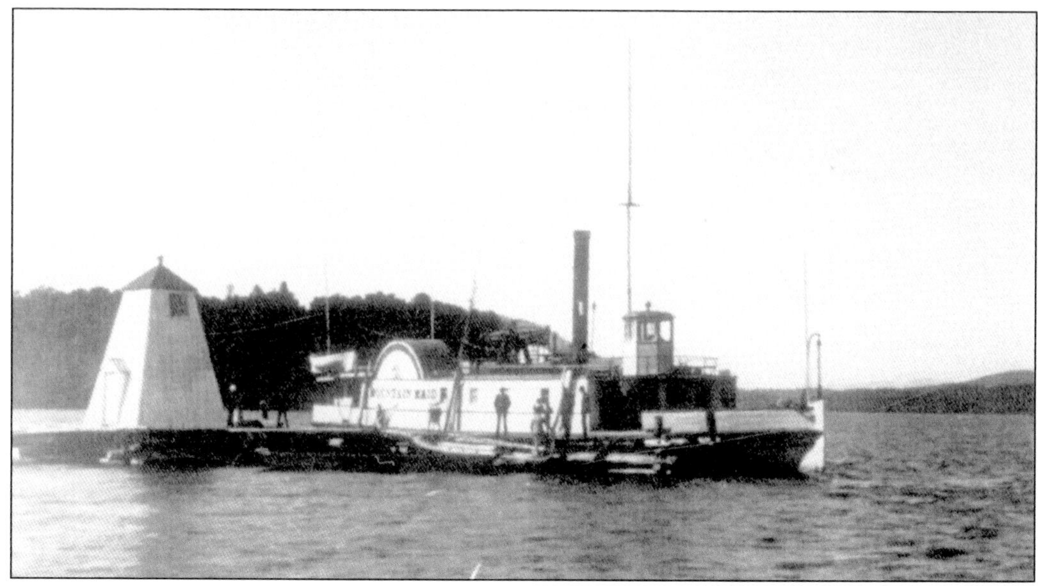

**SMUGGLERS AND CUSTOMS.** With the launching of the *Mountain Maid* in 1850, activity increased on the lake. W.F. Parker, a retired Canadian naval officer, became the first customs officer. When John Carty Tuck took his place, Parker Sr. was enraged to think his son had been replaced by a rebel-dog and noted smuggler. John Tuck's job was to ride the steamer and protect the cargo. Parker Sr. felt that John Tuck was an unaccountable character to be residing in a colony under the queen. (Courtesy of Georgeville Historical Society, Canada.)

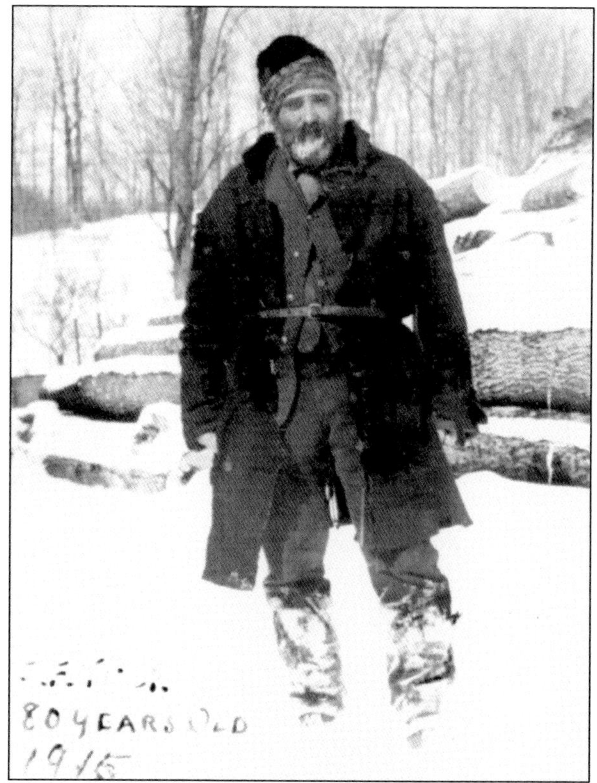

**JOHN F. TUCK.** The son of John C. and Susan Tuck, John F. Tuck was born in 1835 in Georgeville. His father was requested by Captain Fogg of the *Mountain Maid* to be removed as customs officer because of his "insolent abuse." By 1856, customs problems revolved around the fight for the cushy job aboard the *Mountain Maid.* (Courtesy of Potton Heritage Association, Canada.)

**LIGHTHOUSES.** In May 1879, by an act of the U.S. Congress, $5,000 was allocated to build three government lighthouses not to exceed 25 square feet. One was at the site of Steamboat Wharf in Newport; another, the Stake (shown here), was off the west shore of Whipple Point; and the third was at Maxwell Point. Captain Fogg had to pay a light tax of $300 as a user's fee for these lighthouses.

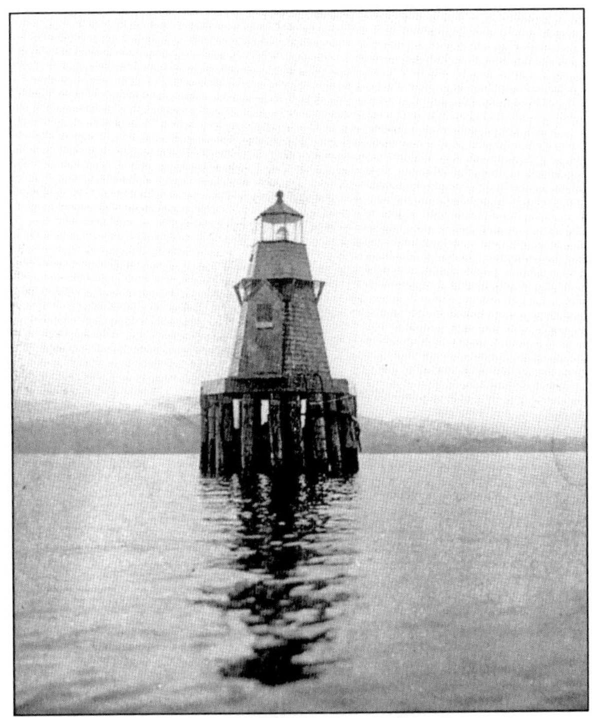

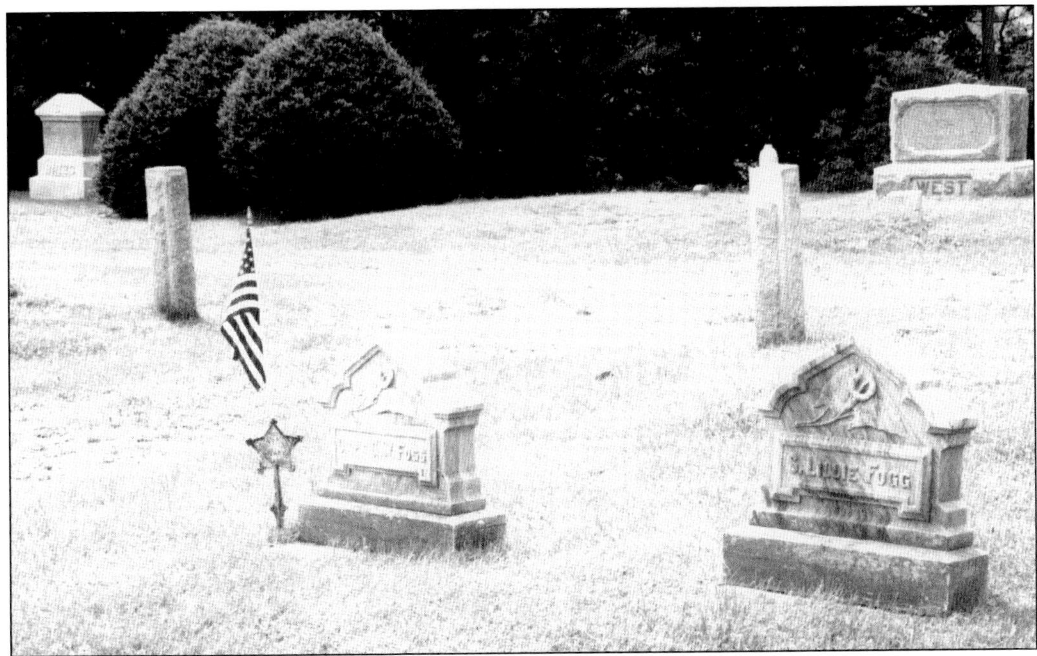


**THE FOGG PLOTS.** Captain Fogg was buried beside his wife, Sophronia (Lilly) Fogg, at the East Main Street Cemetery in Newport, Vermont. Captain Fogg was known as the father of commercial navigation on Lake Memphremagog. He died on April 12, 1885, at his farm of 35 years overlooking the lake. Sophronia had assisted her husband in the management of his steamboats. She died on February 8, 1894, leaving their son, Charles, and their daughter, Nettie. Nettie married in 1893 and went to live at her late parents' home, Lake View Farm.

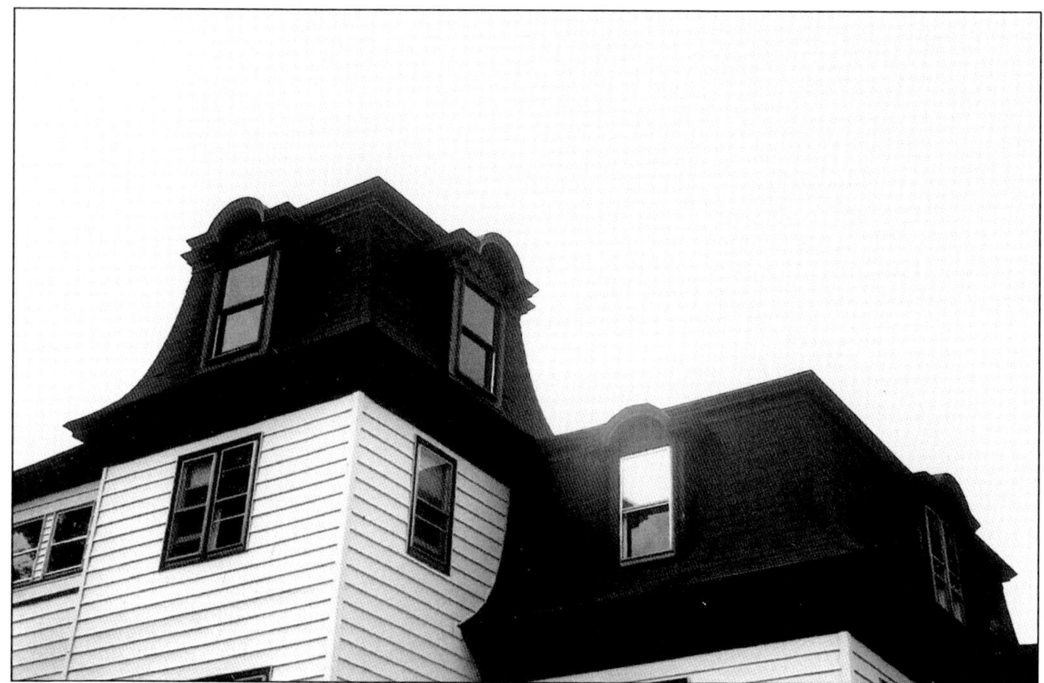

**Lake View Farm.** Captain Fogg's home (above) was purchased in the 1850s. It overlooked the village of Newport and the Memphremagog Hotel. In this view from Prospect Hill (below), his home can be seen at the far right, with a circular driveway extending from the Long Bridge at Railroad Square.

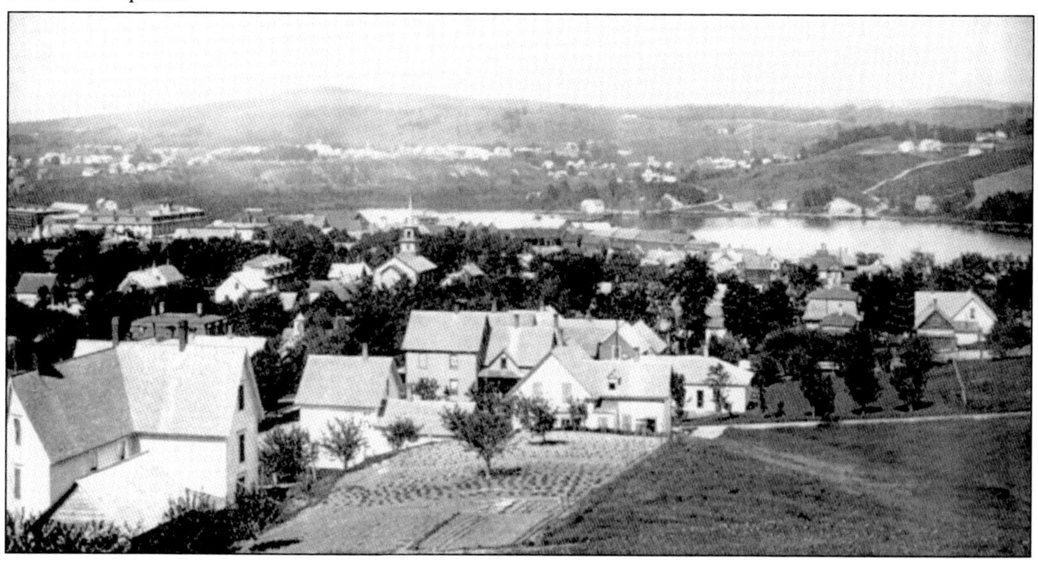

# *Six*

# Twenty Islands

Lake Memphremagog's 20 islands have varied and interesting stories. Some carry legends while others are Indian campgrounds, favorite landmarks, or fishing spots for the communities around the lake. Only five of the islands are on the American side of the border. Province Island is the largest, but only about one-third of its land is in the United States due to the international boundary cutting through it. The early steamboat captains would give a short, sharp blast from the steamer's whistle to inform the passengers that they were crossing the line. The islands of Horseneck, Black, Belle, Cove, and one-third of Province lie within the United States. Two-thirds of Province and all of Tea Table, Loon, Gull, Whetstone, Round, Minnow (Minnie's), Skinners, Long, Molson's, Lord's, Eagle, Threes Sisters, and Charest Islands are in Canadian waters.

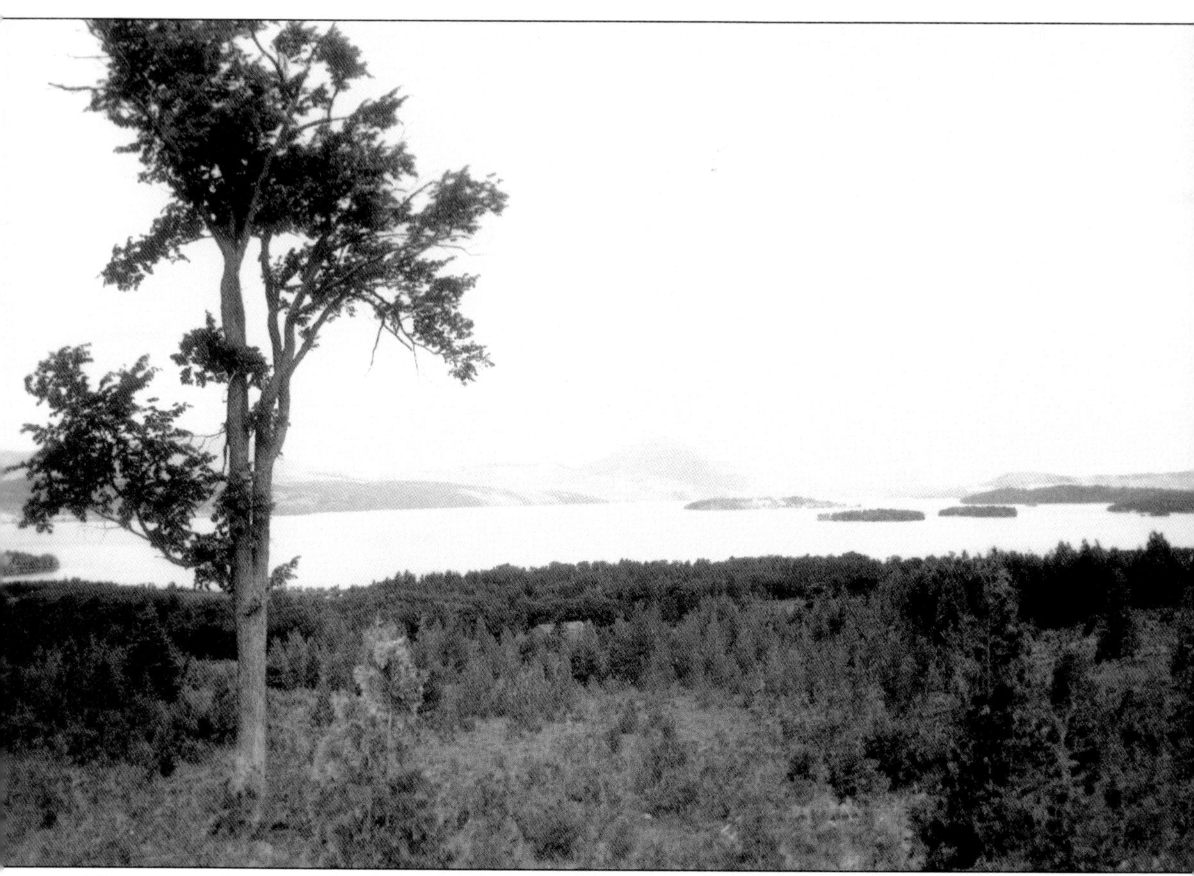

**Horseneck Island.** The first island on the lake, just north of the bluffs on Indian Point, is Horseneck Island, seen here on the far left. This island was once connected to the mainland by a peninsula or neck. It is a favorite spot for fishermen and also a place where sightings of the legendary lake creature Memphre have occurred.

**BELLE ISLAND.** Closer to the Canadian border but still in United States waters are Belle and Black Islands. They are landmarks for the border towns of North Derby, Vermont; Cedarville, Quebec; and Beebe, Vermont and Quebec. Belle Island is 20 acres in size and is known as one of the Twin Islands. In 1865, it was annexed to the town of Derby and was named after George W Bell, a Newport farmer.

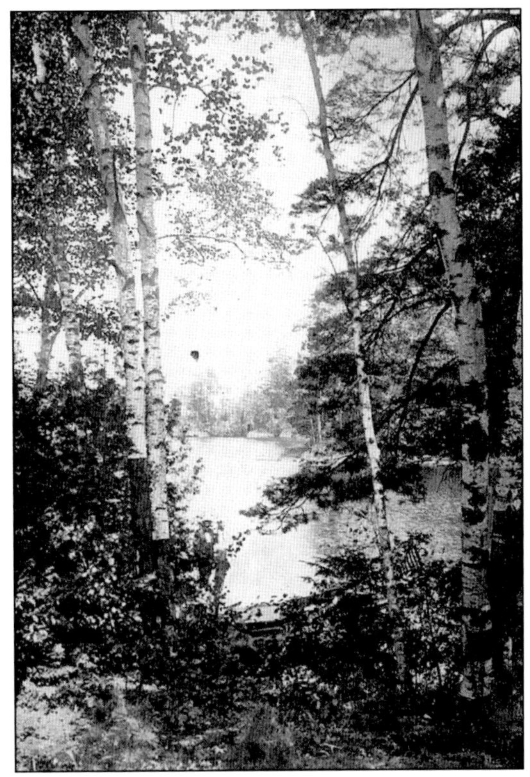

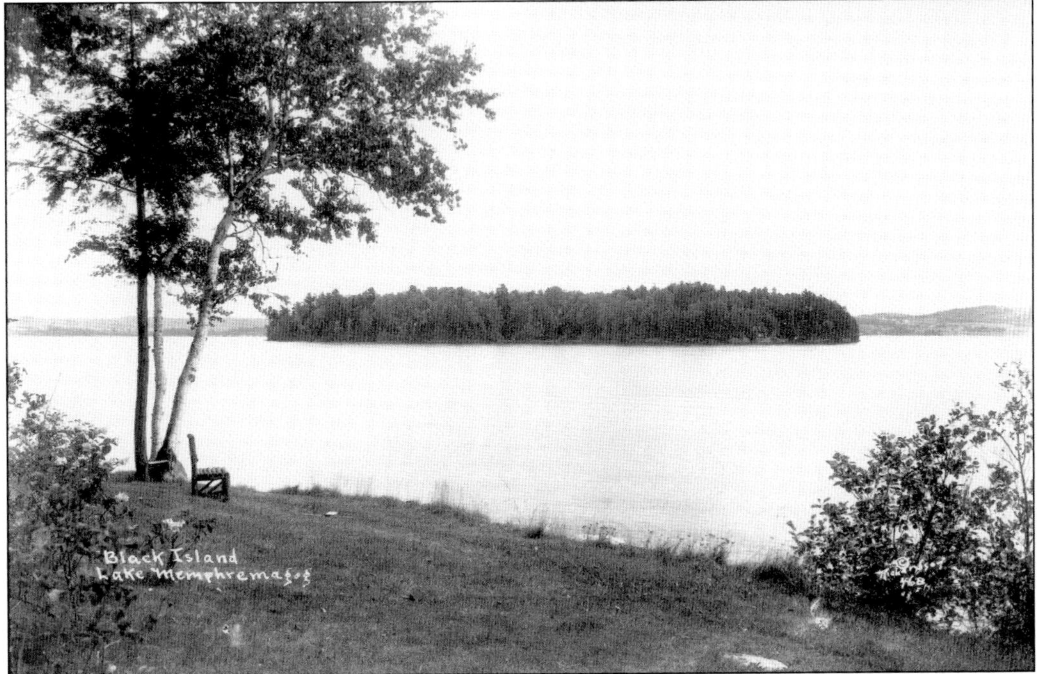


**BLACK ISLAND.** Considered one of the Twin Islands, Black Island is also 20 acres in size. In 1900, Frank Hawes and his family owned and occupied it. Frank Hawes's son Austin was Vermont's first forester.

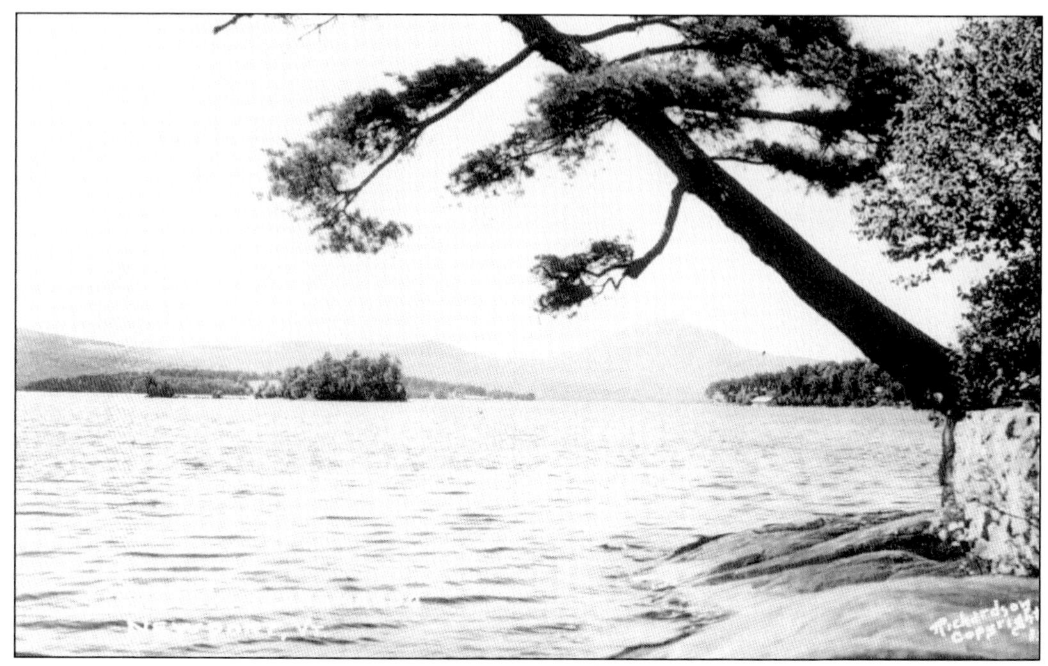

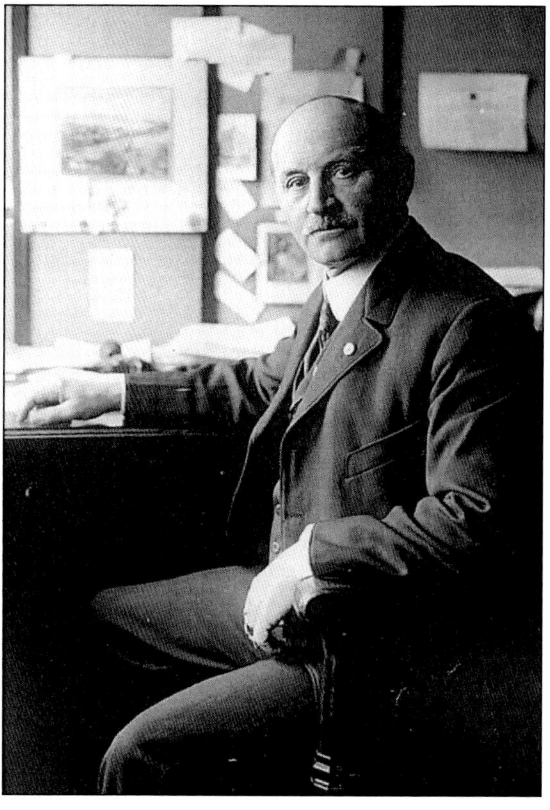

**Cove Island.** Cove Island (above) was also annexed to Derby Township. Businessmen Baxter, Flint, and Pike persuaded old farmer Selon Jackson to sell them his island for $10 each. In 1900, Col. Curtis S. Emery (left), purchased the island and built a cottage in 1910. In 1912, Colonel Emery's daughter Sally married Lt. Henry Flint at Cove Island. After the ceremony, the wedding party was taken by the steamer *Yioco* to Newport for a wedding breakfast at the bride's home. In 1918, Emery became the first mayor of Newport.

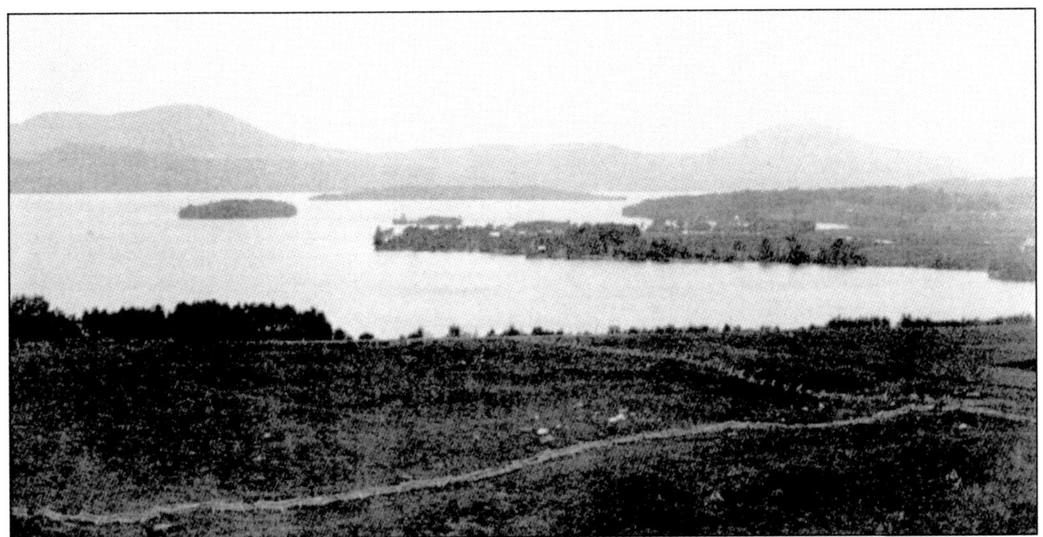

**Province Island.** North of Eagle Point and Lake Park lies the largest island in Lake Memphremagog. Province Island's 100 acres is separated into two countries by the 45th parallel's international boundary, and only one-third lies in American waters. The southern tip, seen here, is only five miles from Newport.

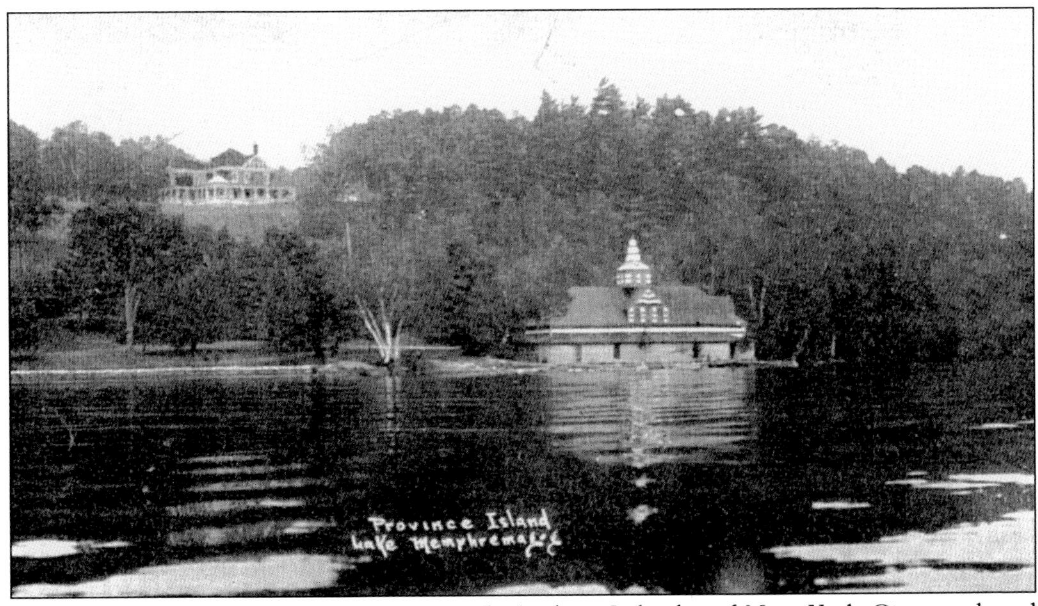


**The Province Island Mansion.** In 1885, Andrew Labriske of New York City purchased Province Island from the Carlos V. Pierce estate. He built a summer mansion in 1886, which was not open to visitors from the mainland. Benjamin Howard bought the island in 1917 with a blank check, and by 1922, telephone, electric services, and piped water had been brought to the island. Therefore, Province Island is also called Howard's Island by some local folks.

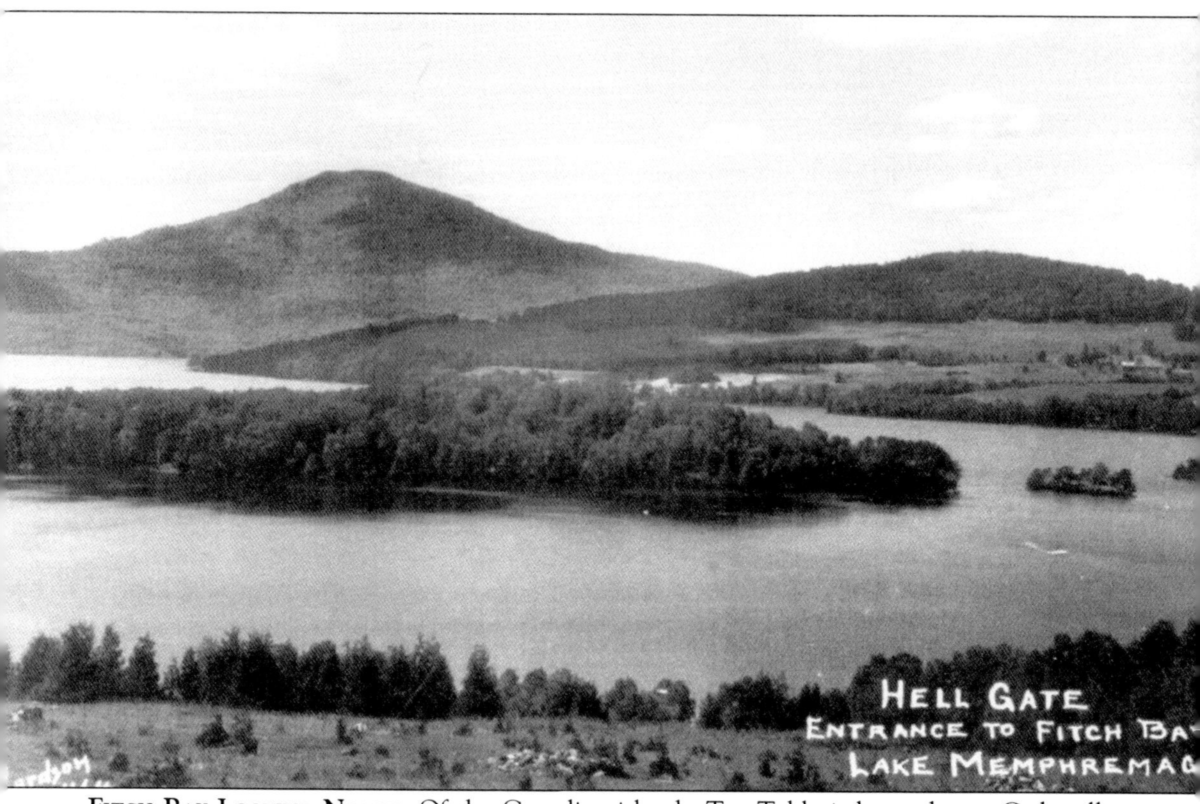


**FITCH BAY LOOKING NORTH.** Of the Canadian islands, Tea Table is located near Cedarville Wharf, Loon is in Fitch Bay, and Gull is north of Whetstone on the east shore. When the water is low, one can wade from one island to another. The 40-acre Whetstone Island stands at the entrance of Fitch Bay and was named for a quarry that furnished whetstones with the quality of imported oil stones. Fitch Bay, the eastern arm of Lake Memphremagog, was named after Col. George Fitch, an early settler who died in 1799.

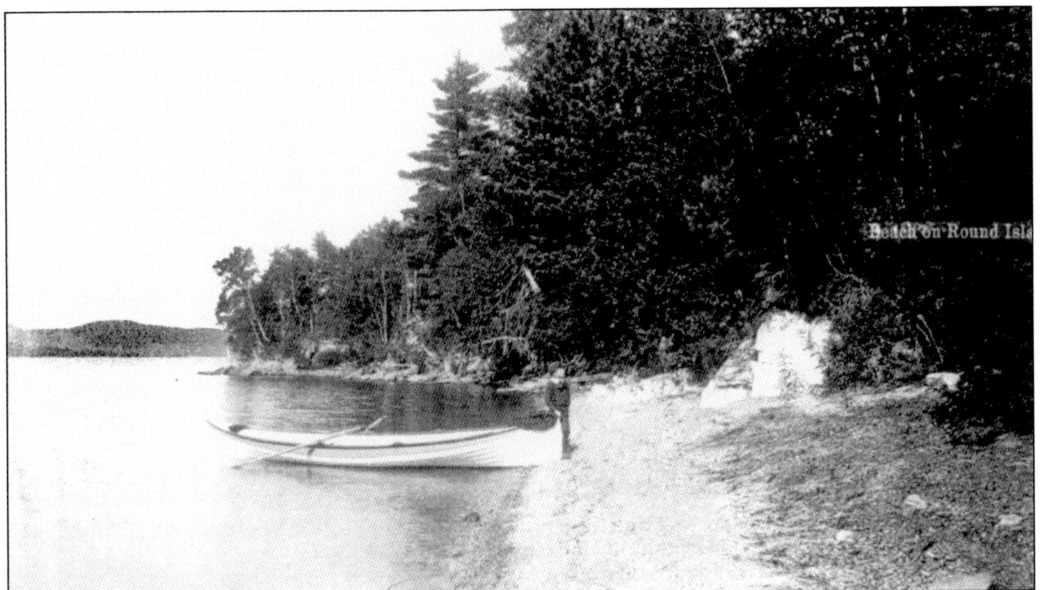


**ROUND ISLAND.** Near the base of Owl's Head on the west shore is 10-acre Round Island. Once covered with white birches and pines, the island was used seasonally by the Abenaki for several generations. Tomahawks, projectile points, and copper fishing hooks have been found here and preserved. Nearby, where the water is very shallow, a sand bar is called the Sunken Island by some.

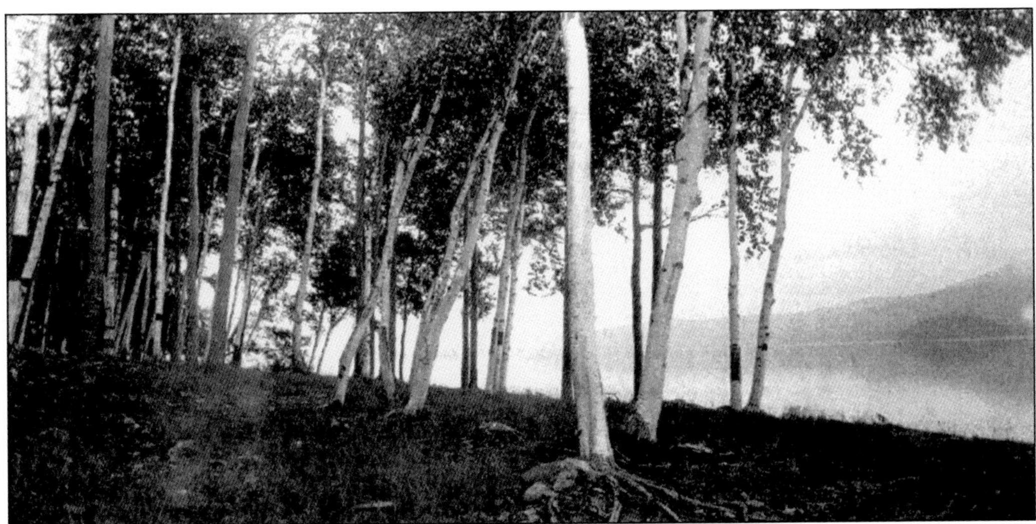

**MINNOW ISLAND.** Minnow Island, sometimes called Minnie's, is off Magoon Point and can be viewed from Bay View Park. Situated on the east shore, this island is half an acre of rocky and barren land once popular with picnickers from Bay View Beach during the late 1800s.

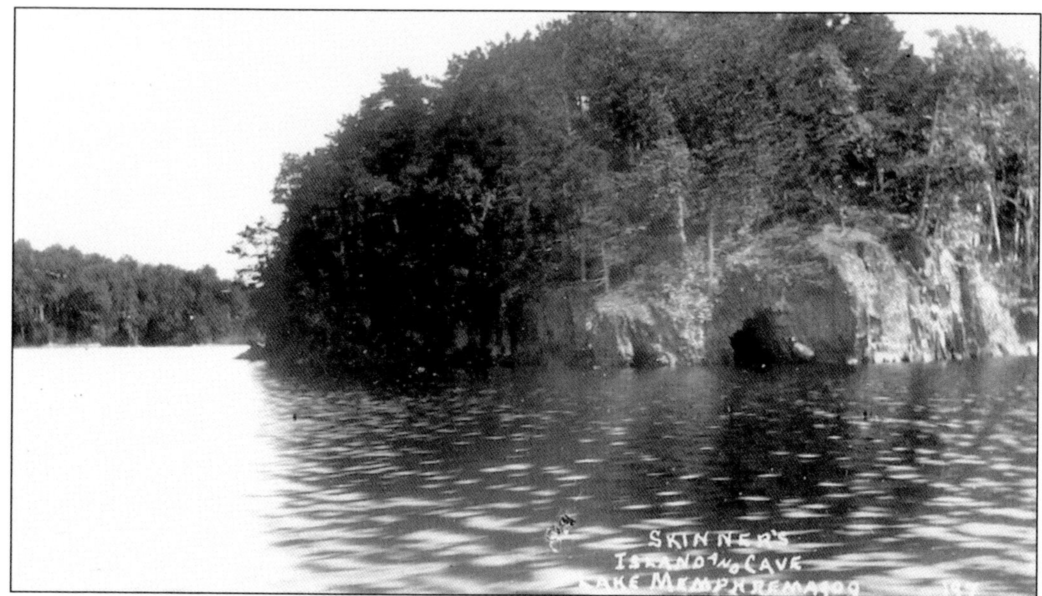


**SKINNER'S ISLAND.** Opposite Magoon Point, the 10-acre Skinner's Island is one of the most famous in Lake Memphremagog. Uriah Skinner, a known pirate and smuggler on the lake, often made his escape by boat, usually at night, disappearing from customs officers and lawmen near this island. The island's rocky overhang and its cave were likely his refuges. The island and its cave are named after Uriah Skinner and his escapades. Legend states that his skeleton was found in this cave.

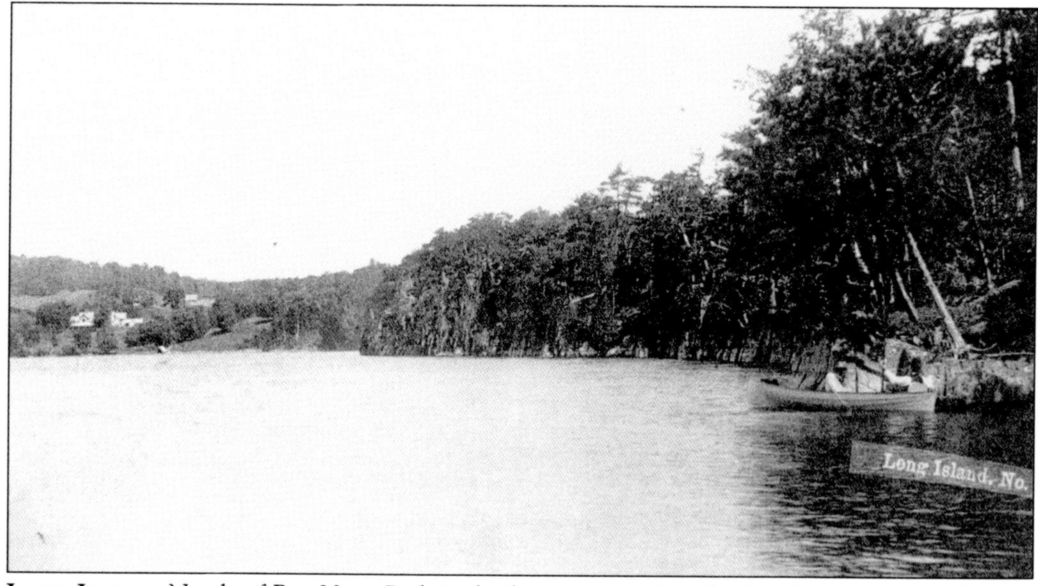


**LONG ISLAND.** North of Bay View Park is the longest island in the lake's waters. Long Island, 40 acres of broken ridges of rock (mostly granite), birch trees, dwarf pines, shrubs, and sandy beaches, was once known as a favorite spot for blueberry picking. On the southern end of Long Island poised on a high ledge is a granite boulder of 10 to 15 tons known as Balance Rock. It is so perched that just a light touch will set it to rocking. Several legends, both Abenaki and European, explain how and why the rock is there.

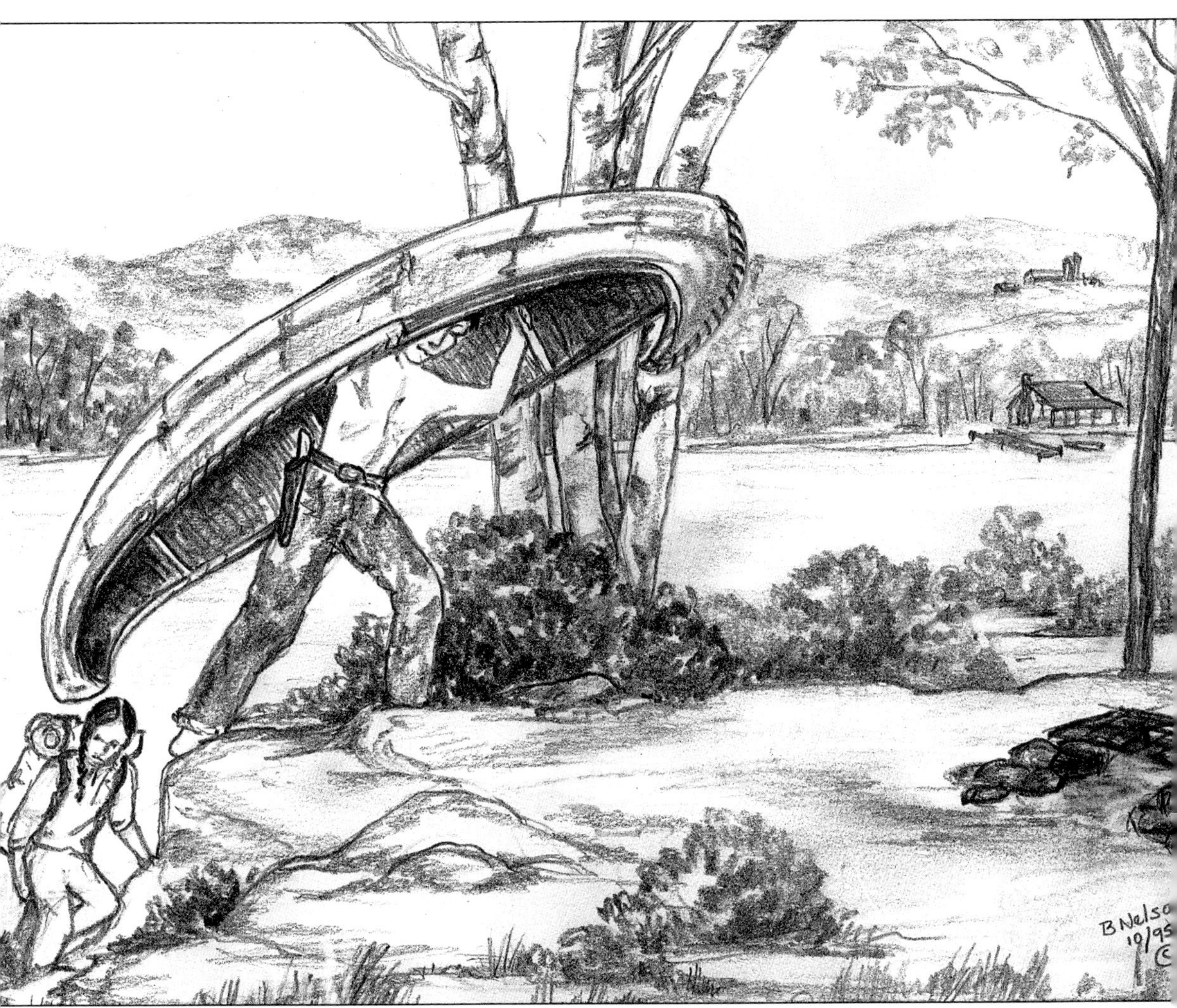


**MOLSON'S AND LORD'S ISLANDS.** South of Belmere Point at Quinn Bay, Molson's Island (50 acres) once had its own lighthouse. Lord's Island, about 25 acres, lies in the narrowest portion of the lake opposite Bryant's Landing on the west shore and is named for Stephen Lord, who settled in the early 1800s. He made the first clearing that furnished good pasturage near where he built his house. On many of these islands, Abenaki descendants still camp and canoe, a modern version of an ancient tradition.

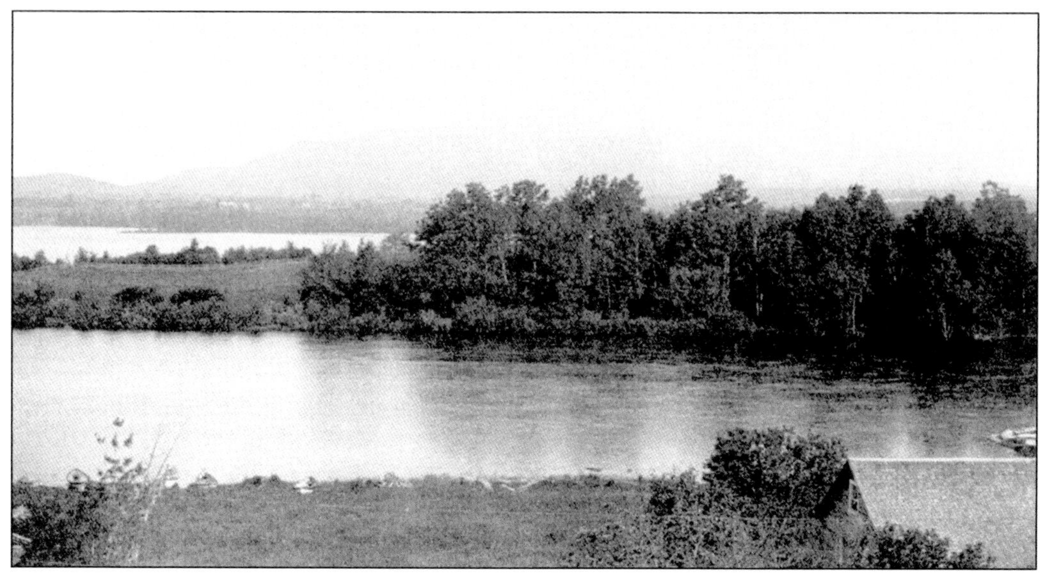

**The Last of the Islands.** Near Magog at the northern end of Lake Memphremagog are the last clump of islands. Eagle, or Eaglet, Island is located near the shores of the Hermitage Country Club property and was once accessed by club members only. The Three Sisters Islands are a group of small, rocky single islands, and Charest, formerly known as Cummins Island, is located off the end of Merry's Point at the mouth of the Magog River. The Magog is Lake Memphremagog's only outlet.

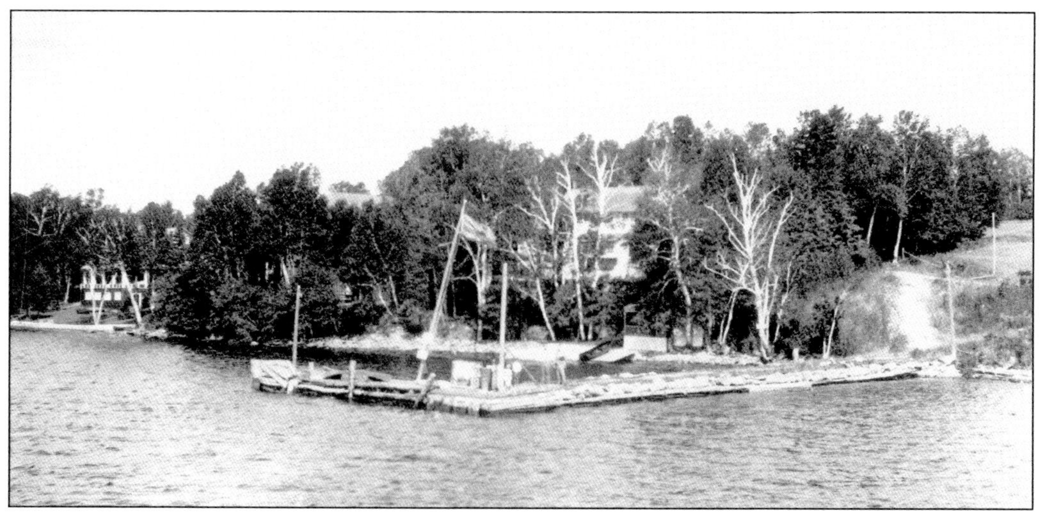

**The Hermitage Country Club.** In 1850, Judge Drummond of Montreal and Major Johnson, a Quebec City harbor master and retired British officer, built a large house called the Hermitage on 180 acres of farmland five miles from Magog. In 1928, the clubhouse burned down. After a $100,000 investment, it was rebuilt. Montrealers constructed summer homes and cottages around the club, and they have been owned by the same families for generations.

## *Seven*

# The Magog Outlet

Long before Capt. Ebenezer Hovey, Nicholas Austin, the Outlet (the early name of Magog), or Magog, this area was the location of one of the main villages of the Abenaki and had been occupied for hundreds of years. In the 1600s, the French asked permission of the Abenaki to build a truckhouse, or trading post, at the outlet of Lake Mamlabegwok. Permission was refused, but nonetheless, trade in pelts and furs was a livelihood on and around the lake. The first recorded settler within the bounds of Magog Township near the outlet was Capt. Ebenezer Hovey, a resident of Hatley. Nicholas Austin of Bolton built a gristmill on the outlet (the Magog River), which was a part of his original grant. Ralph Merry purchased the gristmill in 1798. Many of the early settlers were loyalists who wanted to remain under the British flag. The first school was established *c.* 1818, and the first mail was delivered on horseback by 1823. It was not until 1855 that the township of Magog was formed from portions of Hatley and Bolton. In 1888, the Outlet's name was changed to Magog, which received its charter as a town in 1890.

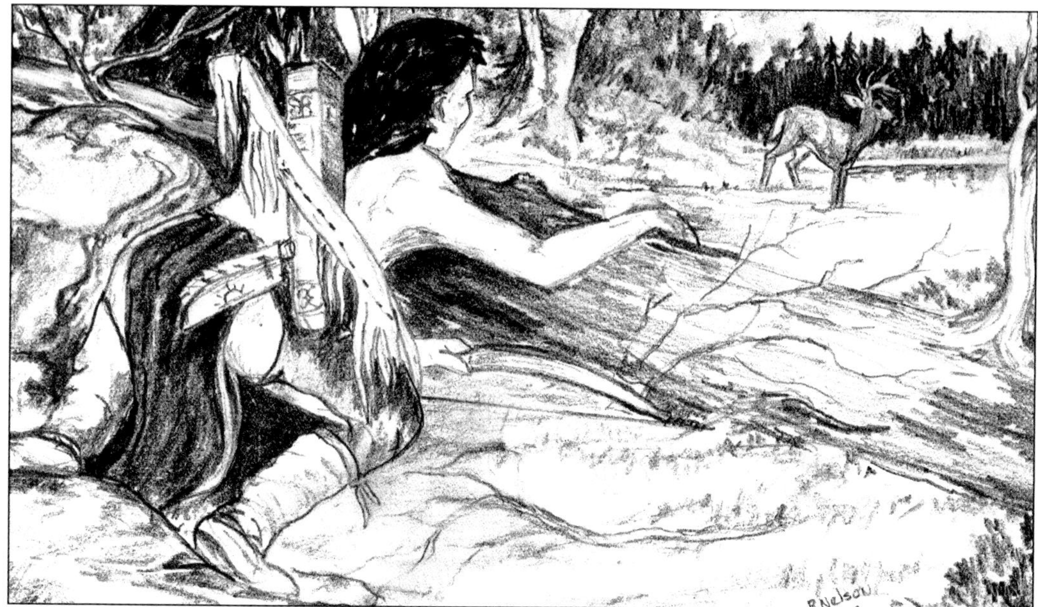

**THE OUTLET'S PREHISTORY.** The area around the outlet of Lake Mamlabegwok was home to the Abenaki Indians for hundreds of years. The location was chosen for its abundance of game, fish, waterfowl, and plants for gathering. Early settlers discovered a permanent fish weir, or fish dam, on the outlet when they first arrived. Another favorable feature was the easy access of waterway travel routes. From here, it was possible to travel via the St. Lawrence to the Great Lakes or to the northern Atlantic; via the Connecticut River to southern New England; or via the Missisquoi to the Champlain and Hudson and down to New York.

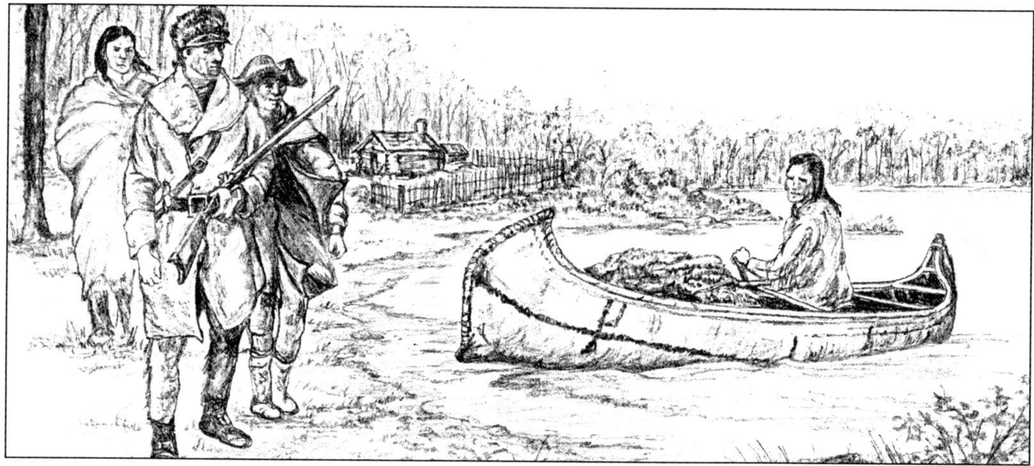

**EARLY CROSS-CULTURAL CONTACT.** Because of its ideal location for waterway travel and the abundance of nearby streams, lakes, marshes, and game, the Indian villages at Magog and Sherbrook were ideal centers for the pelt trade. First to be aware of this were the French, allies of the Abenaki during the French and Indian War. The French were more interested in furs and were encouraged to live with the Algonquians, whereas the English wanted land to settle and did not understand the native way. When France ceded to Britain, the Abenaki were left out of the treaties. Some families remained and adjusted to living and trading with the Europeans, French, and English. The fur trade was Magog's and Lake Memphremagog's first cross-cultural business.

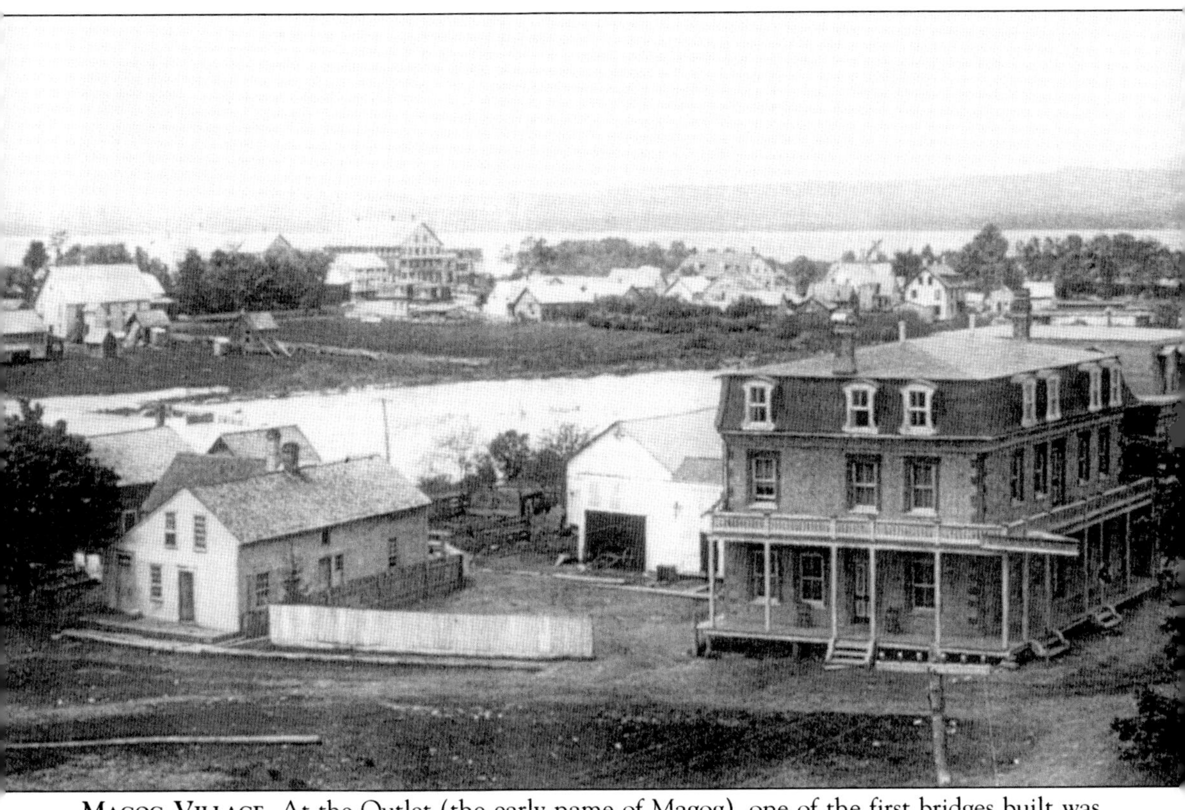

**Magog Village.** At the Outlet (the early name of Magog), one of the first bridges built was pole supported over the Magog River, which is the only outlet for Lake Memphremagog at the northernmost end. This location, where the Cherry River flows in and the Magog drains out, was chosen for the village of Magog. The Magog River flows into the St. Francis River at Sherbrook and on to the St. Lawrence Seaway, a favorite waterway route for the Abenaki. Ralph Merry, one of the first settlers, bought Nicholas Austin's gristmill and built the first sawmill. Merry came to the outlet from Lynn, Massachusetts, and acquired 13,000 acres in 1798. Merry settled here with his wife Sarah (Sylvester) Merry and had nine children, one of which was Ralph Merry IV.

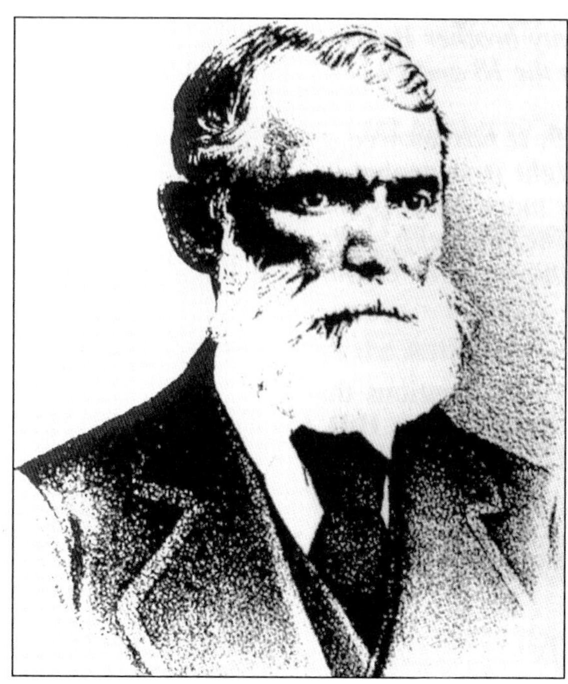

**Ralph Merry IV.** Ralph Merry IV was born in Massachusetts in 1786. He married Ruth Whitcomb and had a family. A man of slight build, only 123 pounds, he taught school from his father's home in 1818 long before the schoolhouse was built. On May 2, 1863, the year of his death, he made one last entry into his diary: "Pray that I may die with a smile on my face." (Courtesy of Stanstead Historical Society, Canada.)

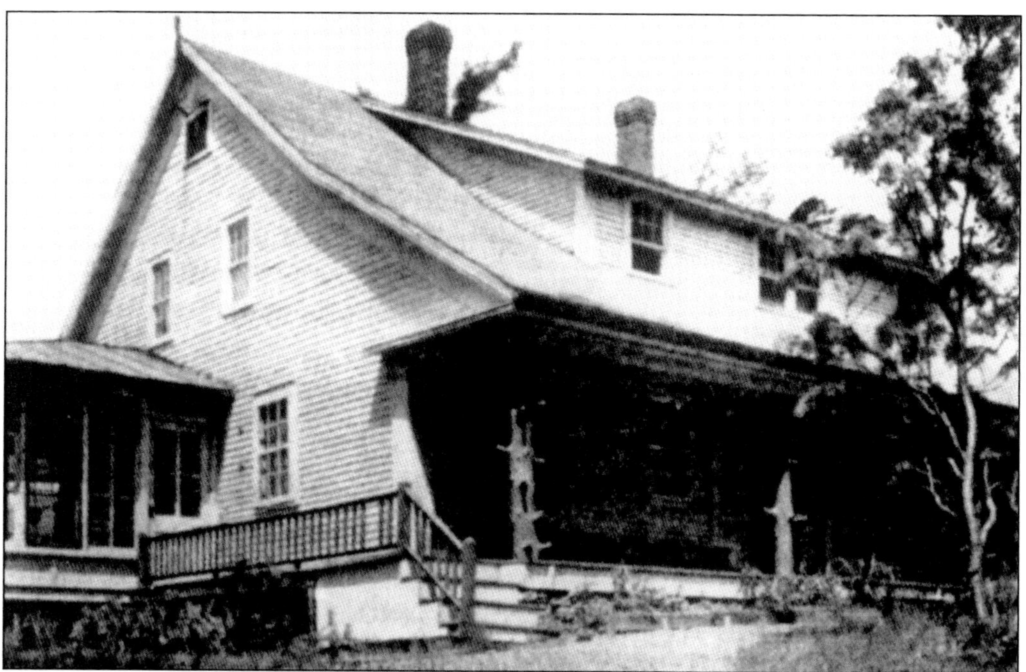

**The Merry Homestead's Secret.** The Ralph Merry IV homestead, built in 1814, still stands today on the corner of Main and Merry Streets. Found under the floorboards during a renovation were some of Merry's diaries. These diaries were hand-sewn and focused on sea serpent sightings witnessed by eight people in 1816. One of these diaries, which revealed the eyewitnesses to be Wadleigh, Rider, Channell, and Merry, was presented to the Stanstead Historical Society by descendants of the Merry family in 1959. Today, the sea serpent is known as Memphre by most local folks. (Courtesy of Stanstead Historical Society, Canada.)

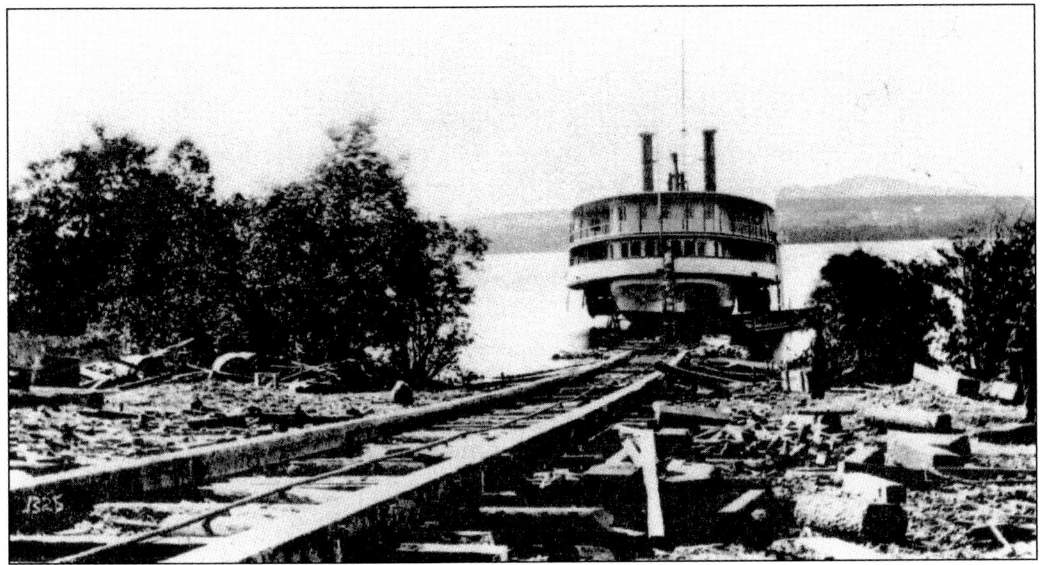

**THE LADY'S FIRST LAUNCHING.** The first launching of the *Lady of the Lake* was at Magog on September 10, 1867. The paddle wheeler only slid into the water and stopped. The passengers who had paid for tickets and the hundreds of spectators were somewhat disconcerted. It took two weeks to disengage her, and on September 26 at 5:00 p.m., she finally left Magog, Quebec, on her maiden voyage to Newport, Vermont. The trip took just two hours.

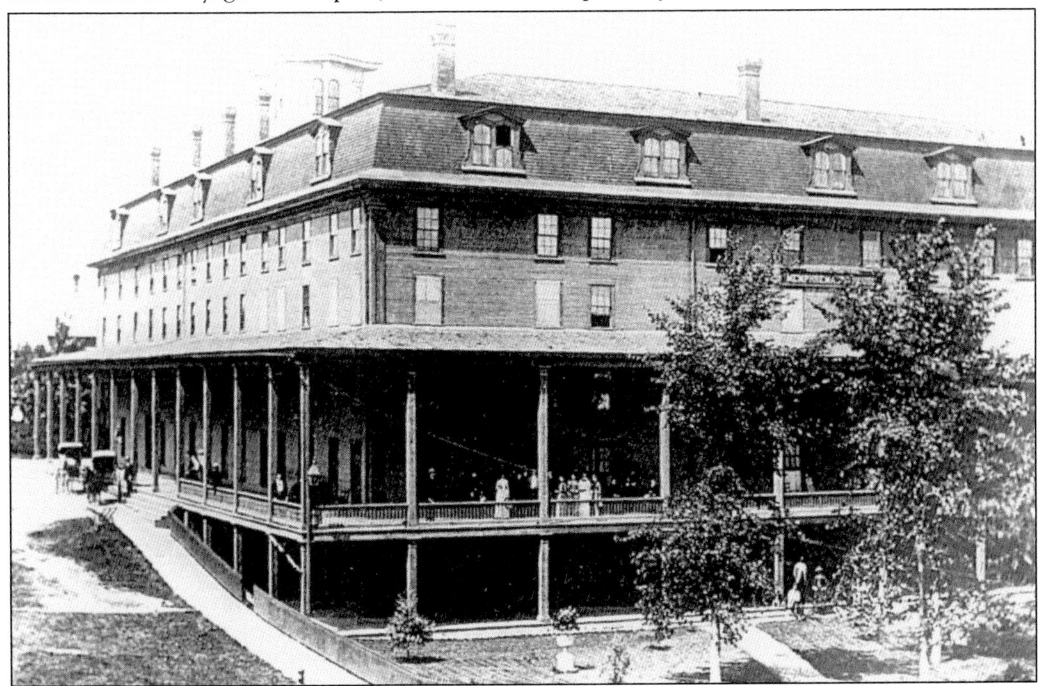

**THE MEMPHREMAGOG HOTEL CELEBRATION.** A crowd of spectators and the hotel's summer guests stayed over to witness the *Lady of the Lake*'s maiden voyage. Peter Porter, a harness maker, suddenly gave a yell, "She's coming!" The steamer was moving to the rhythm of her paddle wheels as she slowly came alongside the wharf and fastened to the pilings. This version was remembered by Charles D. Robinson.

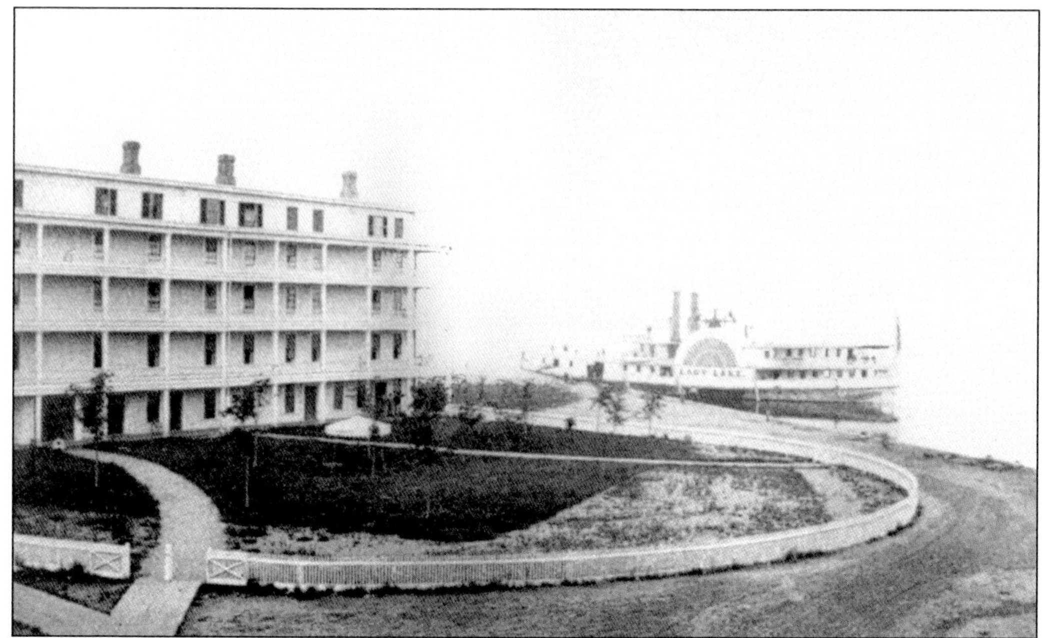

**The Celebration Continues.** Captain Handyside, the *Lady of the Lake*'s first captain, is dressed in a blue uniform with gold stripes on his cap and a big blue boat cloak reaching below his knees. He made his way up the Memphremagog Hotel stairway to the events, which lasted until midnight and celebrated the largest paddle-wheel steamer's maiden voyage to Newport. Capt. George W. Fogg was still in command of the *Mountain Maid* but took over the helm of the *Lady* in 1868.

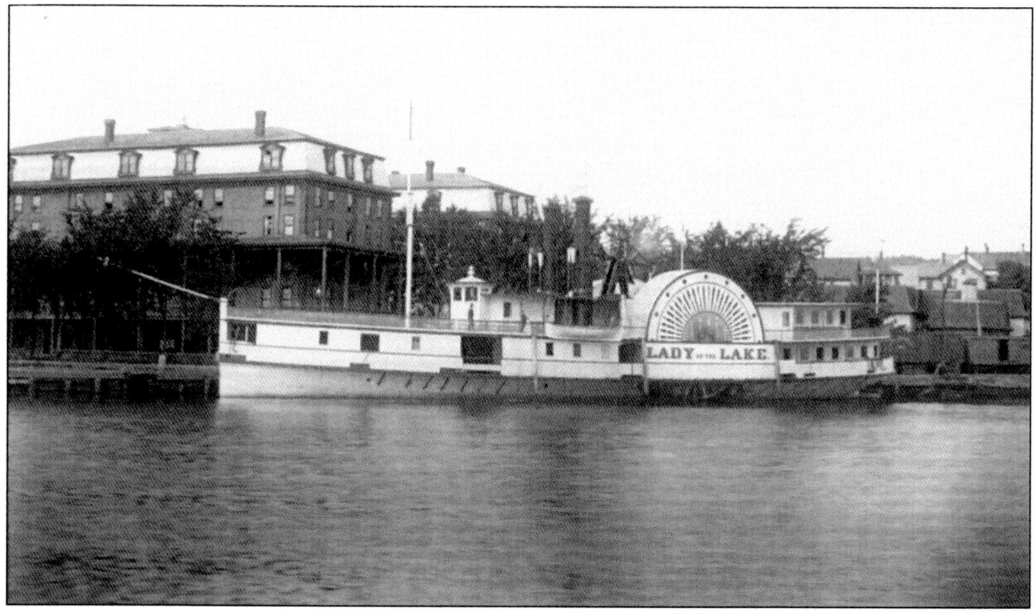


**The Excursion.** The *Lady of the Lake* left Newport's Steamboat Wharf and traveled across the border, its first stop being at Bay View Park on the east shore, before darting back and forth to the lake's other wharves along the way. Then she headed north to the Magog Wharf, a round trip of 75 miles that offered ever-changing views of the lake and its scenery.

# Lake, Mountain and Island Scenery

## * * * * * UNSURPASSED * * * * *

**MORNING TRIP.**

| | | |
|---|---|---|
| Lve. | Newport | 8.00 A.M. |
| " | Mountain House | 8.50 " |
| " | Perkins Wharf | 9.10 " |
| Arr. | Georgeville | 9.55 " |
| Lve. | Georgeville | 10.00 " |
| " | Mountain House | 11.00 " |
| Arr. | Newport | 12 00 " |

CONNECTING WITH

Day Express for White Mountains and all Points South.

**AFTERNOON TRIP.**

| | | |
|---|---|---|
| Lve. | Newport | 1.00 P.M. |
| " | Mountain House | 2.00 " |
| " | Georgeville | 2.55 " |
| Arr. | Magog | 3.55 " |
| Lve. | Magog | 4.00 " |
| " | Georgeville | 5.00 " |
| " | Mountain House | 5.45 " |
| Arr. | Newport | 6.50 " |

CONNECTING WITH

All Trains North and South.

THE FINE IRON STEAMER

# LADY OF THE LAKE,

Commencing June 29, 1891, will run until further notice on

## LAKE MEMPHREMAGOG

Leaving Newport every morning and afternoon (Mondays excepted), sailing among the Islands, passing Skinner's Cave, Balance Rock, and many beautiful residences and spacious grounds, landing at Mountain House, Georgeville and Magog, making a trip of 75 miles, affording ever-changing views of Lake and Mountain Scenery.

## On MONDAYS the Boat will make one trip through the entire length of the Lake,

Leaving Newport 8.00 A.M., Mountain House 8 50 A.M., Georgeville 9.40 A.M., Magog 10.40 A.M. Returning, leave Magog 12.45 P.M., Georgeville 1.45 P.M., Mountain House 2.30 P.M. Arrive Newport 3.45 P.M., in season to connect with the express train for Montreal, *via* the Canadian Pacific Railway.

**SABBATH SCHOOLS AND EXCURSION PARTIES** will be given low rates, and landed at desirable places for Picnics. The boat can be chartered for Excursions The steamer has been thoroughly overhauled, refitted and furnished with all modern appliances for safety and comfort. The Company reserves the right to use the steamer for large excursions, cancelling regular trips such days, without notice.

**A FIRST-CLASS RESTAURANT** has been added, where parties can be furnished with nice warm meals at all hours. Fine Cigars and Confectionery, and views of the Lake, on sale at the news stand. **SEASON TICKETS FOR SALE ON BOARD THE BOAT.**

For information regarding Excursion Rates, etc., apply to

| H. E. FOLSOM, Supt., | D. J. FLANDERS, G. P. A., | C. C. BULLOCK Master, |
|---|---|---|
| LYNDONVILLE, VT. | BOSTON, MASS. | NEWPORT, VT. |

A TIMETABLE. Above is an 1891 timetable for the paddle-wheel steamer the *Lady of the Lake*.

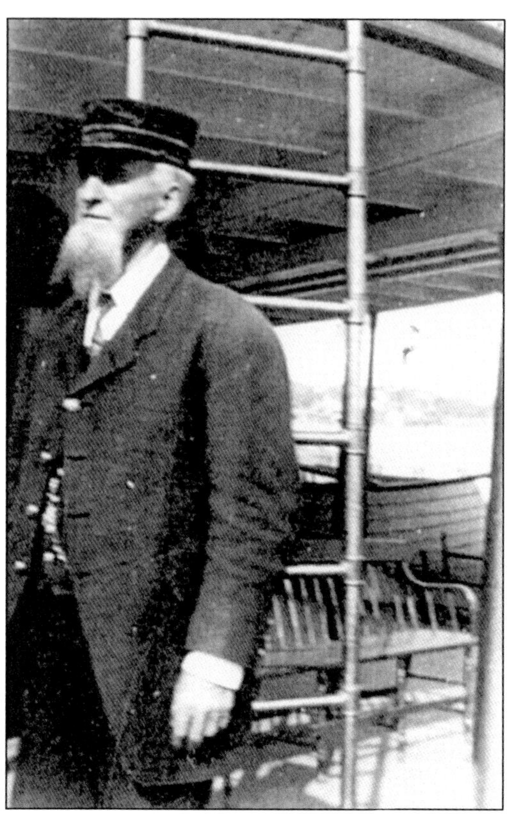

**Capt. Charles C. Bullock.** The last captain to pilot the *Lady of the Lake*, owned by the Boston & Maine Railroad, was Charles Bullock (1837–1916). He was the son of Increase and Harriet (Cross) Bullock. Captain Bullock died on August 23, 1916, in Granby, Quebec. His wife, Betsey (Channell) Bullock, had predeceased him in December 1908, just a month after they had celebrated their golden wedding anniversary.

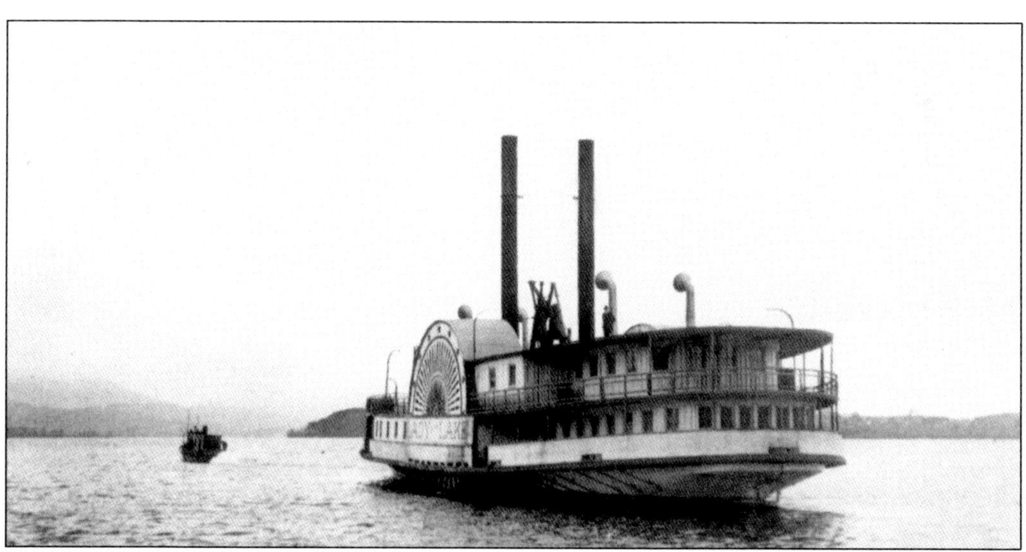

**The Retirement.** After the death of Capt. Charles Bullock in 1916, the *Lady of the Lake* was towed from the Newport Wharf at Railroad Square to the Magog Wharf on October 20, 1917. There she lay idle until Colin C. MacPhearson acquired ownership. He dismantled the lake's largest paddle wheeler, as there was no interest in lake excursions once the automobile was introduced.

## *Eight*

# THE WEST SHORE

The west shore of Lake Memphremagog remained wild longer than the other areas, partly because of the terrain and the mountains. The western shores were frequented the most by the Abenaki and other Algonquian Native Americans, especially those traveling and trading west. The proximity of the Missisquoi River and its wide and winding path through the Green Mountains to Lake Champlain became a destination from the west-shore portage place near Owl's Head. Owl's Head Mountain and its surrounding area were considered sacred lands and were visited often. Early settlers on this side of the lake also had difficulty surviving until gristmills, sawmills, and blacksmiths arrived. Later, the west shore became a favorite tourist attraction due to the Potton Springs and the Mountain House with its mountain trails and magnificent views. The Lake Memphremagog steamers—the *Mountain Maid*, the *Lady of the Lake*, and the *Anthemis*—stopped at western-shore wharves on their daily excursions around the lake.

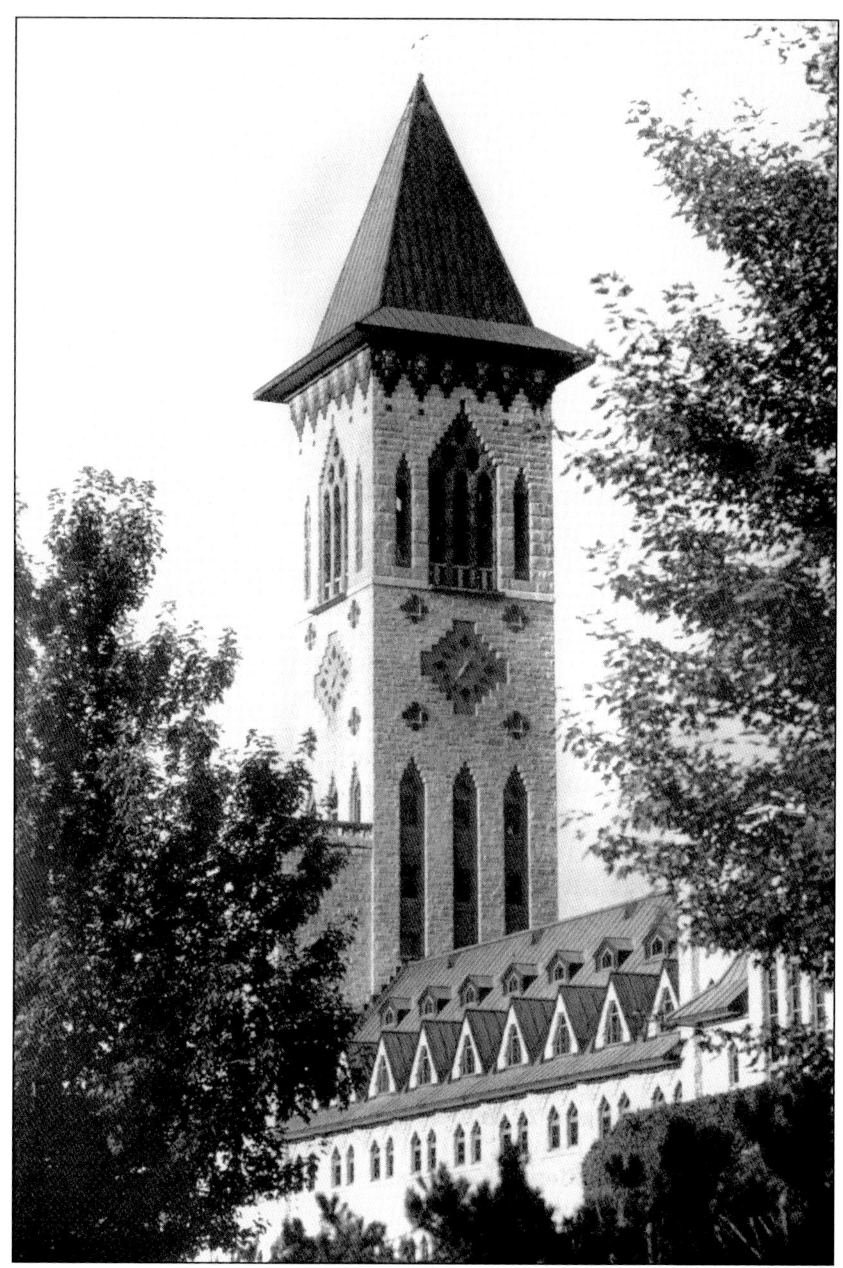

**St. Benoit-du-Lac.** Nicholas Austin, a Quaker and a Tory, was born in England in 1736. He was the first settler to the northern shores of Lake Memphremagog. Arriving from New Hampshire on foot at Duncansboro, he bought a canoe from the local Abenaki. He then paddled up the west shore to Sargent's Bay and finally settled in Bolton Township. Austin was buried in a lone grave in 1821. The abbey, St. Benoit-du-Lac, dates from 1912, when the Benedictine monks moved from France because of laws hostile to religious congregations. They came to the municipality of Austin in Bolton Township at Gibralter Point. The abbey and its farmland is where the monks live a religious life observing the teachings of the Italian St. Benoit De Nursie (480–547 B.C.). The architectural style is due to the arrival, in the 1930s, of Dom Bellot, a Benedictine from France. (Courtesy of St. Benoit-du-Lac, Bolton.)

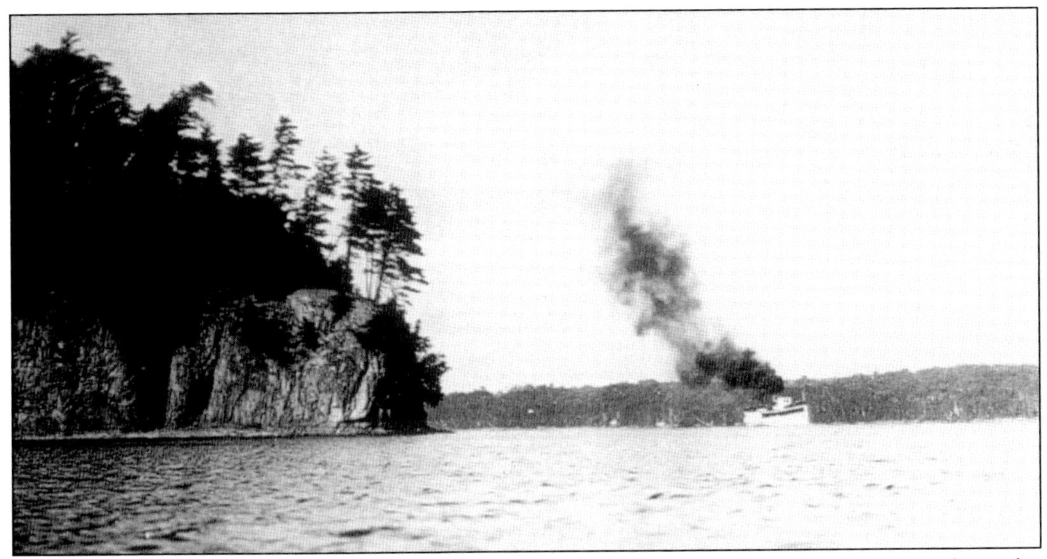

**Gibralter Castle.** On Gibralter Point at the entrance of Sargent's Bay, the waters run deep, the cliffs are high, and the pines stand tall. In 1883, a Montreal capitalist built a five-story summer hotel with a French roof and a cupola dome called Gibralter Castle. Legend tells of the ghost of Gibralter Castle. On certain nights, a bright light shone from the castle dome and cast an outline of a human skull. The building, never completed, was dismantled and shipped to Montreal.

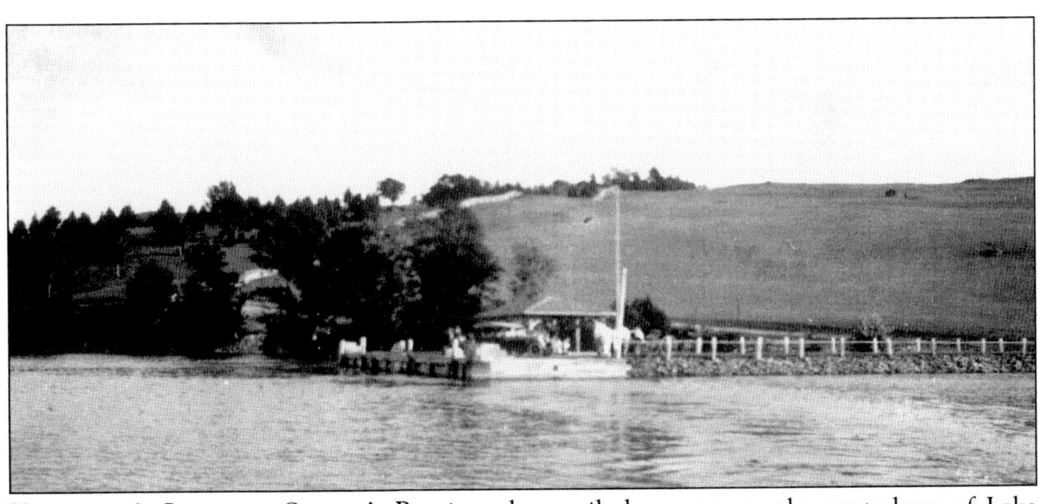

**Knowlton's Landing.** Sargent's Bay is a three-mile-long arm on the west shore of Lake Memphremagog. At Knowlton's Landing, the bay narrows up toward wooded hills with cold water springs in attractive welcome. In the 1870s, Captain Fogg repurchased and rebuilt his *Mountain Maid* steamer here, creating the *Mountain Maid II*.

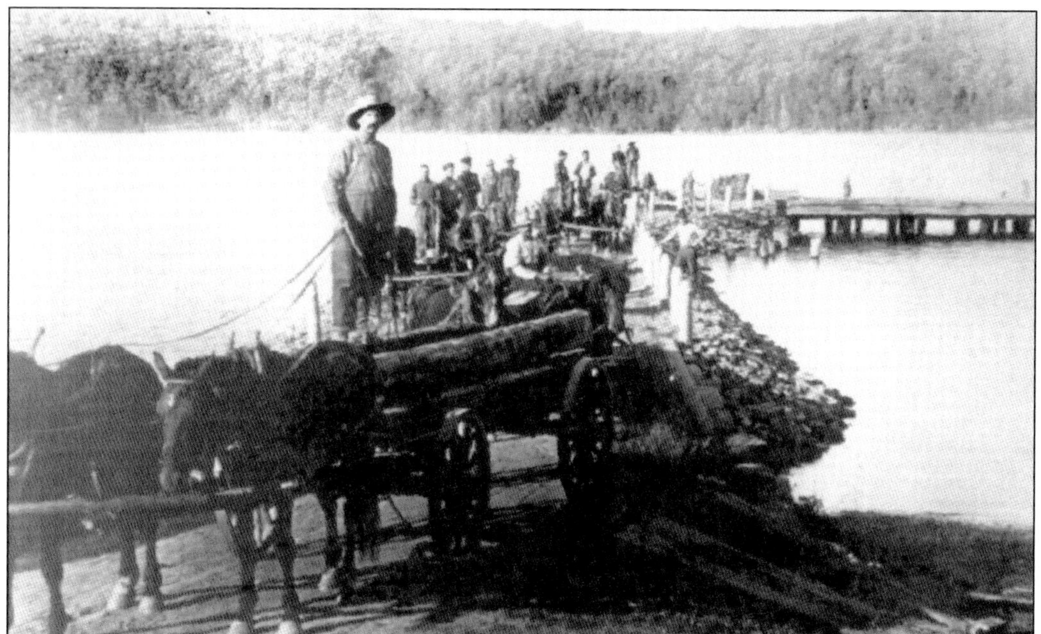

**The Wharf.** This c. 1900 photograph was taken while the Knowlton's Landing Wharf was being built. Charles Ethier is the man on the first horse team. (Courtesy of Potton Heritage Association.)

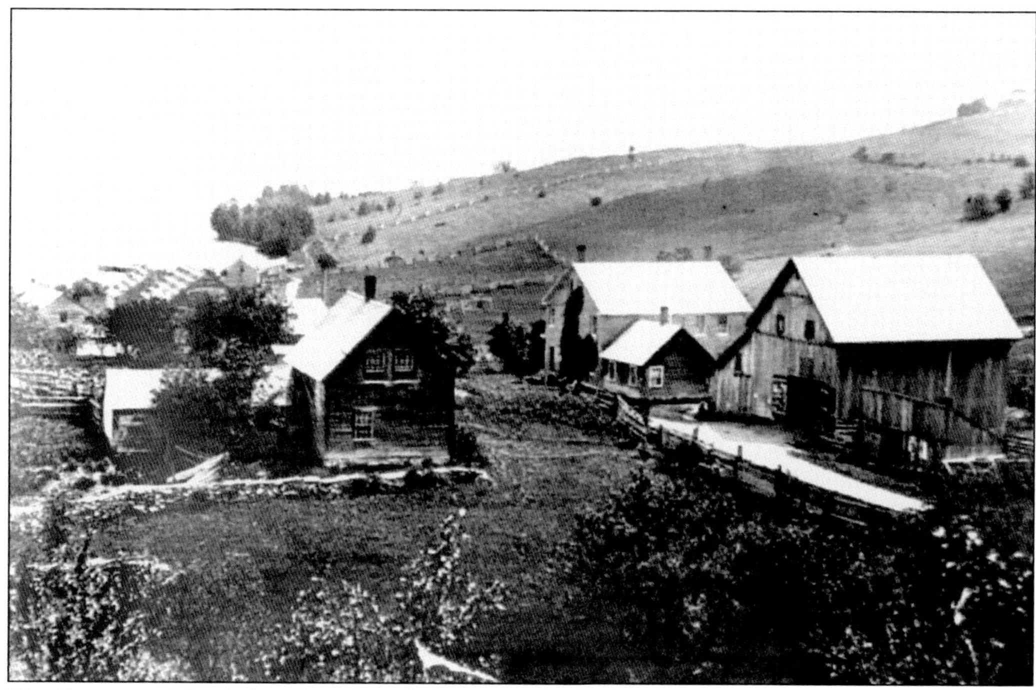

**The Landing.** Nestled at the edge of a cove are the buildings of an early Knowlton's Landing. The end of the wharf can just barely be seen. (Courtesy of Potton Heritage Association.)

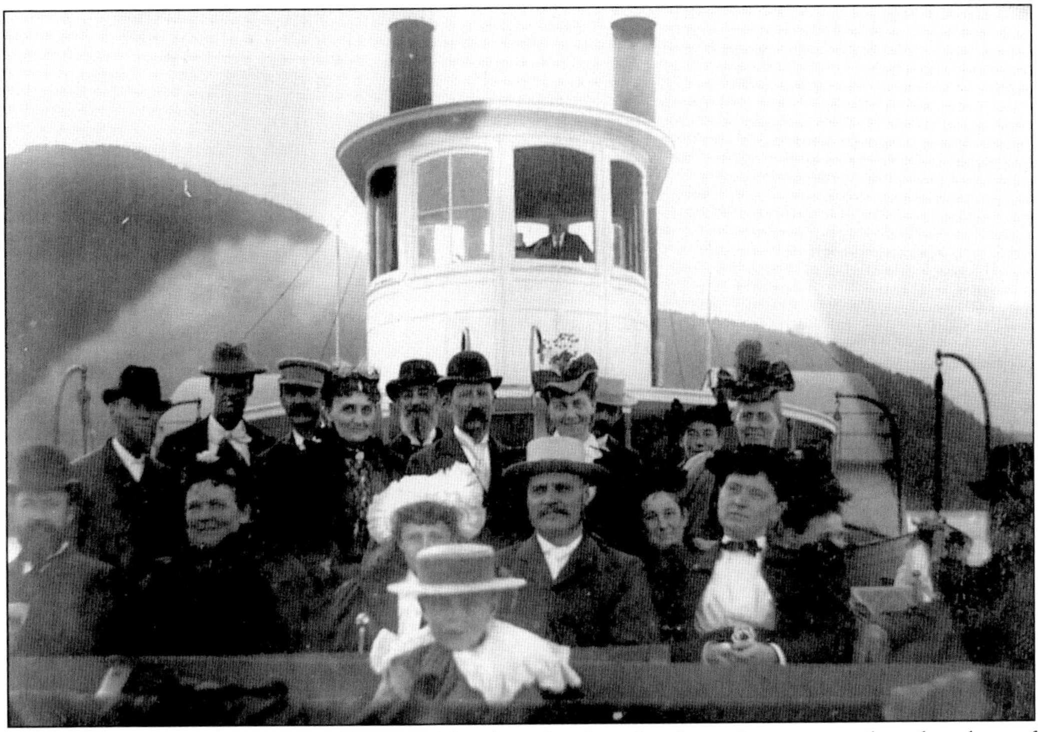

**THE KNOWLTON'S LANDING PICNIC.** The board of trade, later known as the chamber of commerce, was established in Newport, Vermont, in 1892. Its purpose was to secure prosperous enterprises. One hundred members enjoyed the board of trade picnic at the Knowlton's Landing grounds after an outing aboard the *Lady of the Lake*. The band played all day, making the outing a merry one.

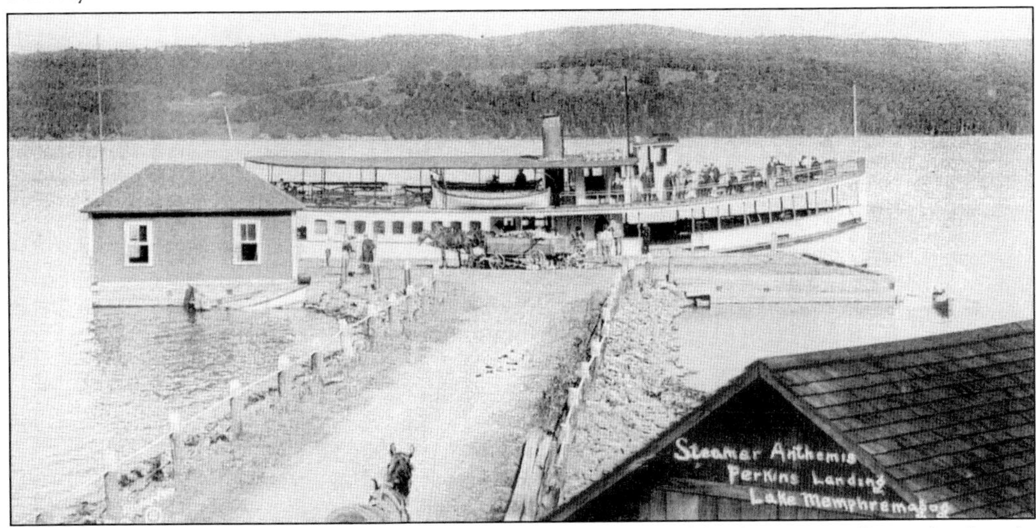


**PERKINS LANDING.** Samuel Perkins settled here in 1840 and built a sawmill on the brook. Perkins Landing and Wharf is sometimes known as Trojan Park. Years later, Capt. George Fogg constructed a sawmill here and employed Alonzo Magoon, a 21-year-old Abenaki descendant. Magoon lived in a shanty and cut wood for the captain's steamboats. In 1875, Magoon was caught in a snowstorm while crossing the lake from Georgeville and died.

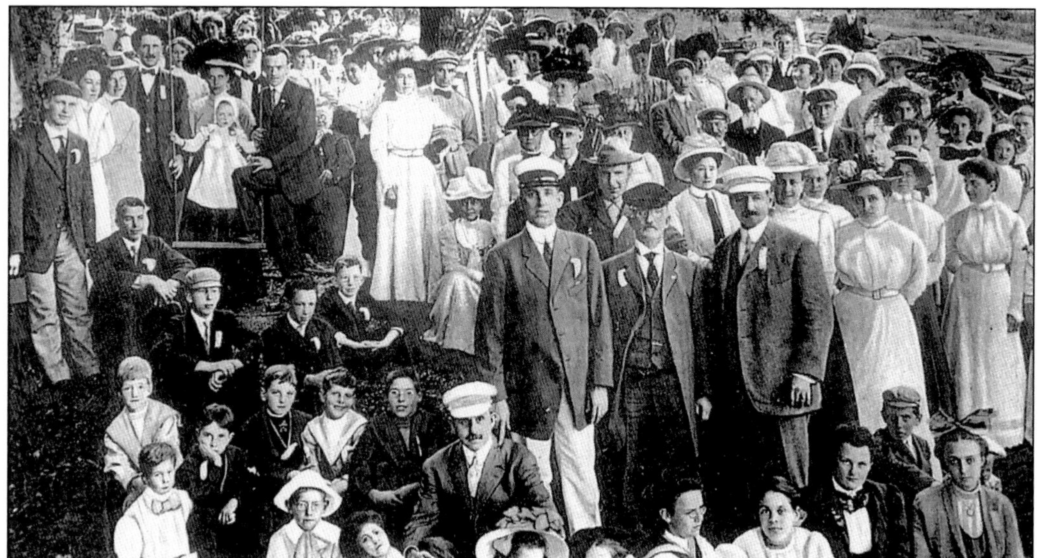

**The Yacht Club Picnic.** The Memphremagog Yacht Club's second annual picnic was held at Perkins Landing in 1908. The yacht club was first organized in 1907 with shares selling for $10 each to fund a first-class clubhouse and boat anchorage at Newport, Vermont, "for pure healthful recreation." Newport businessman Charles Bigelow of Bigelow's Pharmacy is the middle of the three men standing in the front.

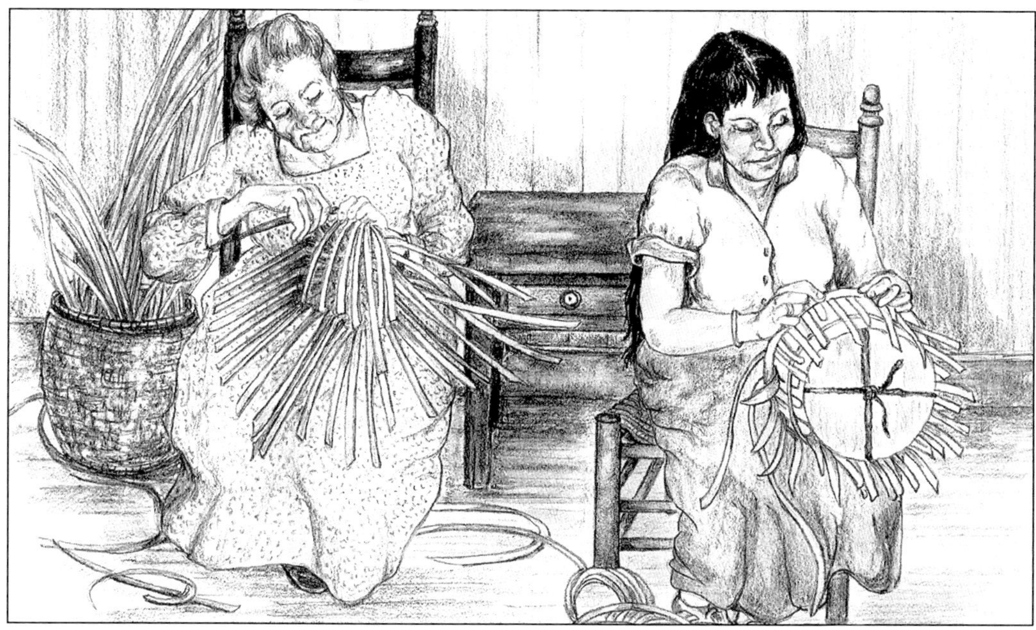

**Ash and Sweet-Grass Baskets.** With the collapse of the fur trade, restrictions on hunting and fishing, and major adjustments to their traditional lifestyle, many Abenaki people turned to making black ash and sweet-grass baskets to sell to tourists and villagers around the shores of Lake Memphremagog. They would make baskets all winter to sell during the summer season, maintaining seasonal rounds. One of the favorite stopover places was Vale Perkins, a traditional travel site. They would set up their baskets on the porch of a big white house owned by the Perkins family and advertise the items for sale.

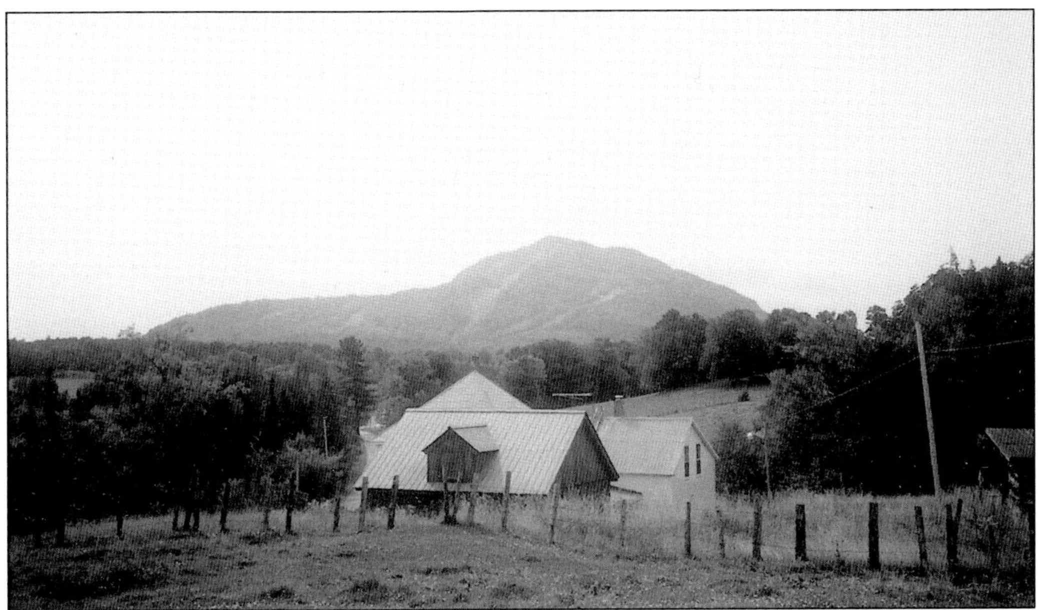

**Vale Perkins.** Near the hamlet of Vale Perkins on the west shore of Memphremagog and overlooked by Owl's Head Mountain is the location of the Potton Stones. This location is at an important prehistoric portage point for the early Abenaki and Algonquian Indians to get to the Missisquoi River. The Missisquoi flows into Lake Champlain and south to New York or north to the St. Lawrence River, an important waterway route for trade and travel.

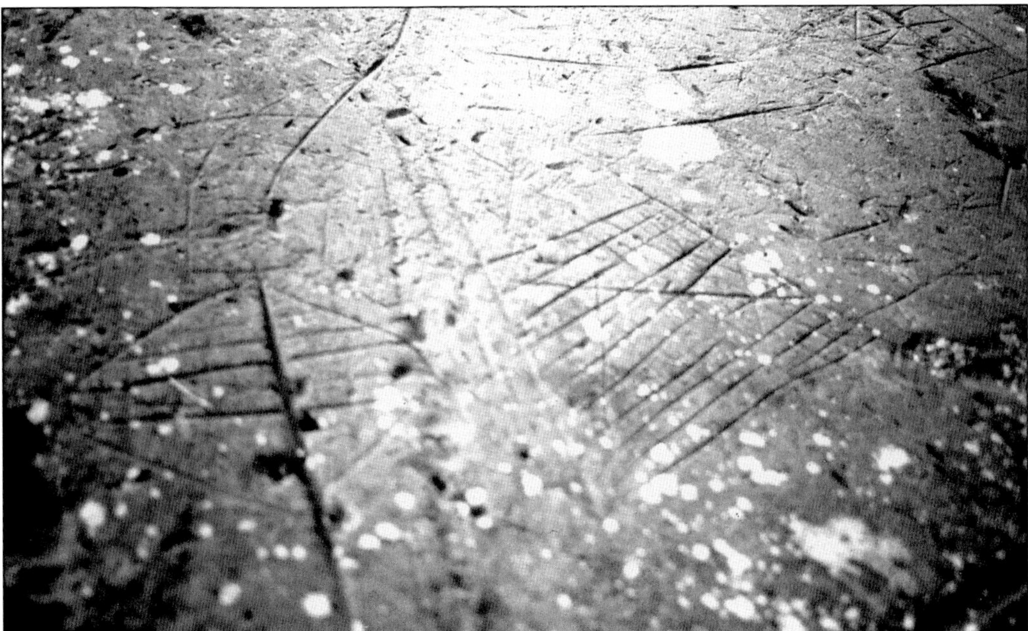

**The Potton Stones.** Along a brook and in a pasture are several areas that bear stones covered in petroglyphs. Many theories have surfaced as to the origins of these carved markings. In reality, they derive from early Native Americans. The markings are Algonquian, more than likely Abenaki, and they relate winter counts, fish kills, village numbers, and other informative communications to other Algonquian travelers and neighboring tribes.

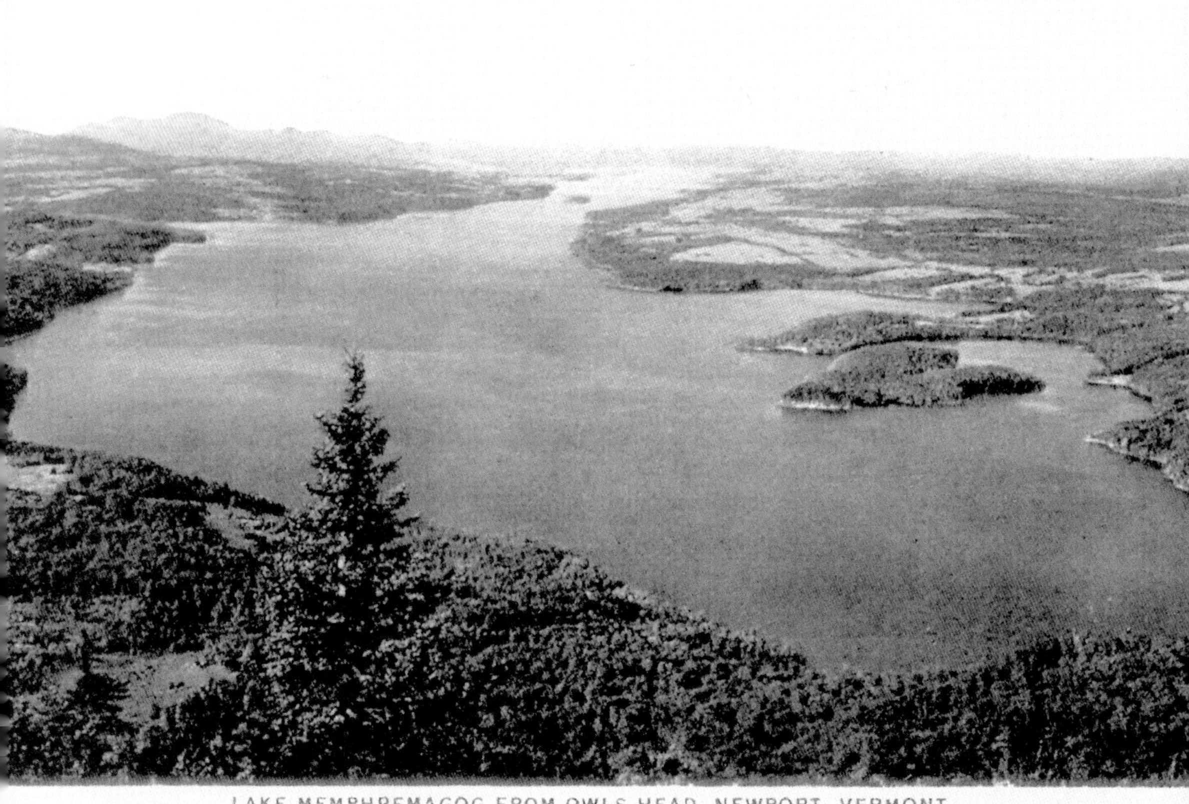


**OWL'S HEAD MOUNTAIN.** The mountain was named by the Abenaki to honor Chief Owl. To them, the jagged profile of the mountain resembled Chief Owl's face when lying in repose. Owl's Head rises 2,480 feet above sea level, and its surface is broken up into deep gorges and ravines. High up is the Eagle's Nest, for many years the home of some of the majestic birds often seen soaring above Lake Memphremagog. There are four chamberlike ravines near the top that have been left from prehistoric volcanic times, one of which is used each summer by the Freemasons.

**The Natural Lodge Room.** In September 1857 at Owl's Head Mountain, the Stanstead Golden Rule Lodge natural lodge room was opened. Seen here at the centennial celebration in 1957, Brother Alfred Pearson of Knowlton stands below the Golden Rule Lodge's No. 5 inscription, where the cabalistic sign of the order is cut into the rock.

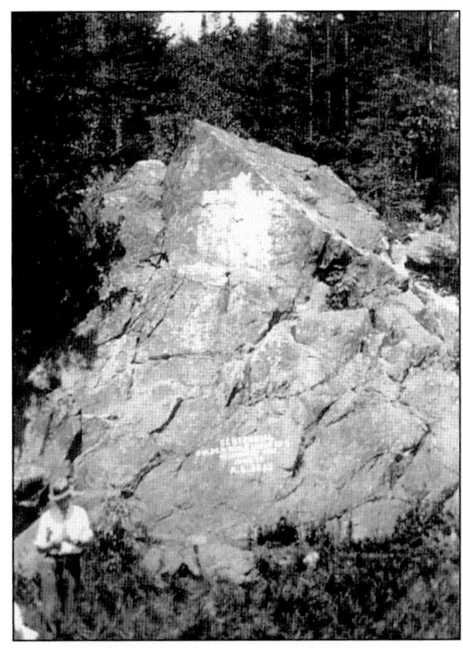

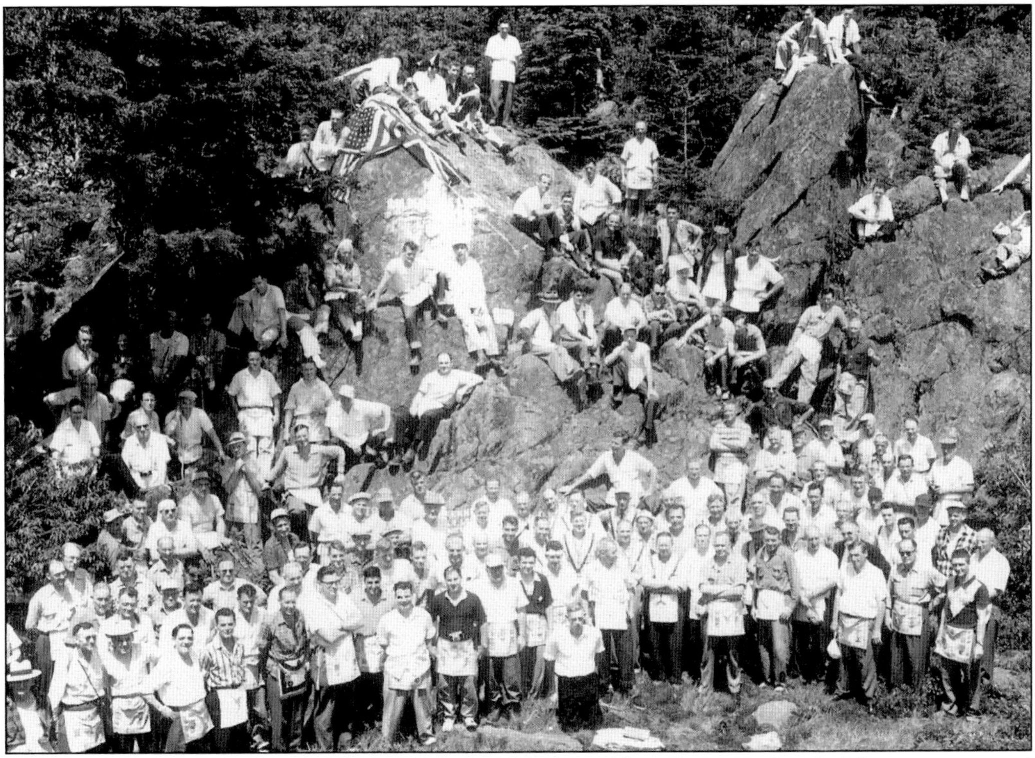

**The Centennial Celebration.** The Stanstead Golden Rule Lodge held its centennial celebration at the natural lodge room that they visit every year in June on Owl's Head Mountain. The open-air lodge room is located near the top of the mountain in a natural amphitheater left by the glacial period of what was once a volcanic rift. This photograph was taken in 1957.

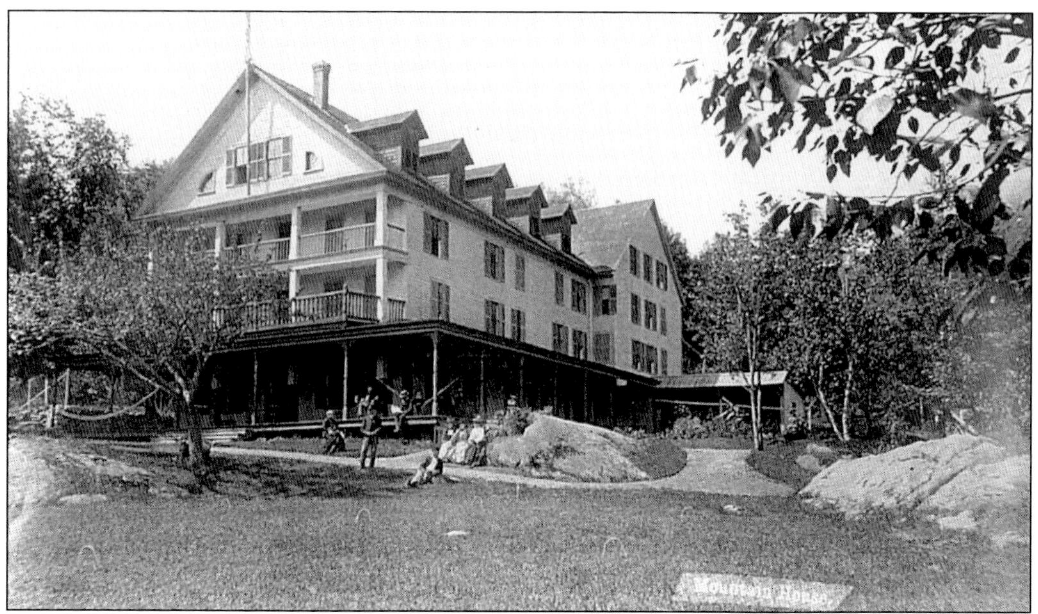


**The Owl's Head Mountain House.** After a fire and renovations, the Owl's Head Mountain House (above) reopened on June 27, 1882. Emmons Raymond of Newport was the owner and appointed E.J. Hill and his wife as managers. The hotel was enlarged to 400 guest rooms, and the dining room (below) was expanded to accommodate more seating. Trails that led from the hotel to the mountainside required the lady guests to shed their hoop skirts in order to make it through their narrow passages. (Below courtesy of Potton Heritage Association.)

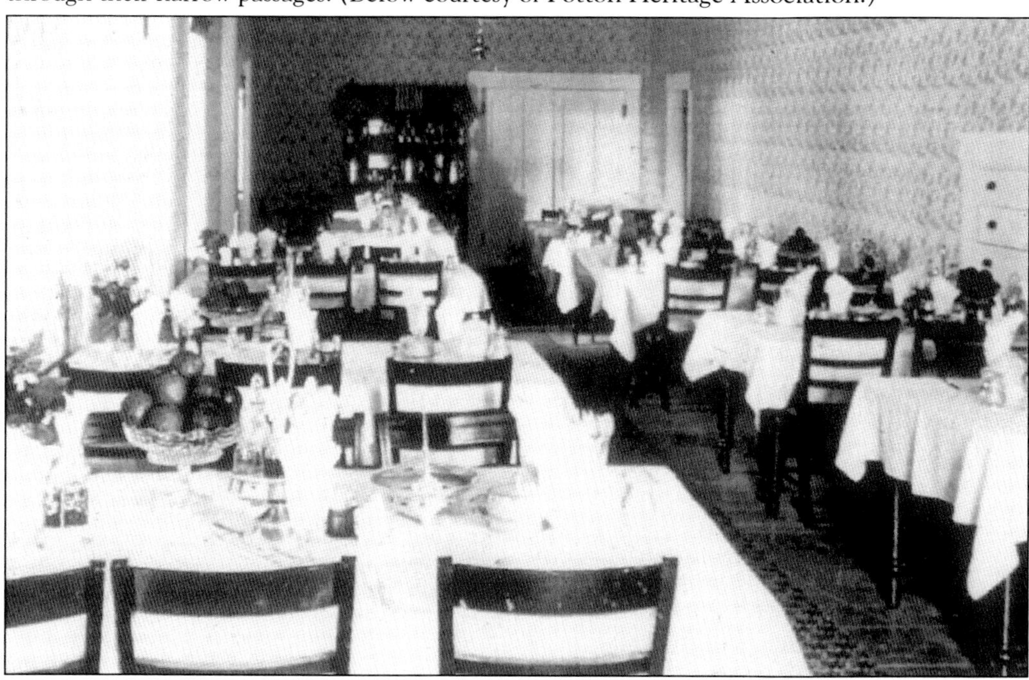

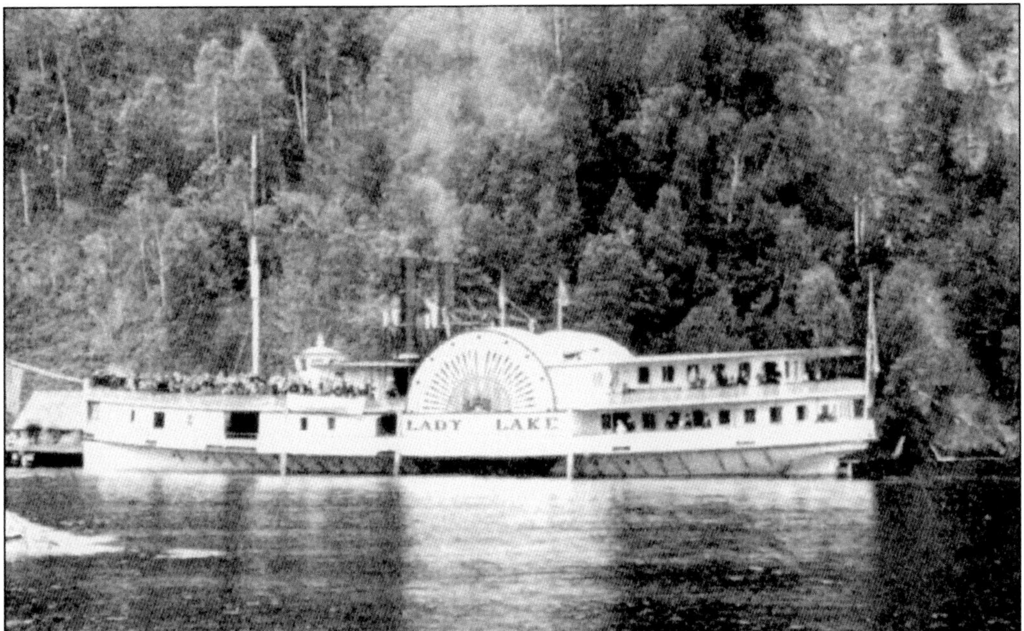


**The Long Wharf.** The Mountain House boasted unsurpassed views of the lake and easy accessibility to the wharf at the water's edge for the lake's steamers the *Mountain Maid* and the *Lady of the Lake*. In 1886, Capt. George Merrill piloted the *Mountain Maid II*, owned by the Central Vermont Railroad, which offered moonlight excursions at 25¢ a ticket from Newport, Vermont, to the Owl's Head Mountain House, returning the following evening. Here, the *Lady of the Lake* is moored at the hotel's Long Wharf. (Courtesy of Potton Heritage Association.)

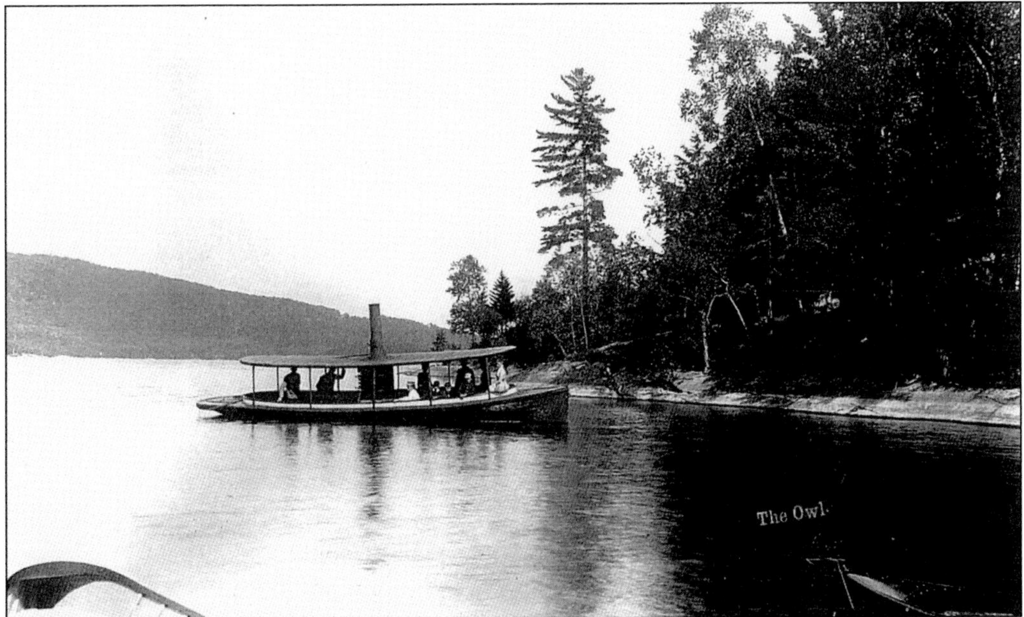


**The Owl.** The Mountain House Hotel had its own steam launch that was used exclusively for the hotel guests. In the 1890s, during the flourishing days of the hotel, the *Owl* connected with the early morning trains and took visitors on excursions around Lake Memphremagog.

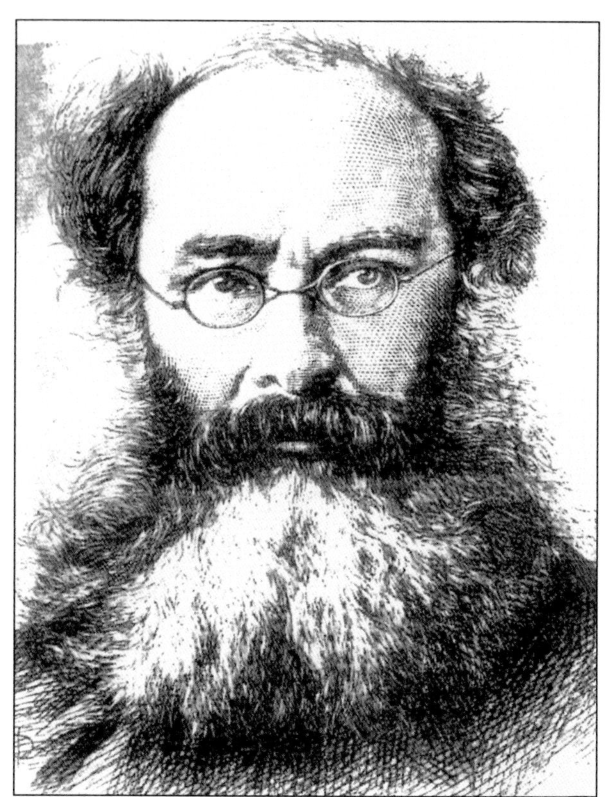

**ANTHONY TROLLOPE.** In 1862, English novelist Anthony Trollope (1815–1882) wrote *In North America* about his visit to the United States. He and his wife traveled to the Memphremagog area in September 1861 and climbed to the top of Owl's Head Mountain. Of that experience he wrote the following: "The Path was thick with trees the whole way, arriving at 5:30 PM we sat down to enjoy the victory and the evening light. On descent after dark we became lost in the rain before men from the hotel with lanterns found us and we all made our way in safety back down the mountain." (Courtesy of *Appleton's Journal III*, 1870.)

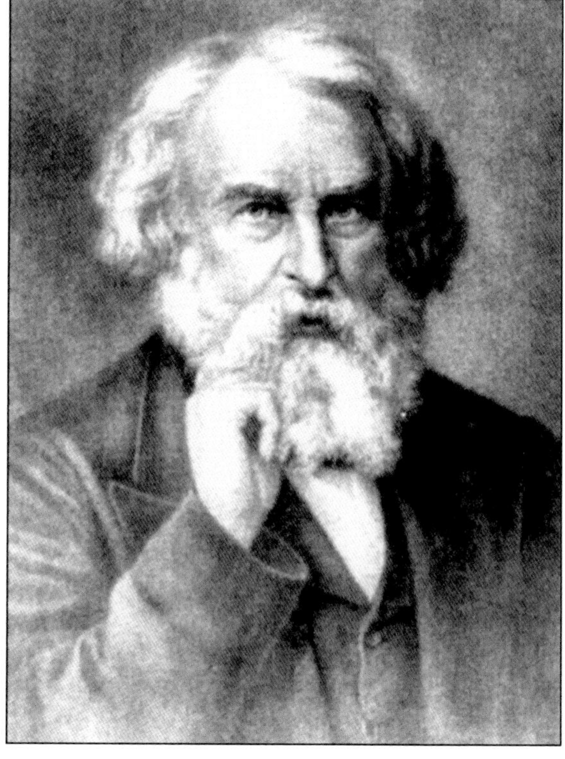

**WILLIAM CULLEN BRYANT.** As a first impression as a guest at the Owl's Head Mountain House, poet and editor Bryant (1794–1878) wrote, "Nature wears her bridal robes, softly colored, fragrant and bright, and we come back to it year after year loving it more and deriving from it the solace that empowers us for renewed toil at the treadmill of city life." Another poem Bryant composed can be found on page 54 of *Beautiful Waters*, volume one, printed in 1926 by William Bryant Bullock. (Courtesy of Goodrich Memorial Library, Newport.)

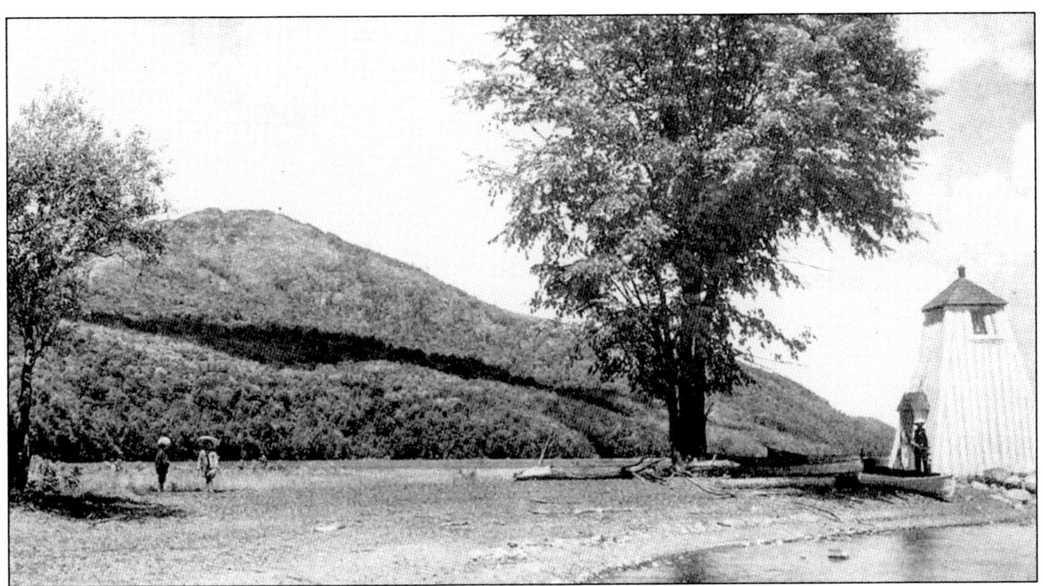

**Lighthouses.** The history of the lighthouses began almost as soon as modern navigation came to Lake Memphremagog in the 1850s. At one time, as many as five dotted the west shore. Capt. George Fogg was one of the first steamboat pilots to pay a light tax for the lighthouse, which was figured according to the steamboat's tonnage. Fogg's tax was about $300 a season. When James Maxfield first settled on his farm, he was paid a stipend by the coast guard to man the lighthouse on Maxfield Point (right) in Newport. He would light the kerosene lantern every evening and turn it out each morning. His son Olin took over as keeper in 1883 and continued until the 1930s, when the new automated iron girder lighthouse was used. This lighthouse was torn down in 2000.

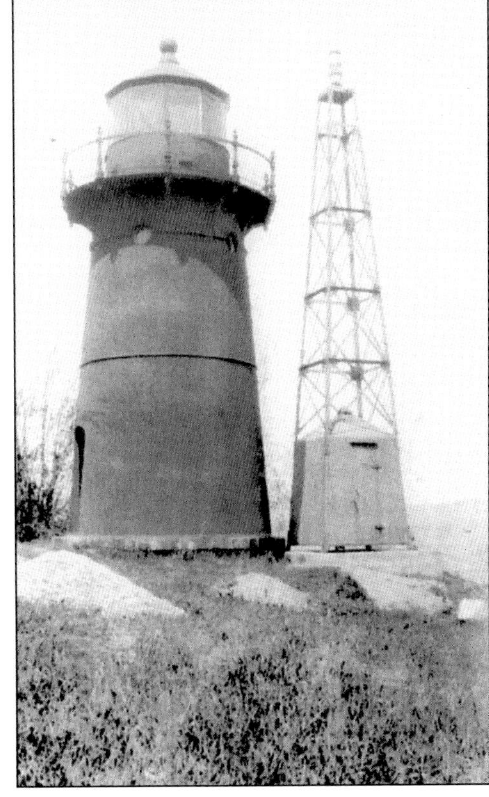

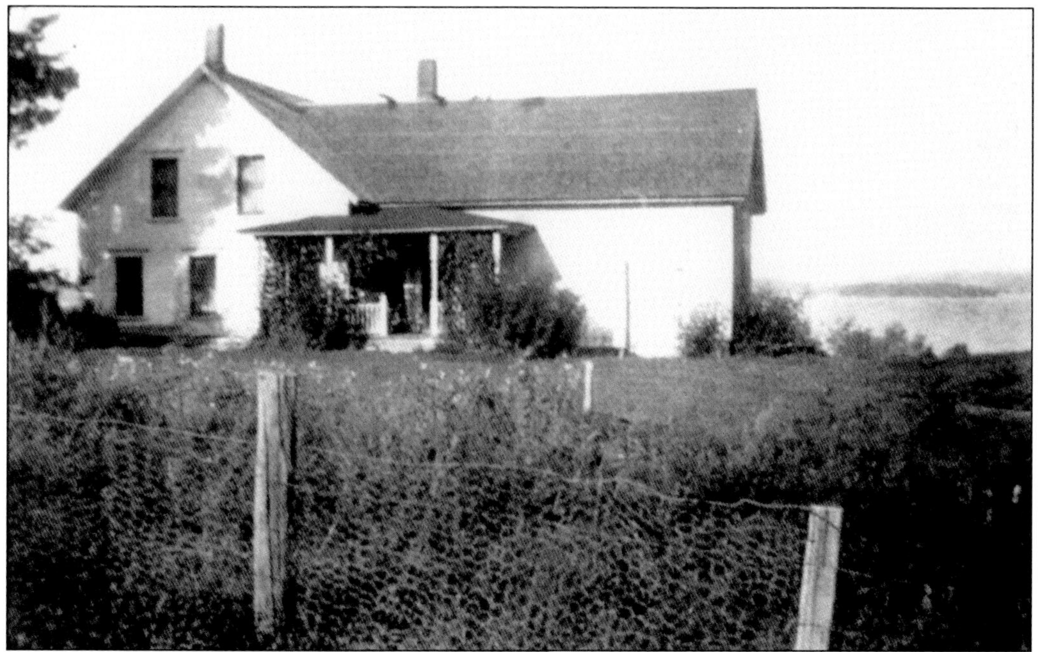

**Maxfield Farm.** In Newport, on the west shore of Lake Memphremagog quite near where the Canadian border separates the two countries, is Maxfield Point. James Maxfield (1837–1896) came from New Hampshire and purchased a 200-acre farm. He married Chorlena Daggett, and they raised a son, Olin. This Lake Road farm was first settled in 1826 by Israel Scott and at one time had a sugar orchard of 500 trees. Olin's son Walter and Walter's wife, Pauline, could not work the farm, so it was sold in 1938 and still remains in that family today.

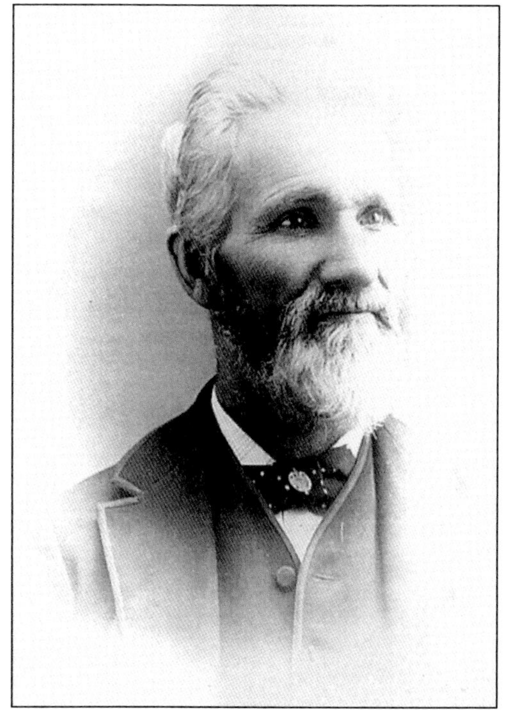

**The Lake Road Pottery Kiln.** Samuel B. Horton, born in 1827 in Stanstead, Quebec, was the son of Abraham and Sally (Bingham) Horton. His uncle Nathanial Horton paid $300 for a piece of land on Lake Road, where he operated an earthenware pottery kiln. He produced jugs and pitchers. Nathaniel sold the business to Eber J. Chaplin in 1807. Samuel Horton lived on Main Street in Newport in 1873 and worked as a foreman of the railroad paint shops. He died in 1904, leaving his wife, Elizabeth (Sevrens) Horton, and two children, William and Jennie.

# *Nine*

# Myths and Legends

There are many stories, tales, myths, and legends surrounding Lake Memphremagog's beauty and mystique. The Algonquian and the Abenaki Indians have creation legends, teaching tales, oral histories, water and island spirit myths, and "little people" stories. Early settlers told myths about wild beasts, forest creatures, and the spirits of the dead. Then came the tales of hauntings, ghosts, mysterious drownings, witches and hermits, strange disappearances, sea serpents, waterspouts, and earthquakes. Even now, we hear about pirating, smuggling, Memphre, and local ghosts. Only a few of these stories are related here, for it is hard to photograph a myth.

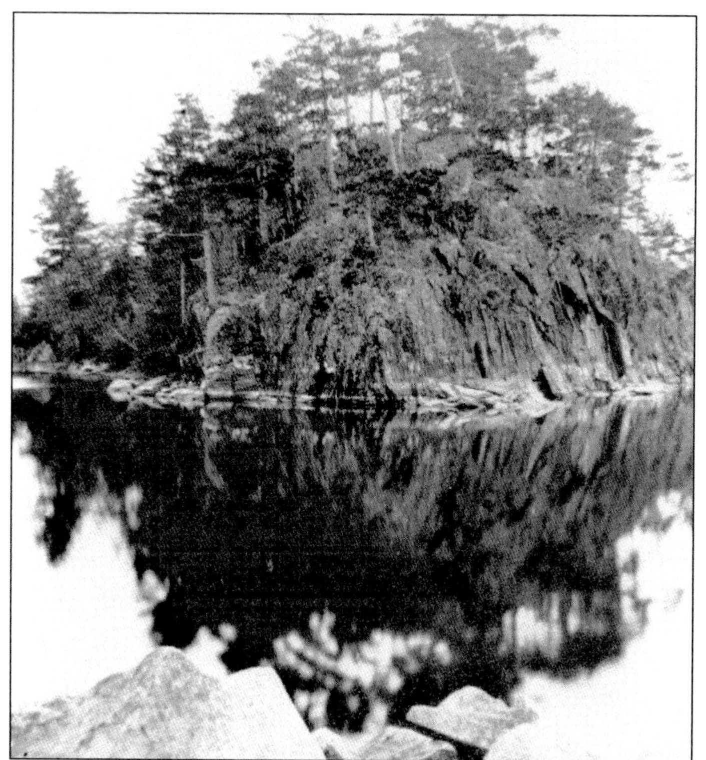

**BALANCE ROCK.** Legend states that the huge boulder on the "Island of Manitou" was once the portal to the afterlife. When Manitou's messenger, a spirit, demanded an Algonquian chief to sacrifice his bride, the chief became despondent and gave himself to the waters of Mamlabegwok. After this tragedy, the huge boulder was mysteriously moved to the southern point of Long Island. According to Abenaki tradition, all traces of the location of the entrance were gone forever. The boulder is precariously balanced and can be easily rocked. It was known to settlers as Balance Rock.

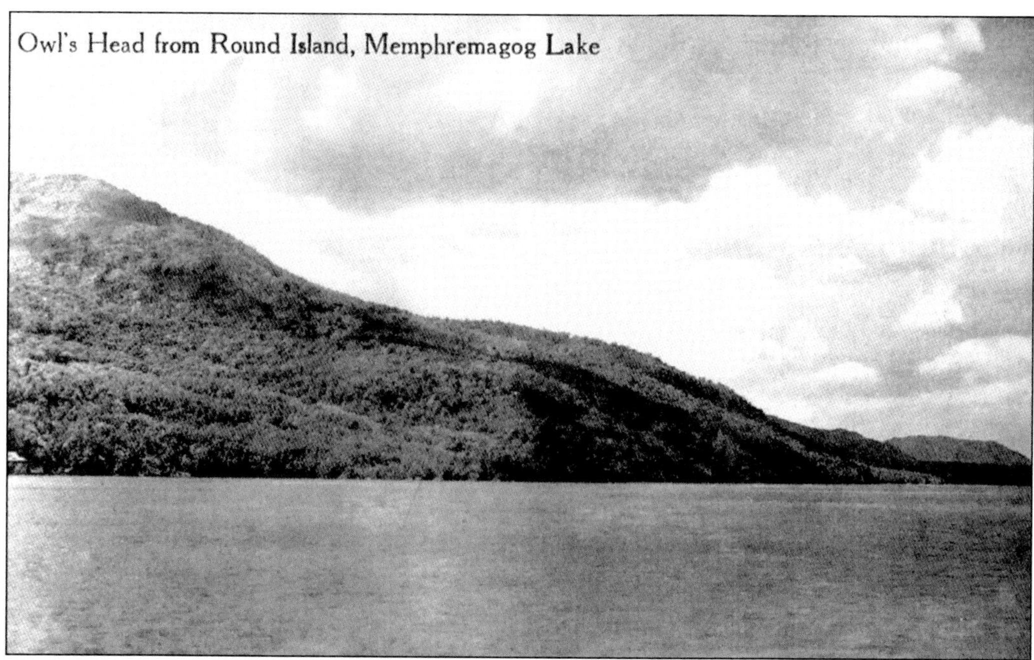


**OWL'S HEAD CAVE.** Abenaki oral history tells that high up on the side of Owl's Head Mountain there is a sacred cave that is well hidden and hard to access. Many people have tried to find it, but those that know have kept its secrets. Round Island, within paddling distance of the mountain and within view from the cave, was a favorite seasonal encampment site for the Abenaki.

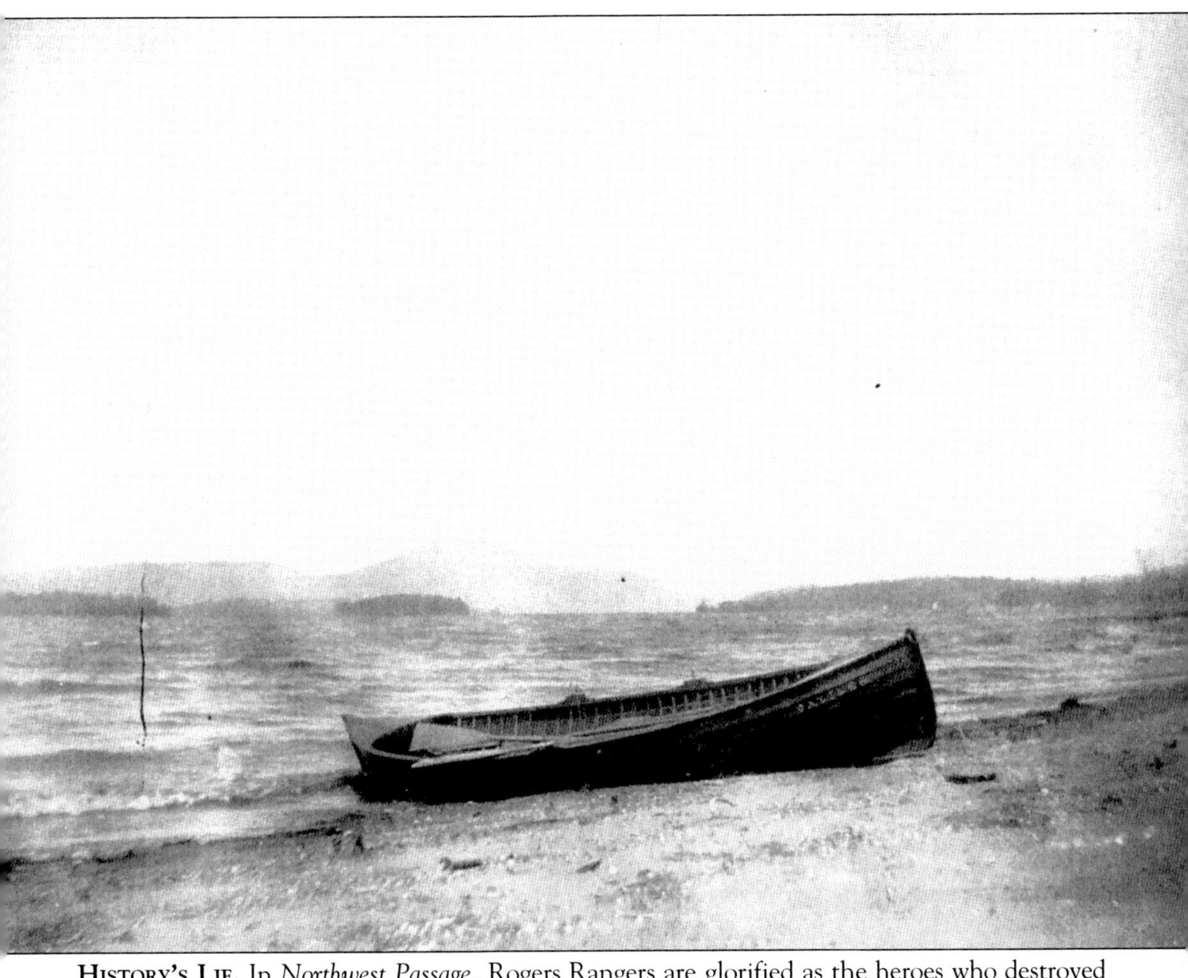

**History's Lie.** In *Northwest Passage*, Rogers Rangers are glorified as the heroes who destroyed Odanak, the Abenaki stronghold and mission village on the St. Francis River. In reality, Robert Rogers took his rangers into a town of women, children, and a few older men to plunder, pillage, and burn in October 1759. Most of the warriors and young men were away fighting with the French at Quebec City or out hunting. On Rogers's flight south, most of his men died of starvation and exposure. When they reached Lake Memphremagog, he abandoned his men, and they split up into small groups to make their own way. Only a handful led by Rogers (he had a young captive Abenaki boy as a guide) made it to Fort No. 4 in Charleston, New Hampshire.

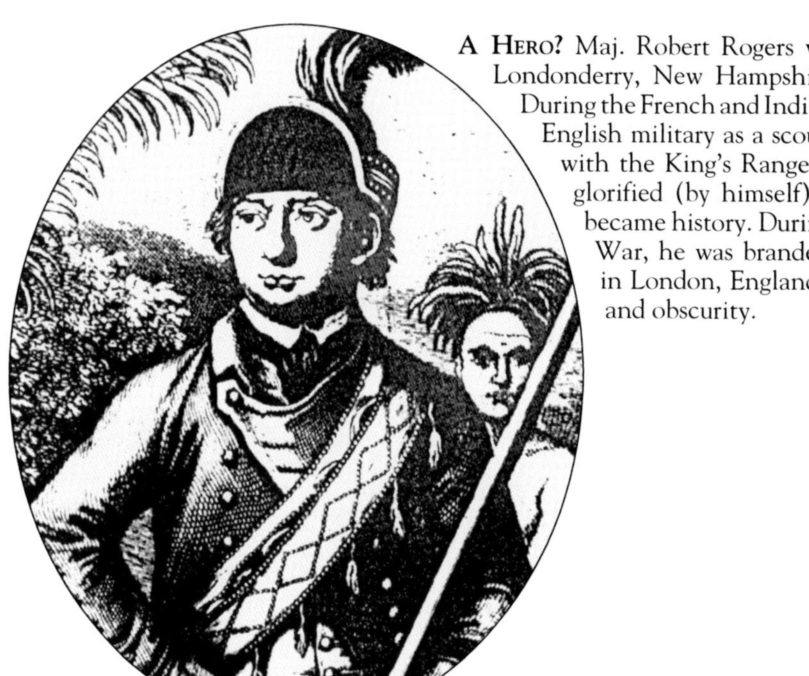

**A Hero?** Maj. Robert Rogers was born in 1727 in Londonderry, New Hampshire, of Irish descent. During the French and Indian War, he joined the English military as a scout and Indian fighter with the King's Rangers. His exploits were glorified (by himself), and his falsehoods became history. During the Revolutionary War, he was branded a traitor and died in London, England, *c.* 1800 in poverty and obscurity.

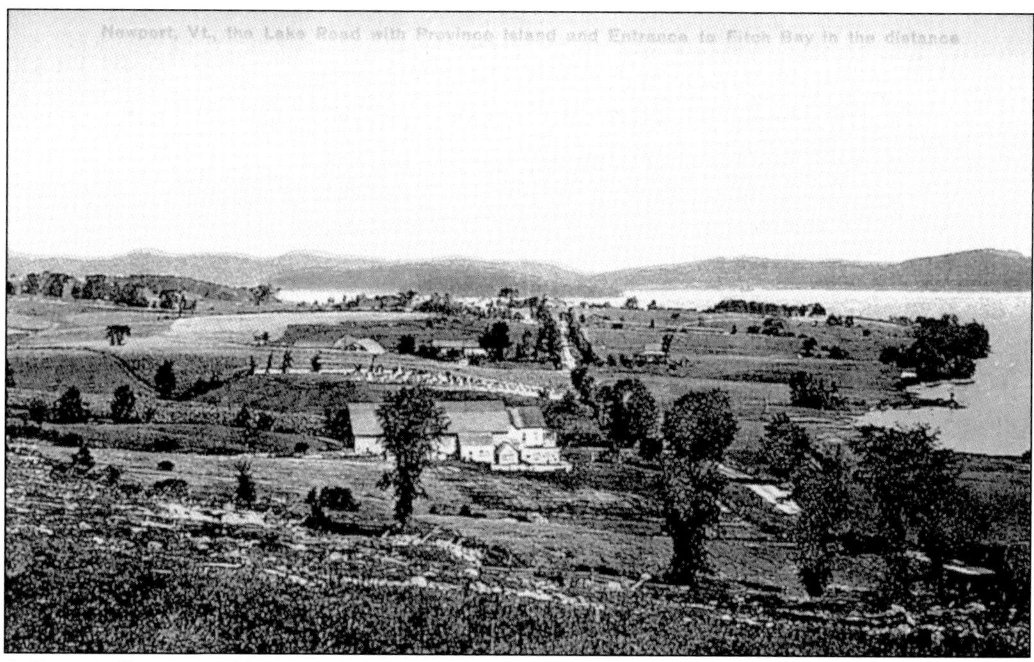


**A Buried Plunder.** Upon arrival at Indian Point on Lake Memphremagog, Robert Rogers left his men to separate and find their own way. He continued on to the Connecticut River with a handful of men. Some of the others crossed the lake to Adams Bay and, because of hunger, exhaustion, and the cold and hard traveling conditions, which caused weakness, they buried their plunder of silver taken from the mission church. It is said the treasure was buried near the Lake Road Cemetery, probably so that the spirits of the dead would protect the booty.

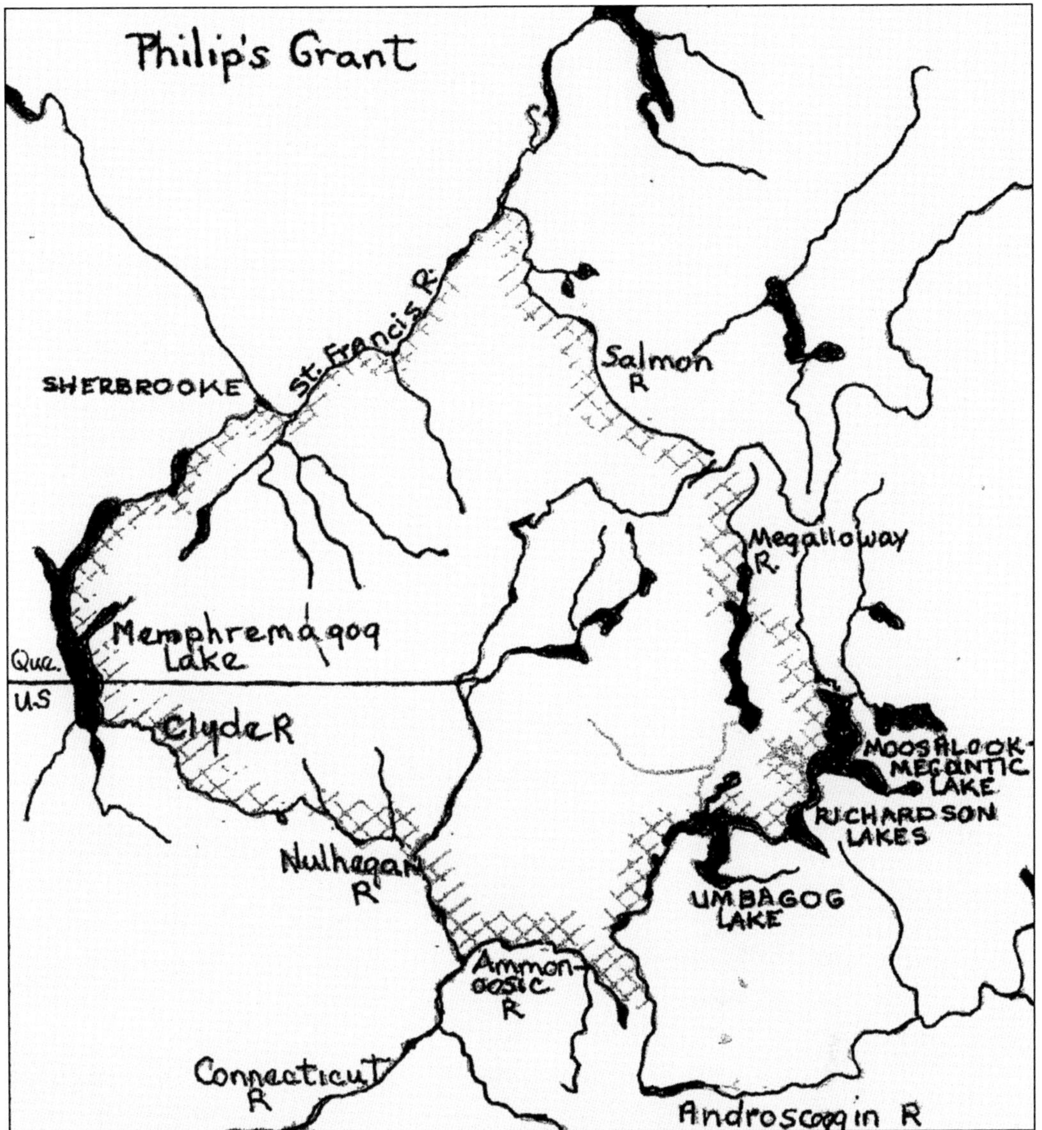


**PHILLIP'S GRANT.** In 1796, Phillip, an Abenaki Indian chief from the St. Francis tribe—the same that inhabited the Memphremagog region—sold some 3,000 square miles straddling the border to four men, Anglo-American land speculators. Thomas Eames and three associates called themselves the Eastern Company. The price was a promise to keep Phillip and his two wives well fed and clothed for the rest of their lives and to allow all other band members fishing and hunting rights in perpetuity. Phillip retired to Odanak, where he later died. In 1798, Abenaki chiefs at Odanak sold virtually the same land to the Bedel Land Company for $3,100. This sale was the basis for New Hampshire's claim to the Indian Stream Territory. At the same time, Canada claimed it. In 1836, Phillip's son Metallak sold part of the grant again. The Abenaki believed land could not be owned, just cared for and maintained. The joke was on the whites. (Courtesy of Bernard Epps and the *Stanstead Journal*.)

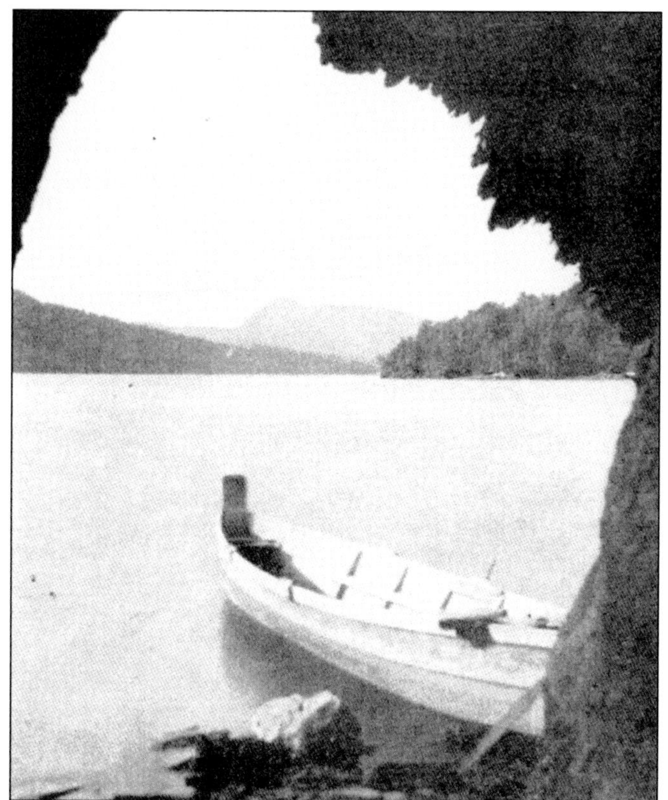

**Skinner's Cave.** Uriah Skinner was believed to be a pirate and a smuggler. He is described as "brawny and brown with very black hair that hangs shaggily down." Of all the smugglers on the lake, he was the hardest to find. On one night all the pursuers found was an empty boat, which they set afloat. Skinner had disappeared. Nearly six years later, a fisherman escaping from a storm discovered a cave on the side of an island and rowed in. When his eyes adjusted to the light, he discovered a skeleton that was believed to be Uriah Skinner, who must have become trapped in his hideout.

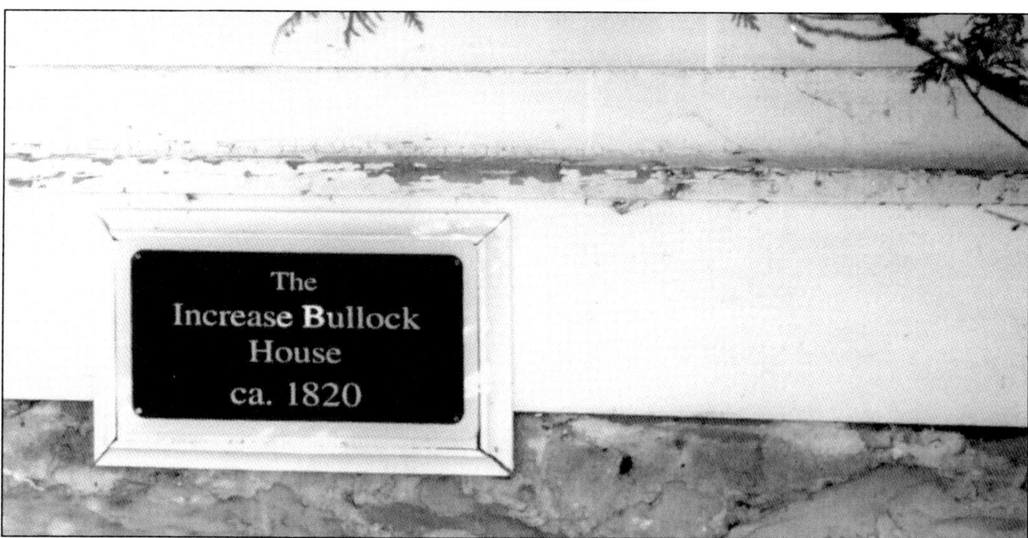


**The Anaconda Legend.** Increase Bullock (1808–1887) and his wife, Harriet (Cross) Bullock, raised five sons. They purchased a home near the lake in Georgeville in 1834, where Increase lived until 1870. He was fascinated by the legendary lake monster, or sea serpent, called Anaconda. He wrote a poem about Anaconda, which was published by his son (by his second marriage) William B. Bullock in his second volume of *Beautiful Waters* in 1938. Another poem about the sea serpent was written by Norman Bingham in 1851 and was published in the first volume of *Beautiful Waters* in 1926.

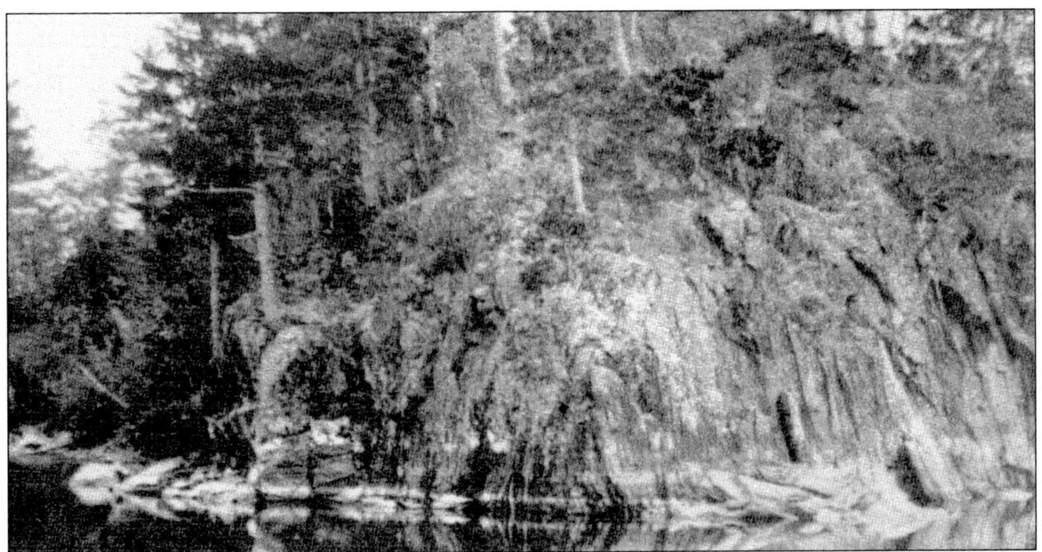

**Uriah Jewett and the Sea Serpent.** During the 1850s, Uriah Jewett entertained the passengers of the *Mountain Maid* by reciting his adventures involving the sea serpent known today as Memphre. Jewett was endowed with a powerful voice and colorful words. His gestures added emphasis to his speech, and he kept listeners spellbound telling of the sudden appearances and disappearances of the serpent into the gloomy depths of his underwater lair beneath Owl's Head.

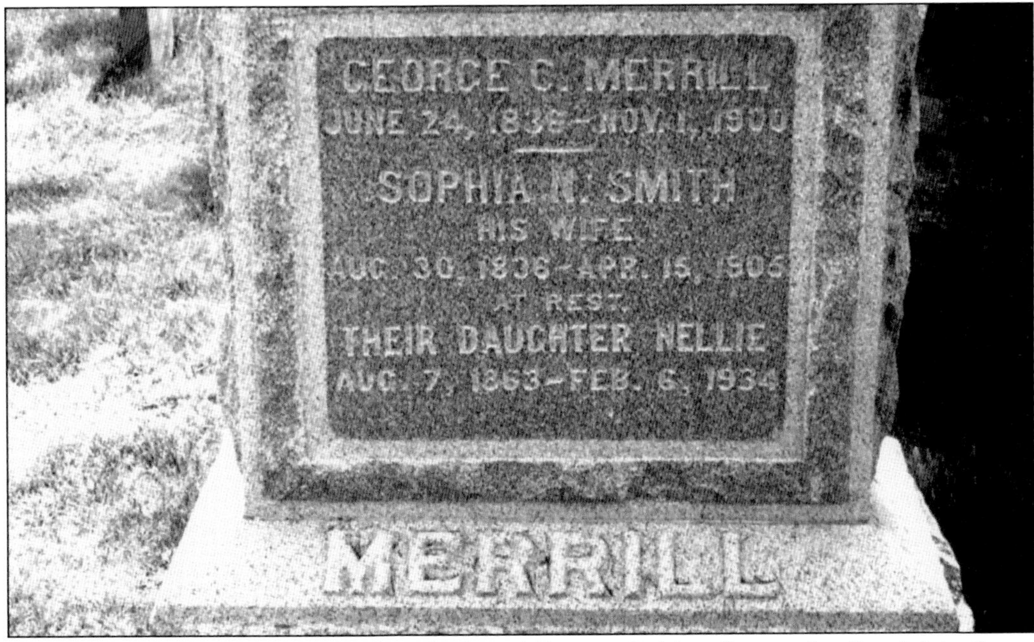


**George Merrill's Notes.** The burial plot of George C. Merrill is at the East Main Street Cemetery in Newport, Vermont. Merrill came to Newport from Georgeville, Quebec, as a purser on the *Mountain Maid I* at the age of 18. His notes and recordings included Uriah Jewett's stories about his encounters with the sea serpent of Lake Memphremagog. Today, the creature is called Memphre and has been seen and documented as recently as May 2003 by the International Dracontology Society of Newport.

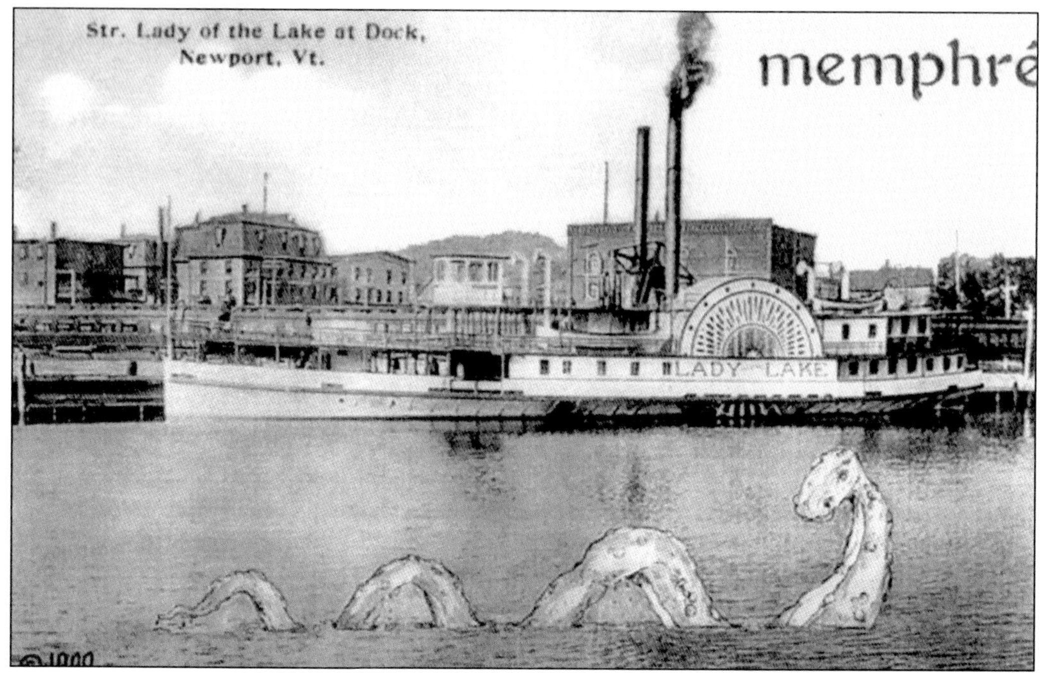


**Memphre.** The sea serpent, or lake creature, was seen and documented as early as 1816. Before that, local Abenaki Indians had their own sightings and stories. Memphre's legends still travel through history, and facts from contemporary eyewitnesses continue to be reported. Sightings often occur near Newport's Railroad Square, where once the *Lady of the Lake* berthed at Steamboat Wharf.

**Memphre's Photograph.** The International Dracontology Society of Lake Memphremagog and Newport's Barbara Malloy, Vermont's first woman dracontologist, took this photograph of the legendary Memphre on July 12, 1989, in South Bay.

*Ten*

# The Return to Newport

Returning to Newport after having explored historic people, sites, and imaginings around the shores of Lake Memphremagog, one comes full circle. This pictorial history has covered the earliest times to the settlement and on to prosperous and thriving communities, from untouched wilderness to lonely settlement, from farmland to summer camps and small cities, and from past to present. One ends the journey of this thumb-through timeline in hopes that the future will be richer because of the knowledge of the past. Lake Memphremagog's legacy and influence make our communities and heritage unique.

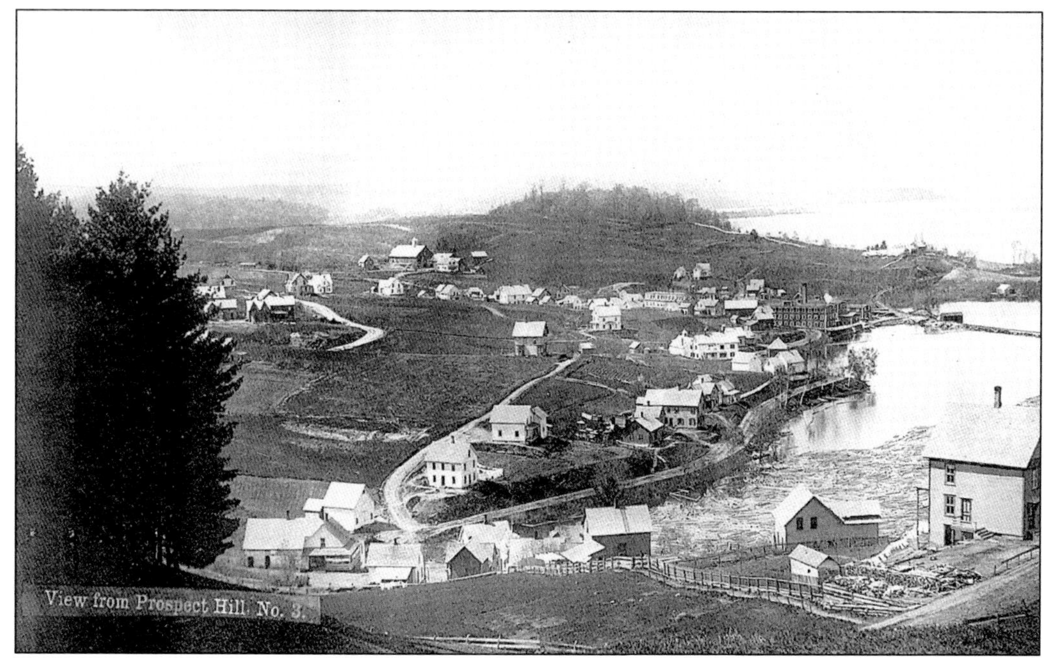


**Batesville.** A hamlet bordering the North Bay of Lake Memphremagog was named after Frank Bates, who built the first industry in the region, a basket factory. In the late 1880s, John Butler built the Memphremagog Veneer Mill, which was later known as the Bates Veneer Mill. Homes were built across the street for his mill workers in 1886, and this hamlet of Batesville was annexed to Newport in 1895.

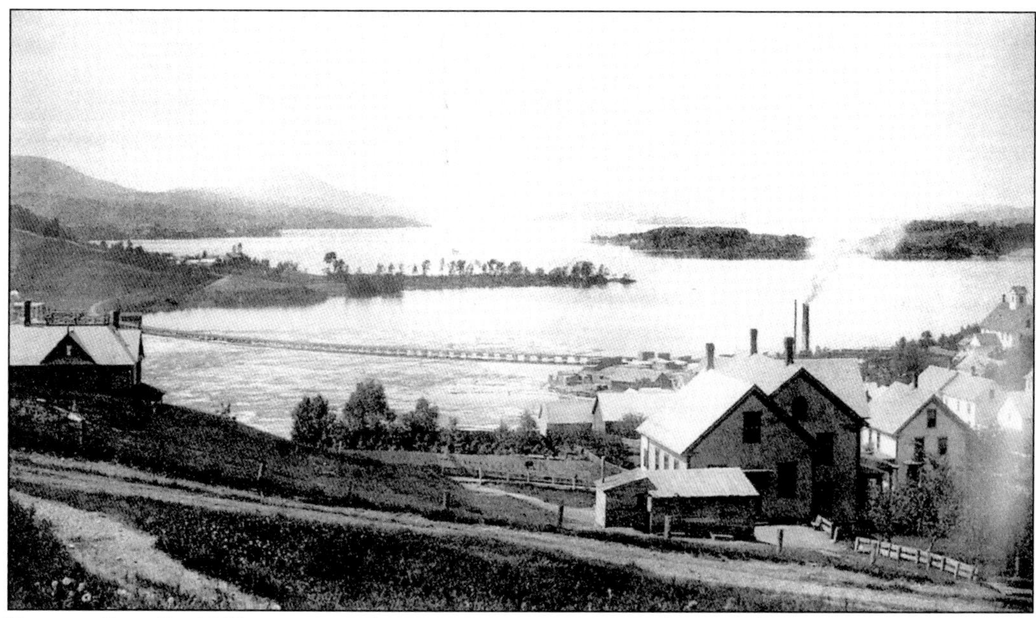

**Prouty Bay.** In 1863, two retired sea captains, Stimson and Winn, built a mill on the North Bay, later known as Prouty Bay. With 40,000 acres of timberland on both sides of the border, logs would be cut and towed to Newport. In 1876, John A. Prouty and Oscar C. Miller purchased the mill and founded the firm of Prouty & Miller.

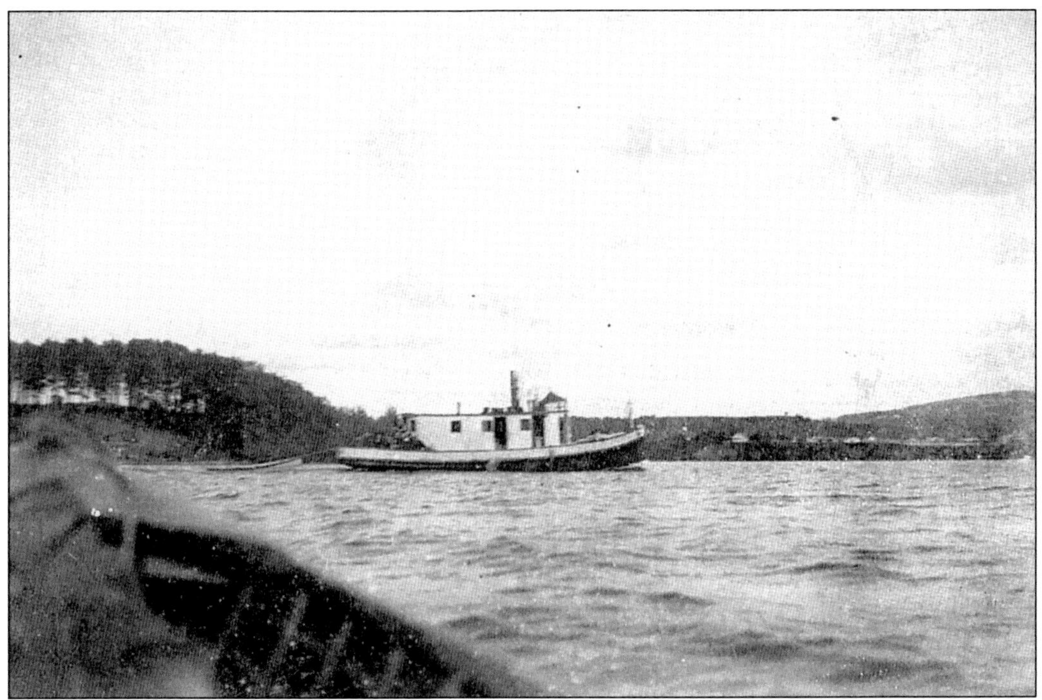

**THE *JOHN A* TUGBOAT.** Along with others, Prouty's tugboat (above) would tow the logs down the lake in large, floating booms to the storage booms covering many acres of water on Prouty Bay (below). John A. Prouty, known as "Colonel" to his men, often hired the second generation of workers in families before he retired in 1889. During the winter months, logs were brought in from Canada by the railroad and were unloaded on top of the ice. In the spring, with the melt, they would be afloat. It was essential that they be kept wet before being hauled out and into the mill's saw rooms.

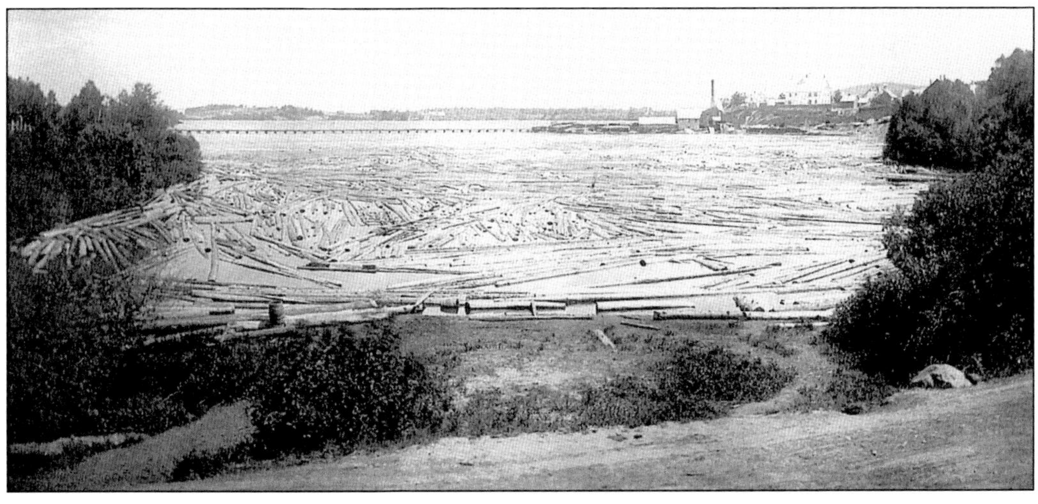

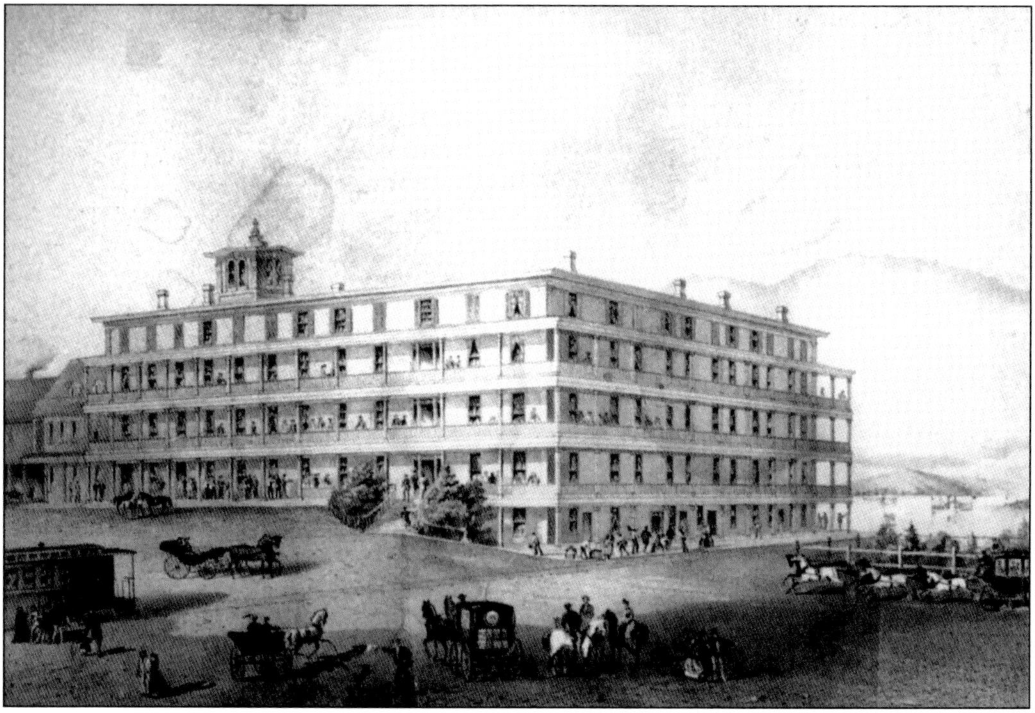

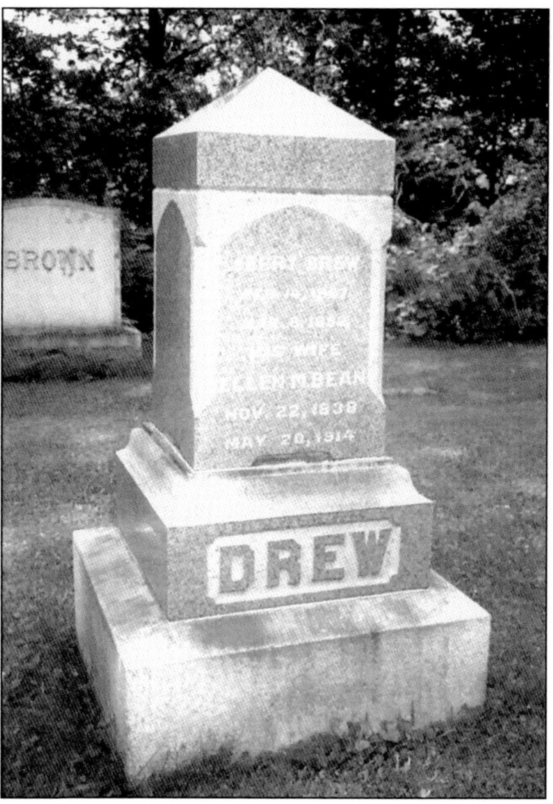


**From Stagecoach to Railroad.** Jerry Drew (1827–1892) owned the old Boston and Stanstead Stage Company. He carried freight, mail, and passengers along the stage route from 1852 to 1858, before the railroad came to Newport. Drew was a handy and skillful driver. With a crack of his four-in-hand whip, his nine-passenger yellow concord coach with a six-horse team would draw up in front of the Memphremagog Hotel (above) in a flourish. Drew, who died on March 8, 1892, and his wife, Ellen (Bean) Drew, are buried at the East Main Street Cemetery (left). In 1863, when the railroad came to Newport, freight, mail, and passengers came by train. Another era had passed.

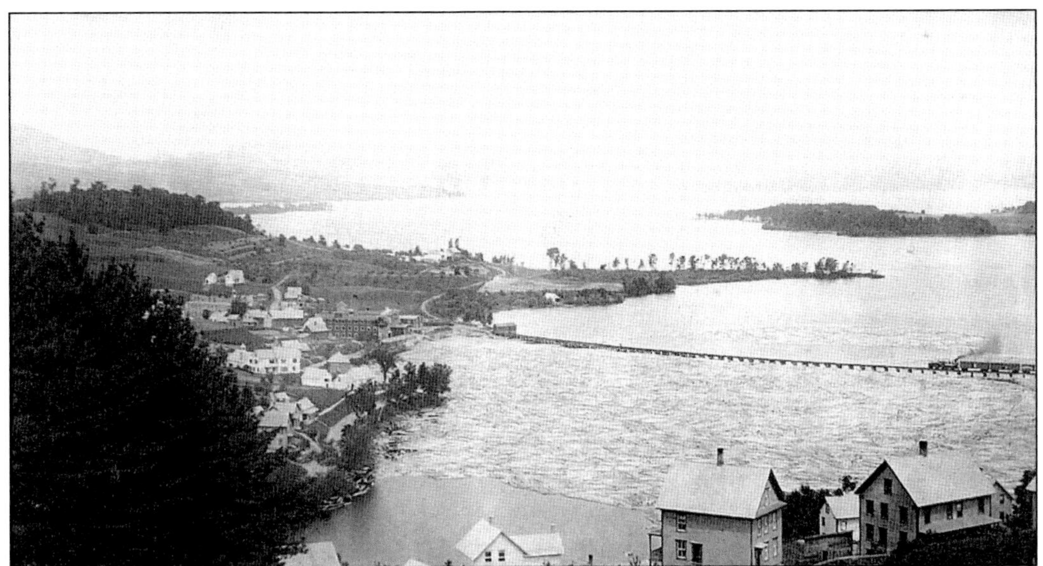

**Early Trains.** During the beginning of the railroad era in 1863, the first train to arrive in Newport village was a Connecticut & Passumpsic wood-burning locomotive that crossed the wooden trestle bridge over South Bay. In 1872, the Missisquoi & Clyde River Railroad, or the Southeastern, crossed over the West Railroad Bridge (above) built over Prouty Bay by Solomon Fields. Eventually, capital stock was sold, and Solomon Fields bought 10 shares (below) signed by Lucius Robinson, president of the railroad. Later, in 1878, Robinson became the first president of the National Bank of Newport.

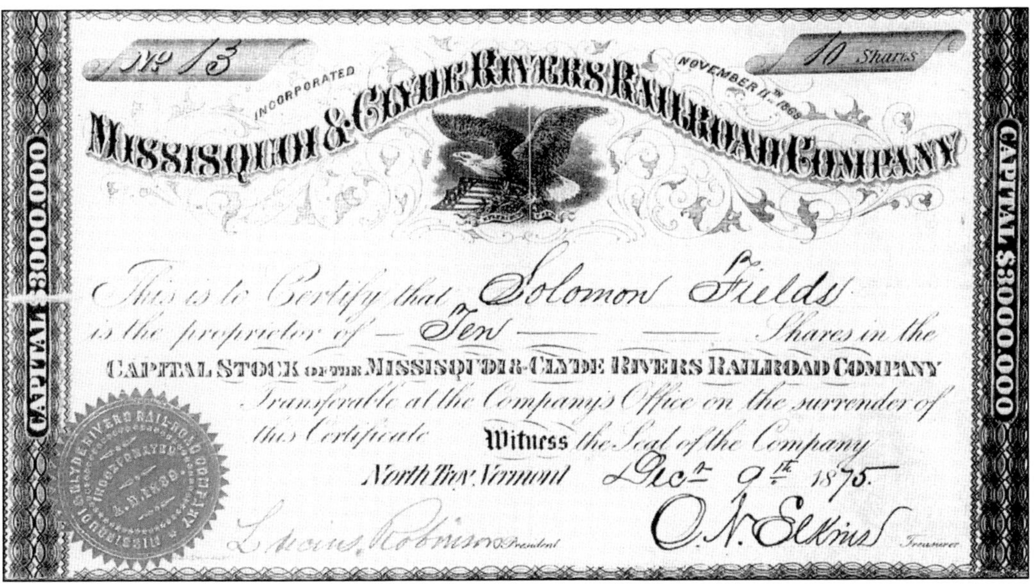

No 13

10 Shares

Incorporated November 11th 1869

Missisquoi & Clyde Rivers Railroad Company

Capital $3000.000

This is to Certify that Solomon Fields is the proprietor of — Ten — Shares in the Capital Stock of the Missisquoi & Clyde Rivers Railroad Company Transferable at the Company's Office on the surrender of this Certificate Witness the Seal of the Company

North Troy Vermont Dec 9th 1875

Lucius Robinson President

O. N. Elkins Treasurer

Capital $3000.000

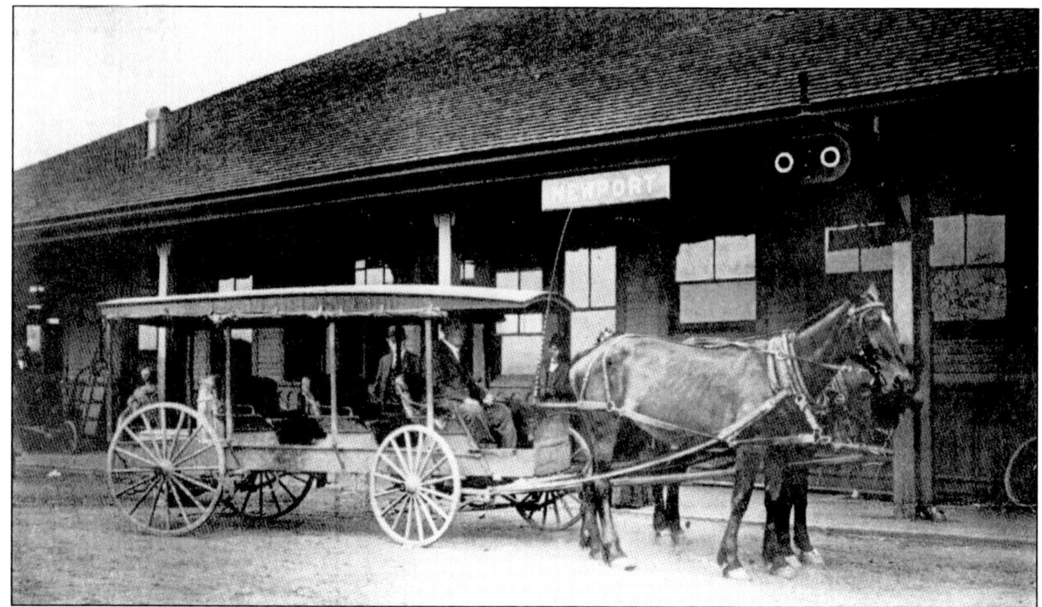


**Passenger Depots.** Newport's first passenger depot was built in 1869 on the south side of Main Street opposite the Memphremagog Hotel. In January 1902, the depot burned down and two passenger railroad coaches were placed on the site to be used for waiting rooms, the telegraph operator, and a ticket office. A new depot was built that same year in front of Steamboat Wharf between the tracks of the Canadian-Pacific and the Boston & Maine. The cost was $10,000. In 1903, piles were driven into the ground to support a new passenger platform.

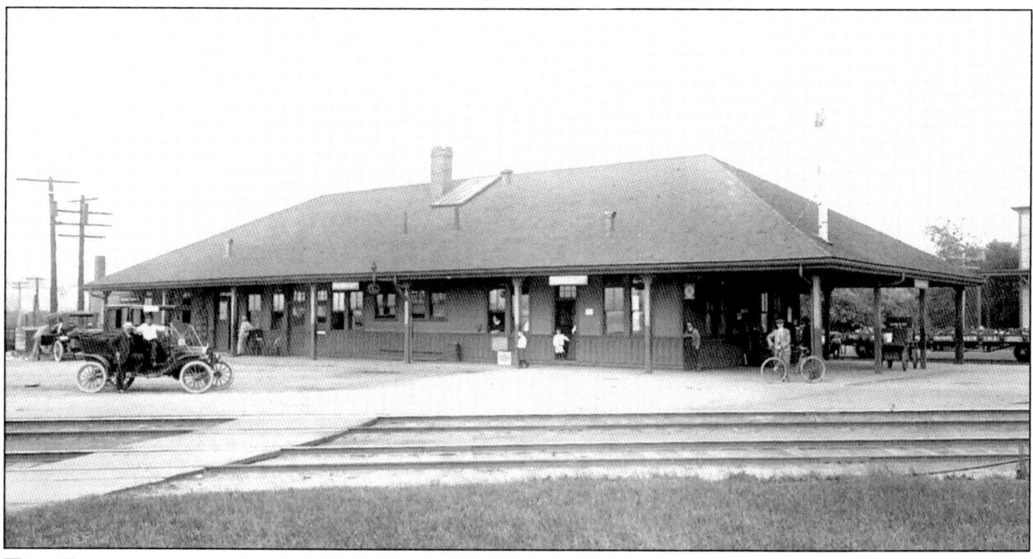

**The End of an Era.** The end of Newport's railroad era began in 1958, when the water tank at the North Yard was torn down. After almost 100 years of service, in January 1965, all passenger service in and out of Newport was stopped. And in July 1966, the Canadian & Pacific Railroad station was dismantled. The railroad brought prosperity and tourists to the local hotels, businesses, and to the lake; it had helped to build Newport. The memories of the iron-horse era will be cherished, as another of Newport's historic landmarks has disappeared from Railroad Square.

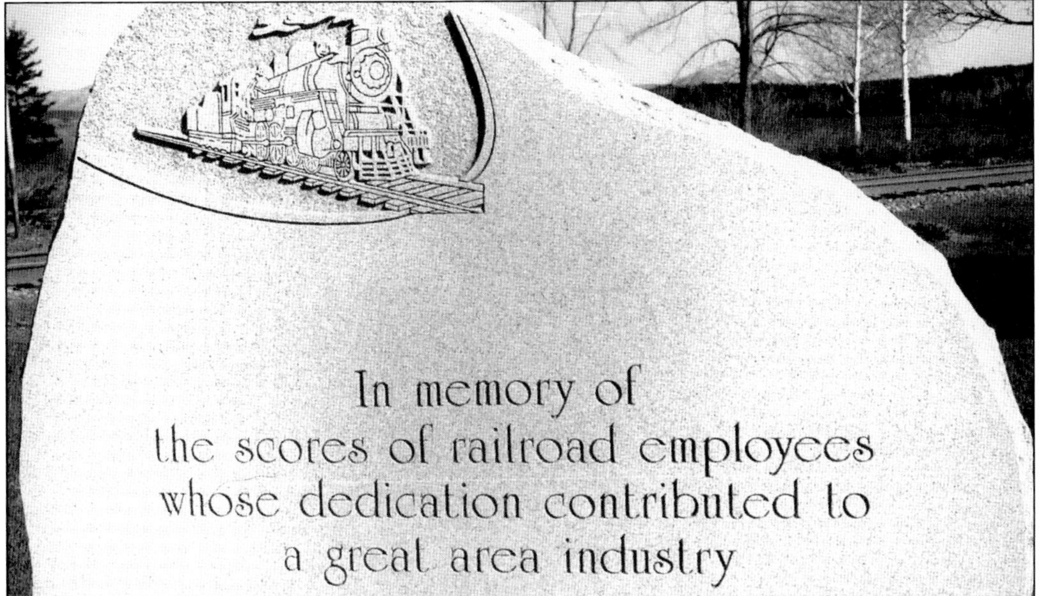


**THE RAILROAD MUSEUM PROPOSAL.** In 1988, former Newport mayor Mel Carter proposed the building of a new depot for Railroad Square to honor Newport's railroad history. The plans called for a museum constructed as a replica of the old railroad station. In 1989, permission was denied, and the fate of a railroad museum ended in controversy. The idea was abandoned.

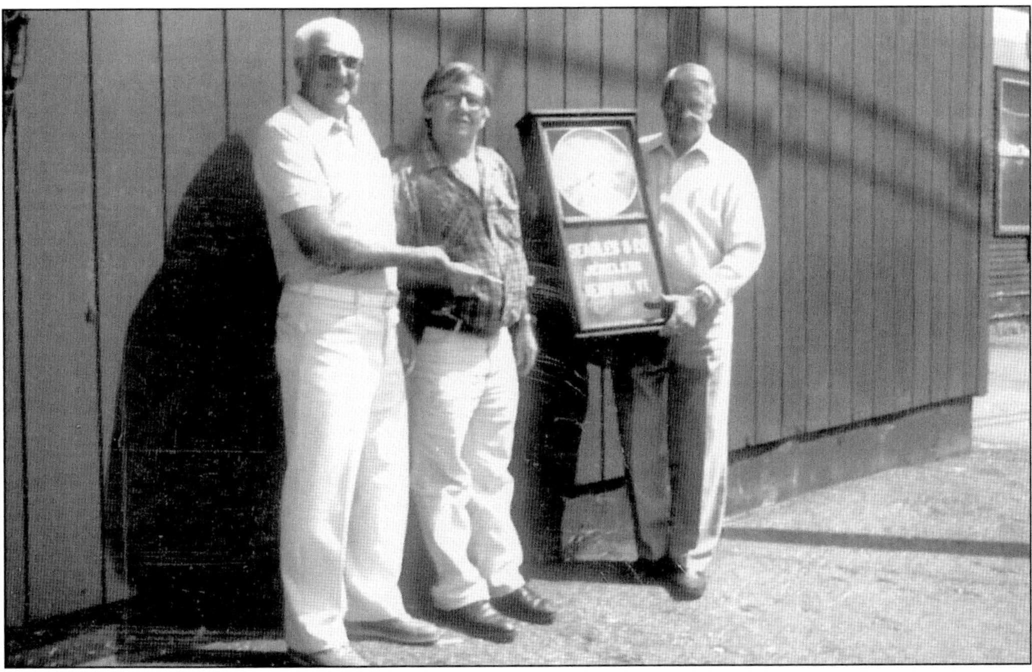

**THE DEPOT'S CLOCK.** In hopes of furthering the cause of Newport's railroad history, Floyd Buck of Wolcott presented to a committee of former railroad men an antique clock that once hung on the walls of the old depot. Pictured here with the clock at the presentation in 1988 are Giles Fugere (left), Floyd Buck (center), and Mel Carter. Newport's railroad history is still in need of revitalization and recognition.

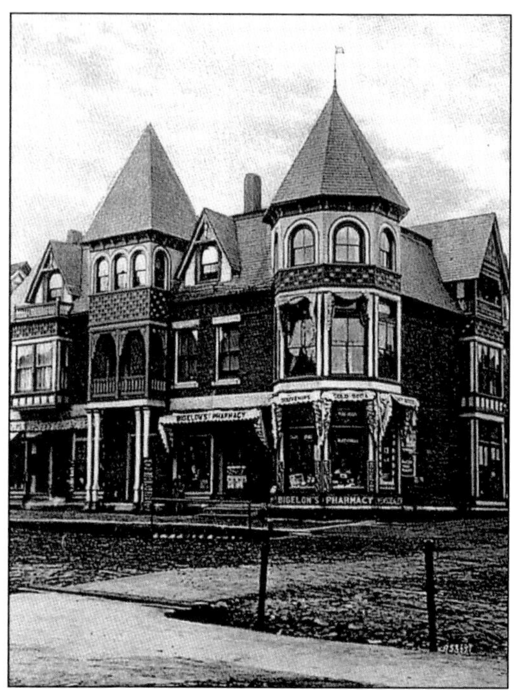


**HALL'S DRUG STORE.** In 1869, James R Hall (1845–1892), the son of Rev. Robert V. Hall, founded Hall's Drug Store. In 1886, he erected a three-story brick building with a slate roof at a cost of $15,000. He and his wife, Amy (Fletcher) Hall (1844–1906), kept their residence on the top two floors of the building, located on the corner of Main Street and North Avenue. They had a fine view of the lake.

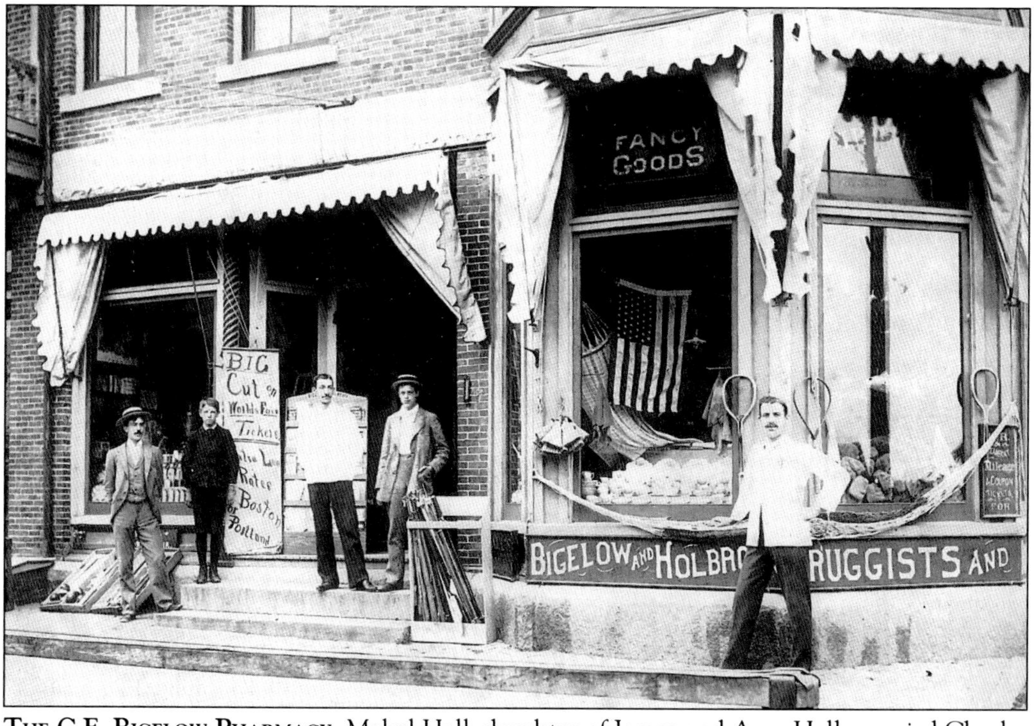

**THE C.F. BIGELOW PHARMACY.** Mabel Hall, daughter of James and Amy Hall, married Charles Bigelow in 1893 with 200 guests present in the front hall of the Main Street residence. After the death of Mabel's father in 1892, Bigelow bought Hall's Drug Store. Bigelow, wearing a white pharmacist's jacket, is seen here on his steps. In 1893, he returned from a trip to Boston with a selection of Christmas goods to sell that made his drugstore the rendezvous of the season.

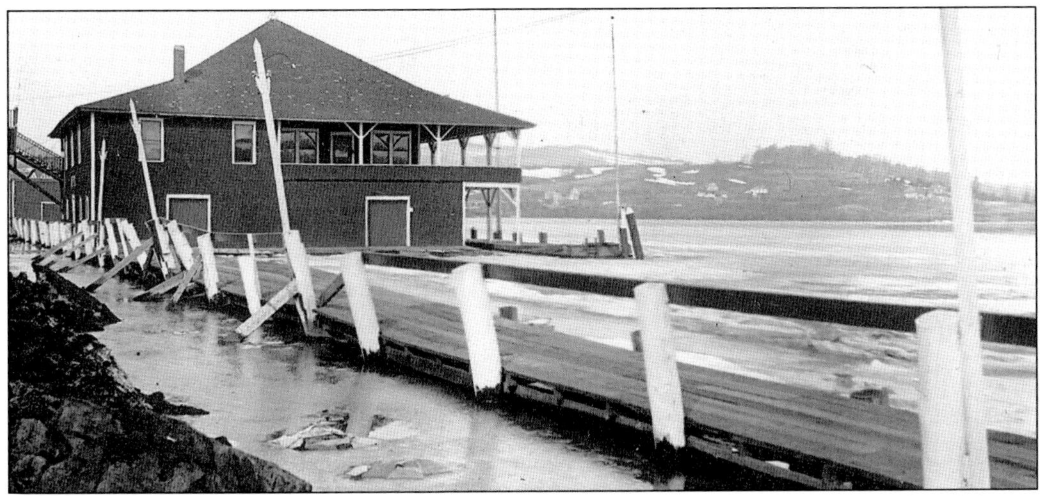

**The Memphremagog Yacht Club.** At a cost of $8,000, the Memphremagog Yacht Club was constructed on piles at the water's edge at the end of Field Street. The open house for its 200 members and the public was held in May 1908. Judge Frank E. Alfred (1853–1921) was the club's first commodore. In May 1946, a fire leveled the timber-dry two-story building. Firemen had to carry the hoses over the Overpass Bridge and were driven back by smoke and flames. The club saw a loss of 20 motorboats and several canoes.

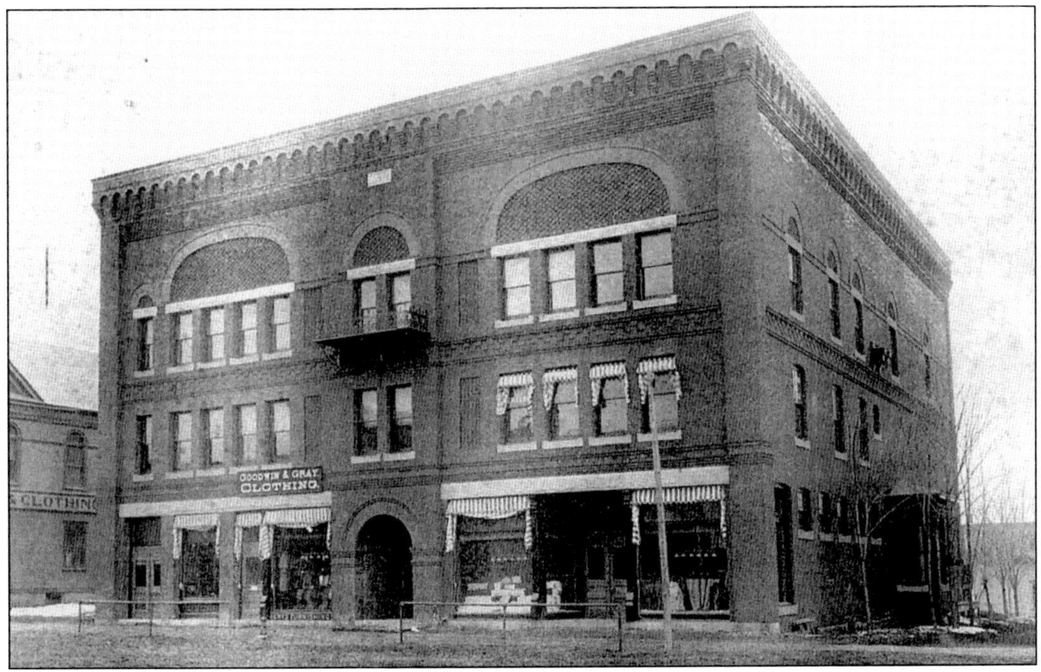


**The Lane & Sons Opera House.** The opera house block was erected in 1892 by Elisha Lane at a cost of $30,000. The mammoth brick building had a general store on the first floor with hitching posts out front to accommodate the horse-and-carriage trade. Located on the third floor was the opera house, which was equipped with a balcony, a stage, folding seats, chandeliers, and footlights. On its stage, plays and minstrel shows, dedication ceremonies, and Newport's first annual town meeting were held. In December 1923, the Lane block burned to the ground, and by 1930, storefronts and the Burns Theater had appeared.

**William Bryant Bullock.** Born in Georgeville, Quebec, he was the son of Increase and Marry Jane (Bryant) Bullock. William (1867–1942) was also the stepbrother of Charles Bullock, the last captain of the *Lady of the Lake* in 1915. William B. Bullock is best known as the writer, printer, and publisher of the two volumes of *Beautiful Waters*. These books are filled with historical sketches and stories of Lake Memphremagog. Nellie (Brainard) Bullock, his wife, was born in Morgan, Vermont. Together they raised two daughters: Martha Esther (born in 1895) and Pauline (born in 1897).

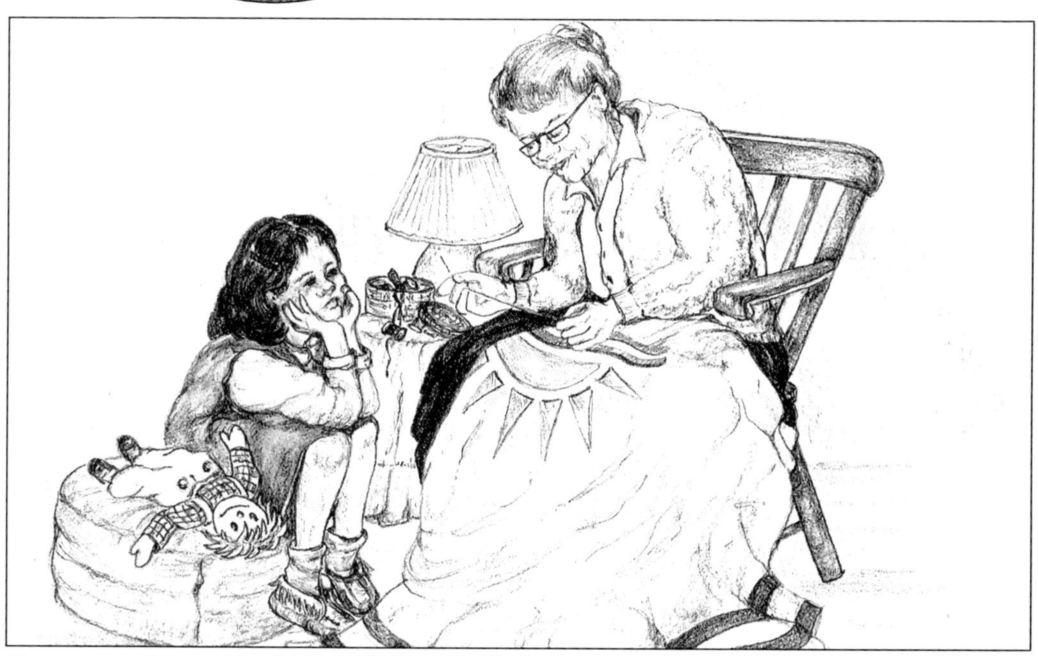

**Continued Teaching.** Just as William Bullock and the authors of this book wish to keep history and heritage alive, so too do the Abenaki descendants. It is important for those who remember and retain the memories of their ancestors—Anglo or Native American, English or French, Canadian or American—to pass on their heritage and history to the younger generations. Without a knowledge of our roots, our culture, and our struggles in growth, we cannot understand or feel confident of our place in the world. Here, an Abenaki grandmother relates family stories as she works on a traditional quilt. The granddaughter exemplifies the cross-cultural younger generation.

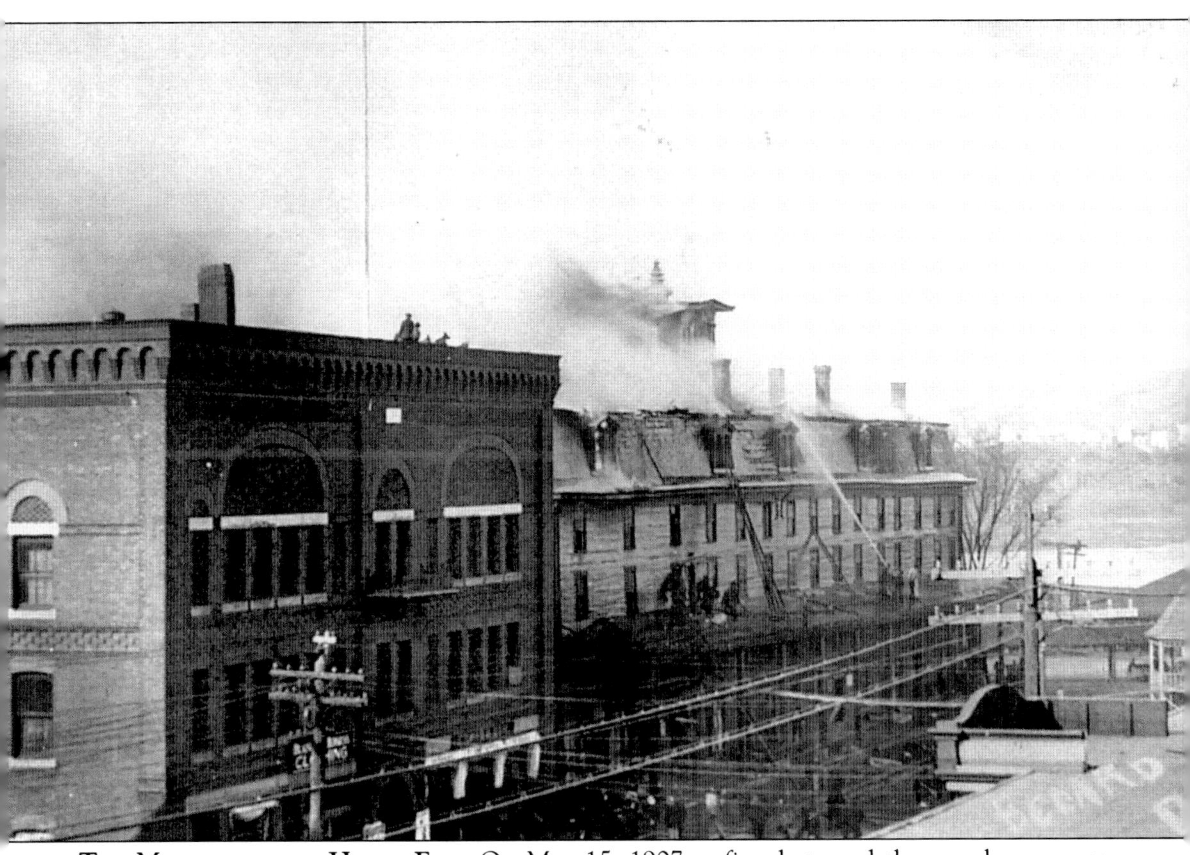

**The Memphremagog Hotel Fire.** On May 15, 1907, a fire destroyed the popular summer resort that stood east of the Lane & Sons Opera House block. When citizens first discovered the flames, their remarks were, "You couldn't burn that down if you tried!" So no one was worried . . . for a while. The minds of the spectators changed when they realized the old hotel was doomed. Then, the *Lady of the Lake* steamer pulled away from Steamboat Wharf to save herself. The hotel had been for sale at the time of the fire, and the owner had valued it and its furnishings at $35,000. Three weeks after the fire an occasional flicker of light could still be seen. Fond memories lingered about the old hotel, the first structure on Main Street once filled with the elite.

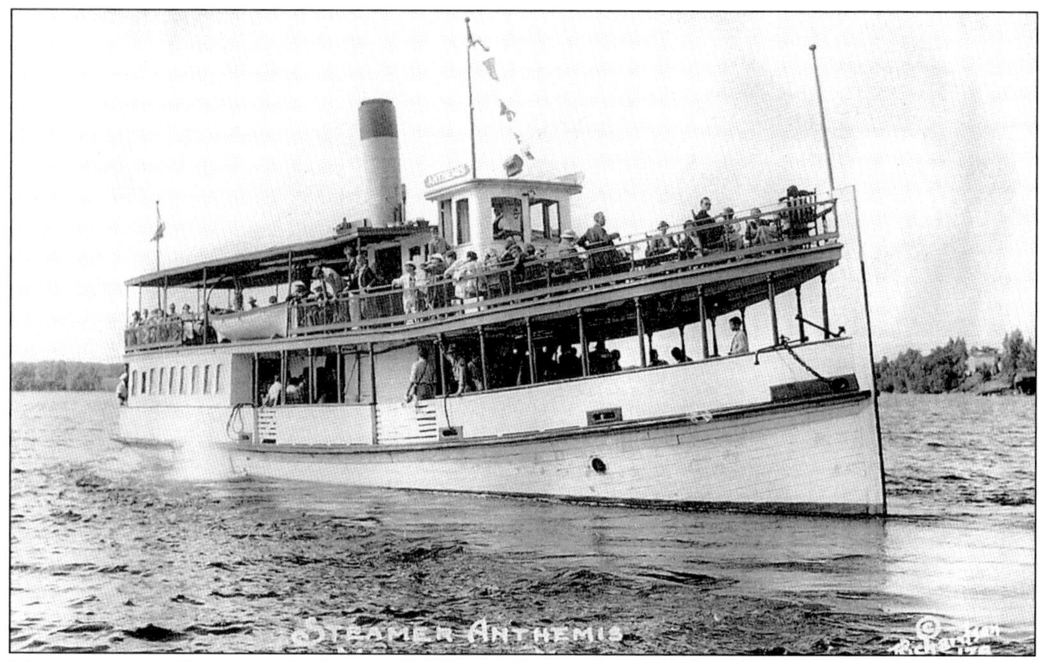


**THE *ANTHEMIS* STEAMER.** Built in 1909, the *Anthemis* was one of the last wood-burning steamers on the lake. It was 100 feet long and could carry up to 300 passengers. The boat was sold in 1947 and, by 1953, was scrapped and laid on its side at the Magog Wharf, sinking in eight feet of water. Capt. Alexander Clarke, the *Anthemis*'s manager, was full of sorrow and regret.

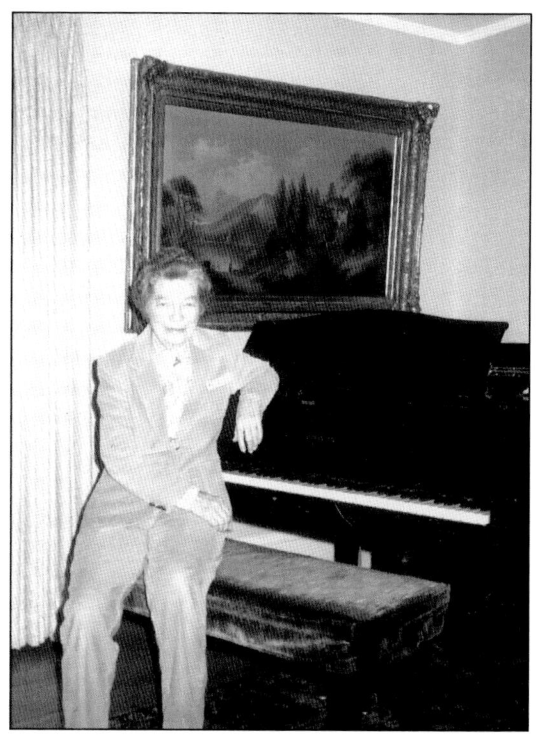

**ELIZABETH MARY CLARKE.** At her Prospect Street home, Elizabeth "Betty" Clarke, the daughter of Capt. A. Clarke (1877–1955) and Bertha (Kirpatrick) Clarke, sits at her piano under a painting of the lake. She came to Newport from Georgeville with her parents in 1930. She will be remembered most for her span of more than 50 years as a Girl Scout leader.

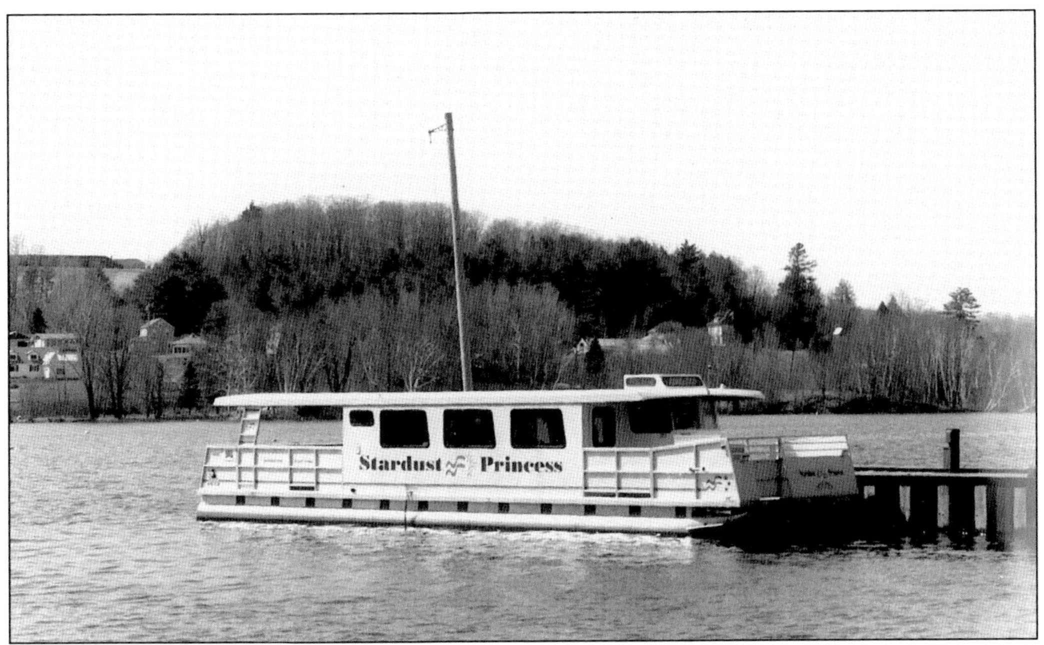


**THE *STARDUST* PRINCESS.** The *Newport Princess*, a 52' paddle-wheeler, arrived in Newport on May 29, 1996. It ran for four seasons until the year 2000. In 2001, the *Stardust Princess*, a 49 passenger 55' air-boat, was the successor to the *Newport Princess* and sailed until 2002. The *Stardust Princess* was the last tour boat on Lake Memphremagog.

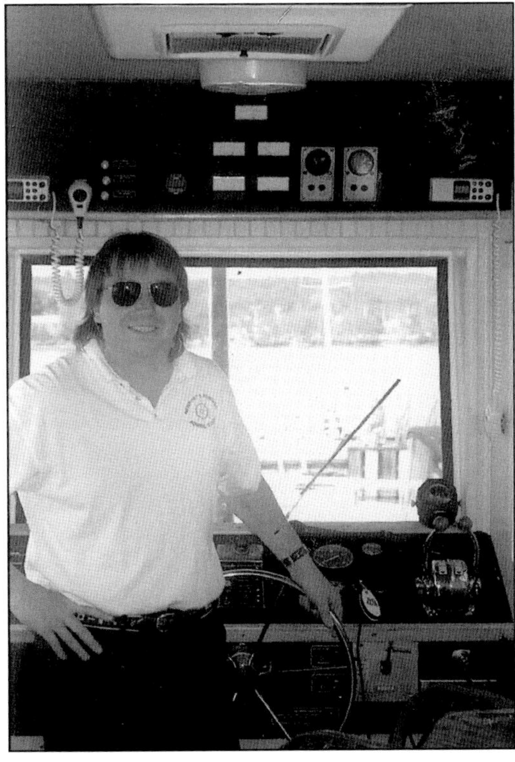

**CHRISTOPHER JOHANSEN.** President and co-owner of the Memphremagog Navigation Company, Chris Johansen took over as captain of the pilothouse on the *Newport Princess* in 1998. During a historic community gathering in Newport in September 1995, he announced that he would bring back paddle-wheel lake cruises to the shores of Lake Memphremagog.

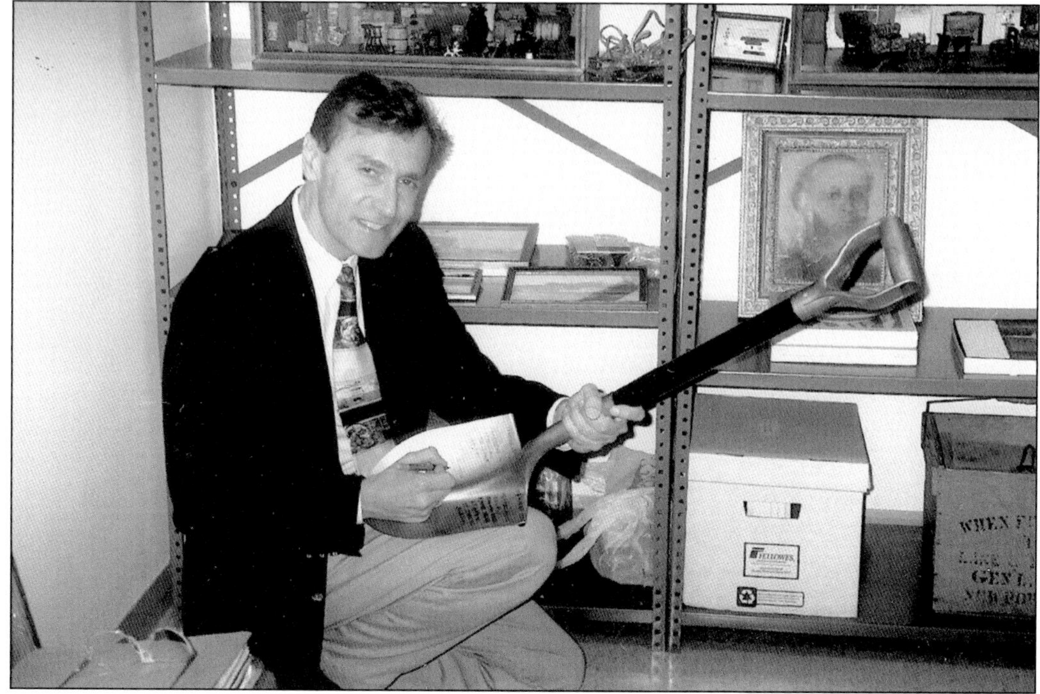

**THE GOLDEN SHOVEL.** Vermont's Sen. Vince Illuzi, mentor to the Memphremagog Historical Society of Newport, signs the "golden shovel" presented to the society by Rep. William Fyfe. The shovel was used in the official groundbreaking ceremony, held in 1997, for the new state office building to be built on the lakefront in Newport. Senator Illuzi was instrumental in helping the society obtain its archival room, exhibition, and showcases in the new building.

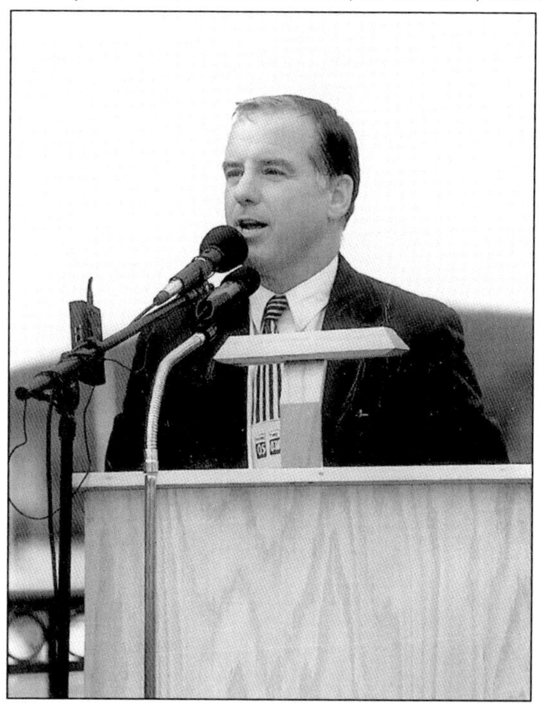

**DEDICATIONS.** Gov. Howard Dean dedicated the Emory-Hebard State Office Building and waterfront development on the shores of Lake Memphremagog on October 1, 1999. The building was named in honor of the late Em Hebard (1917–1993), who ran for state treasurer in 1978 with the slogan "Thrift is still a virtue." On July 28, 2001, the Memphremagog Historical Society and the Alnobak Nebesakiak, along with representation from the state government, celebrated the opening of their second-floor permanent exhibition the Crossroads (the Wabanaki history) and 19th- and 20th-century photographs of Lake Memphremagog and surrounding towns.

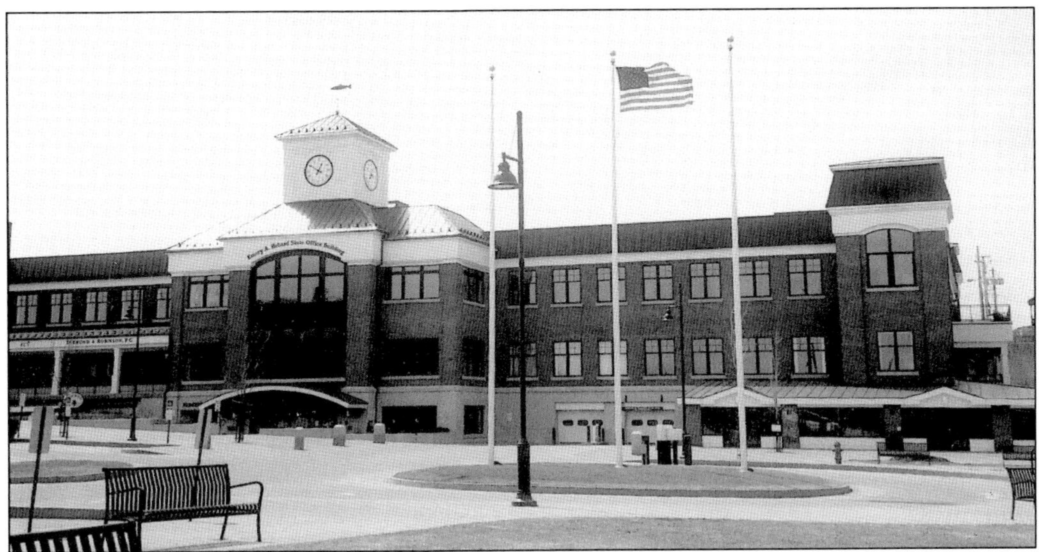

**The Emory-Hebard Building.** The Vermont state government and the Department of Buildings and General Services were responsible for constructing the new state offices. Commissioner Tom Torti and architect John Ostrum worked closely to design the three-story, 95,000-square-foot condominium on a six-acre site. It included a pedestrian walkway and park that link Main Street to Lake Memphremagog. Because the Emory-Hebard State Office Building sits on the site of the Memphremagog Hotel, care was taken to emulate as closely as possible the original architecture.

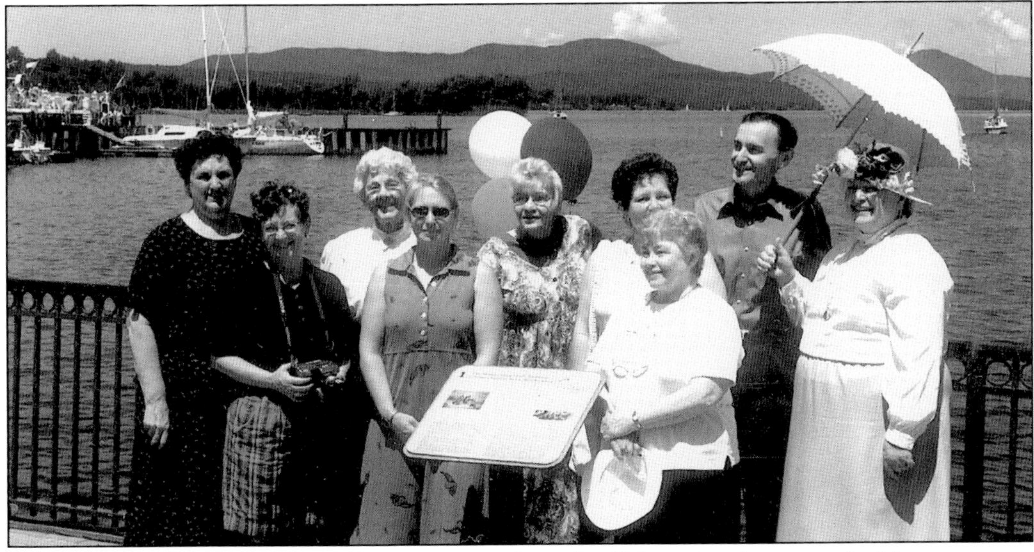

**An Historic Walking Tour.** In an unprecedented collaboration between the Vermont state government, the Memphremagog Historical Society of Newport, and the Alnobak Heritage Preservation Center, the Historic Walking Tour dedication took place on July 29, 2002. The walking tour visits ten historic markers that point out the locations of landmarks at the lakefront and along Main Street in the city of Newport, beginning with the Abenaki presence. The markers are written in both English and French. Shown here at marker No. 1, from left to right, are Barbara Malloy, Sandra McKenny, Steeny Pepin, Kate Chrisholm, Bea Nelson, Nancy McCarthy, Pat Kilbourn, Sen. Vince Illuzi, and June Quigly.

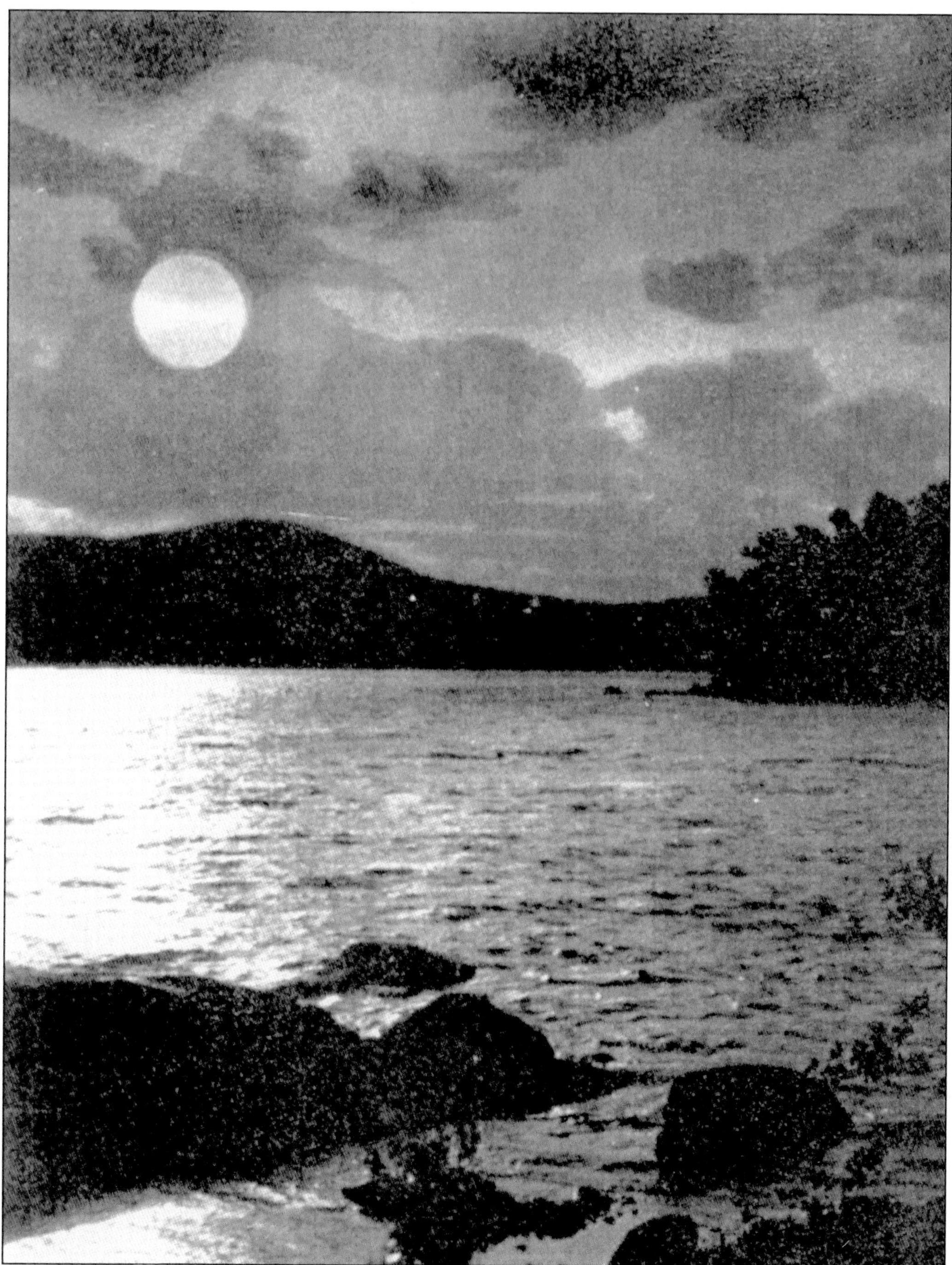

**Time Without End.** Sunsets and moonlight are crowning glories that reflect on the waters of Lake Memphremagog, our Great Lake here on the Vermont-Canada border. Those who called it homeland, those who came to settle, and those ancestors from yesteryear who once dwelled on these shores are now gone. But the sunsets and moonlight reflections will always be here to remind us to reflect on the legacies left behind for us to enjoy and remember, the legacies that transport us into the past around Lake Memphremagog.